R
911
YOU

For Reference

Not to be taken from this room

D1300996

ATLAS OF THE SECOND WORLD WAR

EDITED BY BRIGADIER PETER YOUNG
CARTOGRAPHY BY RICHARD NATKIEL

G. P. PUTNAM'S SONS NEW YORK

Research for maps undertaken by Richard Natkiel.
Text for map sections written by Christopher Chant, Jonathan Martin, and Patrick Scrivenor.

Designed by Rodney Josey.

SBN: 399–11182–4

Library of Congress Catalog Card Number: 73–78626

Printed in Great Britain.

Acknowledgements

The illustrations in this book are reproduced by kind permission of the following:
10: Imperial War Museum. 12/1: Ullstein. 13/1: Keystone. 13/2: Ullstein. 14: Camera Press. 15: Camera Press. 16: Ullstein. 17/1 and 2: Ullstein. 18/1: Camera Press. 18/2: Camera Press. 19/1: Novosti. 19/2: Camera Press. 20: Ullstein. 21/1: Ullstein. 21/2: Paul Popper. 22/1: Keystone. 22/2: Camera Press. 22/3: Keystone. 24: Ullstein. 25: Ullstein. 26: Keystone. 27: Ullstein. 28: Keystone. 29/1: I W M. 29/2: Süddeutscher Verlag. 30/1: I W M. 30/2: Süddeutscher Verlag. 33/1 Süddeutscher Verlag. 33/2: Camera Press. 34: Süddeutscher Verlag. 36/1: Süddeutscher Verlag. 36/2: Süddeutscher Verlag. 36/3: Ullstein. 37: Keystone. 38/1: Ullstein. 38/2: Ullstein. 39/1: Keystone. 39/2: Keystone. 40/1: Sado. 40/2: Sado. 41: Süddeutscher Verlag. 42: Camera Press. 44: Keystone. 45/1: Ullstein. 45/2: Camera Press. 46: I W M/Ballantine Books Photographic Library. 48/1: Ullstein. 48/2: I W M. 19: I W M. 50: Camera Press. 51: I W M. 52: Camera Press. 53: I W M. 54: Ullstein. 55/1: I W M 55/2: Ullstein. 56/1: Ullstein. 56/2: Ullstein. 57: Ullstein. 58: I W M. 59: Camera Press. 60/1: Ullstein. 60/2: Ullstein. 62: I W M. 63: I W M. 64/1: Associated Press. 64/2: Ullstein. 65: Ullstein. 66/1: Ullstein. 66/2: I W M. 67: I W M. 68/1: Camera Press. 68/2: I W M. 69: I W M. 70: Associated Press. 71: I W M. 72: I W M. 73: Keystone. 74: Camera Press. 75: Keystone. 76/1: Paul Popper. 76/2: I W M. 77: Keystone. 78: Keystone. 80: Ullstein. 82/1: Novosti. 82/2: Novosti. 83: Camera Press. 85: Süddeutscher Verlag. 86/1: Ullstein. 86/2: Ullstein. 88: Süddeutscher Verlag. 89: Novosti. 90: Süddeutscher Verlag. 93/1: Novosti. 93/2: Novosti. 94: Associated Press. 96: Camera Press. 97/1: Keystone. 97/2: Camera Press. 99: Paul Popper. 101/1: US Navy/BPC Library. 101/2: Camera Press. 102: Paul Popper. 103/1: Camera Press. 103/2: Paul Popper. 104: I W M/Robert Hunt Library. 105/1: Camera Press. 105/2: Camera Press. 106: US Navy/ B P C Library. 108: B P C Library. 109: Associated Press. 111/1: Paul Popper. 111/2: Sado/BPC. 112/1: Paul Popper. 112/2: Camera Press. 113: Keystone. 114: Camera Press. 116/1: I W M. 116/2: Keystone. 117: Keystone. 118: Camera Press. 120: Keystone. 123/1: Keystone. 123/2: Keystone. 125: Camera Press. 126: Camera Press. 127: Keystone. 128: Keystone. 129: Keystone. 130: Keystone. 131: Keystone. 132: Associated Press. 134/1: I W M. 134/2: Associated Press. 135/1: Camera Press. 135/2: Camera Press. 136: I W M/BPC. 137: Paul Popper. 139: I W M. 141/1: US Navy/BPC. 141/2: US Marine Corps/ B P C. 144: Associated Press. 146: Robert Hunt Library. 147: Paul Popper. 149: Keystone/Robert Hunt Library. 152: Keystone. 154: B P C. 155: Paul Popper. 156: I W M. 157: I W M. 158: Ballantine Books Photographic Library. 159: Robert Hunt Library. 161: Robert Hunt Library. 162: I W M. 164: US Marine Corps/B P C. 165/1: Keystone. 165/2: Keystone. 166: Camera Press. 167/1: Camera Press. 167/2: Keystone. 168: I W M/ Robert Hunt Library. 170: Camera Press. 172/1: Camera Press. 172/2: I W M. 173/1: I W M. 173/2: Camera Press. 174: I W M. 175: I W M. 176: I W M. 177/1: I W M. 177/2: I W M. 178/1: I W M. 178/2: I W M. 181: Camera Press. 182: Keystone. 183: Keystone. 184/1: I W M. 184/2: Paul Popper. 185: I W M. 186: Keystone, 188: Ullstein. 190/1: Novosti. 190/2: Novosti. 191/1: Novosti. 191/2: Novosti. 193/1: Camera Press. 193/2: Camera Press. 194: Ullstein. 195: Ullstein. 196/1: Ullstein. 196/2: Ullstein.

198: Ullstein. 199: Ullstein. 200: Camera Press. 201/1: I W M. 201/2: Camera Press. 202–209: Novosti. 210: Ullstein. 211: Camera Press. 213/1: Novosti. 213/2: Keystone. 214/1: Ullstein. 214/2: I W M. 217/1: Ullstein. 217/2: Novosti. 218: Ullstein. 219: Ullstein. 220/1: Ullstein. 221: Ullstein. 224: Ullstein. 226/1: Camera Press. 226/2: Roger Viollet. 227/1: Keystone. 227/2: Roger Viollet. 228: Keystone. 229: Camera Press. 234: Paul Popper. 235: Keystone. 236: Roger Viollet. 237: Camera Press. 239/1: Roger Viollet. 239/2: Keystone. 240: Keystone. 241: Keystone. 242: Camera Press. 243: I W M. 244: I W M. 246: Keystone. 248: Süddeutscher Verlag. 250: I W M. 252/1: I W M/Robert Hunt Library. 252/2: Ullstein. 253/1: I W M/Robert Hunt Library. 253/2: Camera Press. 254: I W M. 257: Ullstein. 258/1: Süddeutscher Verlag. 258/2: I W M. 259: I W M. 261/1 and 2: Camera Press. 262: Ullstein. 263: Ullstein. 264: I W M. 265: Paul Popper. 267/1: I W M. 267/2: I W M. 268: Süddeutscher Verlag. 269: I W M. 270: I W M. 271: Paul Popper. 274: Robert Hunt Library. 280: I W M/BPC Picture Library.

CONTENTS

INTRODUCTION

THE MILITARY ATLAS is a reference book for the student and historian which provides detailed maps of the military side of the Second World War. It is divided into sections corresponding to the major theatres or campaigns of the war; and within these, the individual battles or phases of battles each have a double-page spread with a selection of maps. Accompanying these are a short explanatory text and illustrations. The introduction to each section has been written to fill in the background to the specific campaign, giving details about the forces and commanders involved, and the particular tactical, geographical and logistical problems with which they were faced.

GERMANY STRIKES IN THE WEST

This is not Peace. It is an Armistice for twenty years.
Marshal Foch on the Treaty of Versailles

Opposite: Bombers of the Luftwaffe over London during the Battle of Britain

In many ways the European armies which went to war in 1939 were still very like those of 1918, in which the majority of the company commanders, and all the more senior officers had served. The most old-fashioned of Germany's opponents was Poland, whose army, for all its gallantry, was completely outclassed by the new *Wehrmacht*. Polish strategy, designed to protect every yard of the frontiers, was to say the least unrealistic. Even so the legacy of the First World War lay heaviest upon the French army. The long slogging match on the Western Front influenced the military thinking of both sides, but more especially the Allies: the Germans who had fought in Rumania and Russia as well as France and Belgium were by no means as committed to ideas of trench warfare. They knew far more about deep penetration and the war of movement. The French, though they had spent a great deal of money on defence, had devoted comparatively little to the air force, and an inordinate amount to their static – and incomplete – defences in the Maginot Line, a system devised for a new Verdun, which the Germans, as it happened, had no intention of fighting. The French actually had rather more tanks than the Germans, but they looked upon them as close support for their infantry, rather than a mobile arm. To a great extent the French army still owed what mobility it had to the horse. But this was true too of the great mass of the German army. The only motorized army on either side was the British Expeditionary Force, which as late as May 1940 had only some fifteen divisions, three of them incomplete, and only one armoured – and that had only two brigades.

At the highest strategic level the French commander General Gamelin, Joffre's staff officer of 1914, attempted to control events from a headquarters so woefully deficient of communications equipment, that he might as well have ensconced himself in a monastery. His plans, moreover, left him no *masse de*

manoeuvre, no reserve, a deficiency which Churchill was to discover when attempting to inspire the French command into launching a counterattack. Controversy will long rage as to the merits of Gamelin and Weygand. Would Gamelin, if left in command, have counterattacked, cutting the exposed lines of communications of the German panzer divisions? Was Weygand too old, and too shattered by what he saw of the German *blitzkrieg* to take effective control? All one can say is that in the fighting *after* Dunkirk, during June 1940, the time when Weygand, now gravely outnumbered, was in command, the French army seems to have inflicted far heavier casualties on the Germans than it did in May.

As for the British the 'miracle' of Dunkirk left them a nucleus for the armies that were to conquer North Africa and play their part from Normandy to the Baltic. Had these troops been destroyed at Dunkirk there would have been little left of the British army. It owed its survival as much as anything to the fact that it was *motorized*: it was so very much more mobile than von Bock's army which was following it up, even if it was outclassed by von Rundstedt's armour that was cutting it off. The miracle of Dunkirk was that the BEF – despite a steadfast rearguard action by the Cavalry Club – went to France in 1939 without a single horse.

The geographical conditions under which the campaign was fought were more or less familiar to the commanders on both sides of the rank of major and above since, with the exception of the Dutch, they had for the most part seen fighting on the Western Front during the First World War. But if the tactical importance of Arras, or Kemmel, or Mont des Cats was well-enough remembered, experience was not always a sure guide. The Ardennes where the French had suffered so heavily in August 1914 were now, on very slender grounds, deemed to be well-

nigh impassable to armoured formations.

The French planners depended to a great extent on their fortifications, especially on the right of their line, between Switzerland and Sedan. To do them justice the Maginot fortresses, for all the faults in their organization, held out without difficulty until the French field armies surrendered. The modern Belgian fortress of Eben Emael, guarding the Meuse and Albert Canal bridges, proof, no doubt, against the techniques which had crushed the Liége fortresses in 1914, succumbed to an airborne *coup de main*. The Dutch depended on the defence of inundations and, everywhere, as the campaign developed the Allies tended to form successive defensive positions along the lines of rivers and canals: there were battles on the Dyle, the Scheldt, the canals round Dunkirk, and the Somme, to name but a few.

The armies of 1940 were armed and organized very much like those of 1918, and, with the exception of the British, they depended in the main upon the horse for their mobility. Both sides were adequately equipped with field and medium artillery, though the Germans by using the Stuka dive-bomber as a form of mobile artillery had the advantage here. It seems also that they were rather better provided with mortars than the Allies. The latter were also short of anti-tank guns, and the majority being 2-pounders were too small to be certain of knocking out a German tank.

With the lessons of 1914–18 both sides had armed their infantry with large numbers of machine guns. The British with the Vickers MMG, the Bren LMG, and a first-class rifle, the Mark III Lee-Enfield, were well-equipped, but unlike the Germans they had as yet no sub-machine gun.

The Allies outnumbered the Germans in tanks, but the latter were greatly superior in their tactical handling. The British, who put very few tanks in the field suffered greatly from lack of

transporters. Travelling long distances
and with no time for maintenance,
they lost numbers of vehicles through
breakdowns. By 21 May, 1 Army Tank
Brigade had only seventy-four tanks.
Of these fifty-eight were Mark I and
sixteen Mark II. The former had
heavy armour, one 7·9-mm machine
gun and was very slow. The latter was
much bigger and had, in addition to
the machine gun, a 2-pounder gun.

Opposite above: German assault troops during
the invasion of Norway

Above: The BEF arrives in France in 1939

Right: German troops parade past the Arc
de Triomphe

THE RISE OF GERMANY

The Nazi party came to power in Germany in January 1933 pledged to tear up the Treaty of Versailles which had drastically cut down the size of Germany. The country would be restored to its 'rightful' place as the most powerful in Europe and all those Germans living in areas outside the Reich would be incorporated into the 'Greater Germany'. The treaty had limited Germany's armed forces to a 100,000-man army with no tanks, a small navy, and no airforce. But, under General Hans von Seeckt, the army was organized as a highly-trained, professional framework for a much larger force which could one day be raised by conscription. Development of tanks and military aircraft went ahead under various disguises – much of it undertaken in the Soviet Union – and civilian flying schools built up a pool of trained pilots. Thus in the spring of 1935, Hitler was able to announce that Germany repudiated the Treaty of Versailles, that she now had an airforce, and that conscription would be introduced to bring the army up to 300,000 men.

The Western democracies, Britain and France, made no effective protest and this convinced Hitler that they had lost the will to act decisively. In March 1936 he openly proved this by reoccupying the Rhineland – against the advice of his generals who knew that the army was still undertrained, underequipped, and far smaller than that of France.

In March 1938, with the apparent approval of the bulk of her population, Austria was annexed to the Reich. Once again, Britain and France made no effort to prevent it. Despite warnings, their governments were determined to avoid war and preferred to give way to Hitler rather than run any risks. But in the autumn of 1938 the Führer made his first overt move against an independent state, when he demanded that the Sudetenland – the western border of Czechoslovakia – with its 3,000,000 Germans should be annexed to the Reich, because its inhabitants were being maltreated by the native population. Czechoslovakia was a model democracy, prosperous and socially advanced, with large well-equipped armed forces and defences which would have proved a difficult opponent for the Germans. The government prepared to resist, but, as Hitler had foreseen, under pressure from Britain and France an 'honourable' solution was found guaranteeing 'peace in our time'. The Sudetenland with all of the Czech frontier defences was handed over to Germany. Hitler had removed a potentially difficult threat on his southern flank and was further convinced that he had nothing to fear from France and Britain. In March 1939 he completed the occupation of Czechoslovakia, but now at last the Western democracies had realized the true nature of his plans and begun to rearm. However, it would take time to redress the years of inactivity and the German forces were now more than equal in strength to their probable opponents. Hitler was ready to turn on his next victim – Poland – where the Danzig corridor cutting off East Prussia from the Reich presented an inviting excuse for intervention.

Left: Troops marching past Hitler during a Nazi rally in Nuremberg in 1936

ORKNEY IS.
Scapa Flow
BERGEN
NORWAY
OSLO
SWEDEN
STOCKHOLM
FINLAND
HELSINKI
Lake Ladoga
LENINGRAD
NORTH SEA
EDINBURGH
BALTIC SEA
COPENHAGEN
TALLINN
ESTONIA
RIGA
LATVIA
MOSCOW
RUSSIA
DUBLIN
GREAT BRITAIN
NETHERLANDS
AMSTERDAM
LONDON
MEMEL
LITHUANIA
KAUNAS
KÖNIGSBERG
EAST PRUSSIA
SMOLENSK
MINSK
Belorussia
HAMBURG
BERLIN
DANZIG
Vistula
Bug
WARSAW
BRUSSELS
BELGIUM
COLOGNE
Rhine
Rhineland
GERMANY
POLAND
KIEV
PARIS
LUX
Sudeten-land
PRAGUE
Dniepr
Ukraine
Maginot line
Siegfried line
CZECHOSLOVAKIA
LVOV
FRANCE
BERNE
MUNICH
VIENNA
BERCHTESGADEN
AUSTRIA
BUDAPEST
ODESSA
SWITZ
GENEVA
HUNGARY
RUMANIA
BORDEAUX
MILAN
BUCHAREST
BLACK SEA
MARSEILLES
BELGRADE
SPAIN
ITALY
YUGOSLAVIA
Danube
SOFIA
BARCELONA
Corsica
ROME
ADRIATIC SEA
BULGARIA
ISTANBUL
Sardinia
NAPLES
TIRANE
ALBANIA
ANKARA
GREECE
TURKEY

0   MILES   400
0   KILOMETRES   600

August 1939

German expansion in Europe

Right: German troops cross the border during the annexation of Austria in March 1938

15

THE POLISH CAMPAIGN

German troop carriers cross the Polish frontier

Hitler's forces conquered Poland in eighteen days. It was not Polish morale that failed, they were simply not strong enough. Against nine armoured divisions the Poles could pit a dozen cavalry brigades and a handful of light tanks. Even in artillery and infantry the Germans outnumbered the Poles by at least three to two. In any case the defending army was not given time to complete its mobilization and the German fleet commanded the Baltic as effectively as the Luftwaffe did the sky. In addition the Germans had a new concept of war – blitzkrieg.

The basis of the blitzkrieg was surprise, speed and terror. Armoured forces were used to break through the enemies' defences and then to drive deep into his rear surrounding large pockets of troops, ignoring and by-passing stubborn defences, and disrupting communications. The German plan (**Map 1**) aimed for two massive pincer movements from north and south, which would break up the Polish armies, forcing them to fight individual survival battles rather than a co-ordinated defence.

At dawn on 1 September 1939 the Germans launched their invasion (**Map 2**). Two army groups swept across the borders supported by a massive air offensive which destroyed

the bulk of the Polish airforce within two days. The Poles were unable to contain the armoured thrusts, and by 8 September the Germans were in the outskirts of Warsaw. General Kutrzeba, whose forces at Kutno had been by-passed, drew in troops from Torun and Łodz and boldly counterattacked the main German advance towards Warsaw with twelve divisions (**Map 3**). But by the 19th the battle of the Bzura was over.

Meanwhile the battle of the Vistula was being fought out. Lemberg fell on the 12th and on the 17th the German pincers closed near Brest-Litovsk. The Russians had crossed the eastern frontier on the 17th, taking Vilnyus the next day. The Polish government fled to Rumania but Warsaw held out till the 27th. On 28 September the victors arranged a fifth partition of Poland (**Map 4**). The Russians annexed 77,000 square miles, leaving the other 73,000 with most of the manufacturing areas under the 'protection' of the Reich.

③
BALTIC SEA
LITHUANIA
KAUNAS
VILNYUS (VILNA)
■ **KÖNIGSBERG**
DANZIG
EAST PRUSSIA
MINSK
BYDGOSZCZ
TORUŃ
Vistula
BIAŁYSTOK
Narew
XIX Pz Corps
RUSSIA
POZNAŃ
MODLIN
Bug
WARSAW 27 Sept
BREST-LITOVSK
KUTNO 17 Sept
GÓRA KALWARIA
PINSK
Pripet
Pripet Marshes
ŁÓDZ
WŁODAWA 17 Sept
XVI Pz Corps
LUBLIN
KOVEL
RADOM
CHELM
GERMANY
P O L A N D
SANDOMIERZ
San
ŁUCK
ROVNO
ZHITOMIR
KRAKÓW
PŘZEMYŚL
LVOV 22 Sept
C A R P A T H I A N   M T S
Dniestr
RUMANIA

GERMAN ATTACKS 15/27 SEPTEMBER
POLISH BZURA POCKET
RUSSIAN ATTACKS 17/27 SEPTEMBER

MILES 200
KILOMETRES 300

④
BALTIC SEA
LITHUANIA
DANZIG
■ KÖNIGSBERG
EAST PRUSSIA
VILNYUS (VILNA)
BIALYSTOK
To Russia
R U S S I A
GERMANY
Vistula
Bug
WARSAW
BREST LITOVSK
To Germany
KRAKOW
San
LVOV
MILES 200
KILOMETRES 300
HUNGARY
RUMANIA

October 1939

German expansion in Europe

Right: General von Blaskowitz negotiating the terms of Polish surrender

Below: A squadron of Stukas in flight. German control of the air enabled them to devastate the Polish defences

THE FINNISH CAMPAIGN

On 30 November, Russia invaded Finland. The troops of five armies crossed the frontier on four main fronts (**Map 1**) but soon found themselves bogged down in the deep snow and wooded terrain. Tanks and transports were forced to stick to the forest roads, and were ideal targets for Finnish ski troops who harassed the flanks, shot up convoys, and cut off formations. By the end of January, the Russians had made deep penetrations in the north of the country but on the Karelian Isthmus they had been unable to breach the Mannerheim Line. At the beginning of February, they launched a major assault (**Map 2**) preceded by a massive bombardment. By the middle of the month a breakthrough had been achieved and Finland was forced to surrender, ceding the Karelian Isthmus and considerable territory in the north. The Russian losses were about 200,000 men killed, about 1,600 tanks and 684 aircraft destroyed. The Finns lost 24,923 men killed and sixty-one aircraft.

Below: German specialists installed these obstacles on the Soviet–Finnish border

Below right: Finnish soldiers on the northern front

RUSSIAN ATTACKS: 30 NOV, 1939/31 JAN, 1940
FINNISH COUNTERATTACKS 27 DEC/5 JAN
[IV] FINNISH ARMY CORPS
CEDED TO RUSSIA AT DATES SHOWN

MILES 150
KILOMETRES 200

BARENTS SEA
NORWAY
Rybachiy Pen
PETSAMO
1947
NAUTSI
104 Div
MURMANSK
Fourteenth Army
L Inari
Murmansk Railway
KIRUNA
GÄLLIVARE
KEMIJÄRVI
SALLA
1940
122 Div
88 Div
WHITE SEA
SWEDEN
Ninth Army
LULEÅ
KEMI
163 Div
44 Div
SUOMUSSALMI
Soviet Karelia
54 Div
OULU
KUHMO
RUSSIA
GULF OF BOTHNIA
155 Div
139 Div
LIEKSA
ILOMANTSI
75 Div
Eighth Army
VAASA
TOLVAJÄRVI
KUOPIO
[IV]
KOLLAA
SUOJÄRVI
56 Div
18 Div
KITELÄ
PORI
MIKKELI
L Saimaa
PITKÄRANTA
1940
SALMI
168 Div
TAMPERE
LAKE LADOGA
LAHTI
[III]
VIIPURI
TAIPALE
TURKU
Vuoksi
KOIVISTO
[II]
ÅLAND IS.
HELSINKI
PORVOO
SUURSAARI
Mannerheim Line
Thirteenth Army
PORKKALA
1947-55
LENINGRAD
HANKO
1940-41
GULF OF FINLAND
Seventh Army
Estonia
KARELIAN ISTHMUS
①

Above: Russian troops fighting on the Karelian Isthmus

Below: Finnish soldiers with a captured Russian tank

THE INVASION OF NORWAY

The German invasions of Denmark and Norway began on 9 April 1940. Denmark was swiftly overrun and a ceasefire agreed by the evening. German naval landings took place at five points on the Norwegian coast and two parachute drops were made. The naval force attacking Oslo was fired on by shore batteries and the cruiser *Blücher* sunk and the pocket battleship *Lützow* damaged. The expedition was forced to land on the east bank of the fjord and move overland to the capital, but their attack combined with that of six companies of paratroops swiftly captured the city. Kristiansand, Stavanger, Bergen, Trondheim, and Narvik all fell with only minor fighting.

The Allied reaction was hampered by lack of reserves trained for landing. British, French, and Polish forces landed at Harstad and Bodö to recapture Narvik and further south at Namsos and Åndalsnes to attack Trondheim. However, the southern forces soon found themselves under heavy German attack and had to be evacuated in two weeks. The northern forces captured Narvik on 28 May, but events in France made it necessary to withdraw them in June.

German soldiers practising advance over rocky terrain in preparation for the invasion of Norway

GERMAN
- SEABORNE LANDINGS AND ATTACKS
- Group I — PARATROOP LANDINGS
- NAVAL GROUPS

ALLIES
- 1 Div — NORWEGIAN DISPOSITIONS
- LANDINGS AND ATTACKS
- WITHDRAWALS

0 — MILES — 150
0 — KILOMETRES — 200

9 April
Gneisenau damaged by Renown

Narvik: 8 April
2 British destroyers sunk by German troop-ferrying destroyers.
10/13 April, 10 German destroyers sunk

✗ 8 June
Glorious sunk, Scharnhorst damaged in naval action

9 April 1940
German forces land simultaneously at Oslo, Kristiansand, Stavanger, Bergen, Trondheim & Narvik

8 April
Hipper sinks destroyer Glowworm

15 April
British, French, Polish
Br 24 Gds Bde
8 June
HARSTAD
BJERKVIK
NARVIK
6 Div
28 May
French & Norwegian forces take Narvik
Germans advance to relieve their force at Narvik
TROMSÖ
Bardufoss
Lofoten Islands
VESTFJORDEN
Ofotfjord
Group I
15 May
BODÖ
Saltfjord
30 May
31 May
MO-I-RANA
14 May
MOSJÖEN
10 May

NORWEGIAN SEA

16/17 April
Br 146 Inf Bde
2/3 May
NAMSOS
STEINKJER
19 Apr
Trondheim-fjord
Group II
Vaernes
HEGRA
TRONDHEIM
5 Div
DRAGSET
29 Apr

SWEDEN

18 April
Br 148 Inf Bde
MOLDE
ÅNDALSNES
30 Apr
2 May
ALESUND
1 May
DOMBÅS
KVAM
GUDBRANDSDALEN
25 May
LILLEHAMMER
21 Apr
TYNSET
RENDAL
24 Apr
ØSTERDALEN
Glomma
RENA
19 Apr
ELVERUM
HAMAR
L. Mjösa

NORWAY

GOL
1 May
Randsfjord
2 Div
HÖNEFOSS
Fornebu
OSLO
1 Div
KONGSBERG
Oslofjord
HALDEN
12 Apr

9 April
Heavy cruiser Blücher sunk by shore batteries

BERGEN
4 Div
10 April
Light cruiser Königsberg bombed & sunk
Group III
Group V

27 Apr
ARENDAL
11 April
Heavy cruiser Lützow damaged by torpedo

STAVANGER
Sola
3 Div
KRISTIANSAND
Jösenfjord
SKAGERRAK
16 February 1940
Altmark boarded
9 April
Cruiser Karlsruhe torpedoed & sunk
Group IV
KATTEGAT
AALBORG

9 April 1940
German forces occupy Denmark

COPENHAGEN
DENMARK

May 1940

German expansion in Europe

Right: German troops in a burning Norwegian village

Below: HMS *Glowworm* photographed from the bridge of the *Hipper* shortly before she was sunk

MILITARY BALANCE IN THE WEST

For six months after the fall of Poland, the armies on the Western Front remained practically motionless; the Allies waiting for the Germans to move, and Germans regrouping after their Polish victory. The key to Allied strategy was the Maginot Line which was still uncompleted as it only reached to the Belgian border. They were thus painfully aware of the gap and mesmerized by their memories of the Schlieffen Plan of 1914 – the massive sweeping thrust through Belgium which aimed towards Paris, and their Dyle Plan was designed to counter such an attack by pivoting forward into Belgium with their right

flank hinged on Sedan and the hilly Ardennes (small map). Unfortunately, the Germans' leading planner, General Manstein had foreseen this reaction; and had realized that the Ardennes were certainly not impassable. His plan relied on an attack on the Low Countries to draw the Allies forward, and then a thrust through the Ardennes, breaking the Allied hinge near Sedan, aiming for the sea near Calais and cutting off the troops who had moved forward into Belgium.

Theoretically, the two sides were fairly equally matched (main map): the Allies had a total of 149 divisions facing 136 German divisions, and about 3,000 armoured vehicles against approximately 2,700. But the Allies were still wedded to outmoded ideas of positional warfare, their armour was assigned to the infantry divisions and spread out along the front. General Gamelin only maintained a small reserve. In contrast, the German armour was organized as a virtually independent Panzer Group, and was assigned to von Rundstedt's Army Group A which would have the job of making the vital thrust through the centre of the Allied line. The Germans also had a massive superiority in the air – more than 2,000 bombers against the Allied 800 and 4,000 fighters against 2,500.

NORTH SEA

GREAT BRITAIN

NETHERLANDS

IJsselmeer

Reserves
42 divisions

Reserves
2 divisions
AMSTERDAM

THE HAGUE
UTRECHT
ROTTERDAM

Dutch Army
8 divisions + res

Waal

BREDA

Maas

Army Group B
(Bock)
29½ divisions, inc 3 armoured

OSTEND

DOVER

ANTWERP

Albert Canal

GERMANY

AACHEN

DUNKIRK

Reserves
4 divisions

Scheldt

BRUSSELS
Dyle

LOUVAIN

WAVRE

LIÈGE

**Supreme Commander,
Armed Forces – Hitler**

OKH (Army High Command)
C in C, Brauchitsch

French Seventh Army
(Giraud)
7 divisions, inc 1 light
mechanised and 2 motorised

BAILLEUL

MAULDE

Meuse

NAMUR

Belgian Army
18 divisions + res

M

Army Group A
(Rundstedt)
45½ divisions, inc 7 armoured
and 3 motorised

ABBEVILLE

Somme

BEF
(Gort)
9 divisions

Ardennes

SEDAN

LUX

LUXEMBOURG

Rhine

French 1st Army Group
(Billotte)
22 divisions, inc 2 light mechanised

LONGUYON

West Wall (Siegfried Line)

GHQ
C in C, Gamelin

North-East Front
C in C, Georges

Meuse

Brit

Maginot Line

Army Group C
(Leeb)
19 divisions

PARIS
VINCENNES

FRANCE

HAGUENAU

French 2nd Army Group
(Pretélat)
35 divisions + 1 British

Seine

Reserves
22 divisions, inc 3 armoured

for 1st Army Group

against outflanking attack
on Swiss border

French 3rd Army Group
(Besson)
14 divisions

General reserve

BASLE

SWITZERLAND

BERNE

0   MILES   100
0   KILOMETRES   160

Far left: Part of the Belgian defences
along the German frontier

Above left: French troops moving forward
heavy artillery. Much of French equipment
dated from the First World War

Below left: A French lookout waits for
the enemy

THE GERMAN ASSAULT IN THE WEST

The campaign in the West falls neatly into two parts: the battle of the Low Countries and the battle of France. The first began abruptly on the morning of 10 May 1940 when the Germans struck with air attacks and parachute landings on Dutch airfields and bridges (**Map 1**) and their troops moved into Holland and Belgium. Both countries called for help from France and Britain, and the Allied army began its planned move forward to cover Brussels. The Dutch, however, despite flooding and demolitions were swiftly forced back into 'Fortress Holland'; on the 14th Rotterdam was blitzed and the Dutch forces surrendered after suffering 25 per cent casualties.

Meanwhile, the Germans had captured Fort Eben Emael on the 11th, and their Panzer divisions had thrust through the 'impassable' Ardennes (**Map 2**) to reach the Meuse. The first three bridgeheads were secured by the morning of 14 May, and were not counterattacked; a 50-mile breach was appearing at the hinge of the Allied line between Sedan and Dinant. After a brief disagreement between Kleist and Guderian as to whether to stop and consolidate, the Panzers again moved forward on the night of 15/16 May, heading behind the BEF and the French First and Ninth Armies which were forced to fall back from Belgium (**Map 3**). By the 20th the German tanks had reached the sea at Noyelles and established a corridor between the Allied forces. On the 21st the Allies made a vain attempt to cut this corridor near Arras, but this failed, and on the 22nd the Germans turned north to drive towards the Channel ports but, partly thanks to Hitler and partly to von Rundstedt, halted the next day and did not move forward until the 25th. The Allies fell back around Dunkirk, and after Boulogne had fallen on the 25th and Calais on the 27th, the decision was taken to evacuate as many Allied troops as possible by sea.

Right: German troops in action at the Aisne, 1940

German soldiers fire
a howitzer in May 1940

DUNKIRK AND THE FALL OF FRANCE

The failure of the Germans to close in on the Channel ports and the determined defence of Calais till 27 May (**Map 1**) enabled the Royal Navy to begin the evacuation of the BEF from Dunkirk (**Map 2**). In the nine days before 4 June, 338,226 men, including 120,000 French, were rescued. The Luftwaffe attempted to annihilate the operation but the intervention of the RAF, which shot down 179 aircraft for the loss of 29 between 27 and 30 May, limited the destruction to six destroyers sunk and nineteen seriously damaged as well as numerous smaller craft.

Dunkirk gave the French in the south some respite. General Weygand now attempted to organize a system of defence on the Somme and the Aisne, but the majority of the French army had lost all confidence in their leaders and themselves. Nor were the remaining Allied forces in any condition to help them. The 51 Highland Division surrendered at St Valery-en-Caux on 12 June. The 52 Division and 1 Canadian Division had to be evacuated.

The Germans were across the Seine by 10 June (**Map 3**) and on that day Mussolini declared war and Italian troops moved a short way into France, meeting stubborn resistance. On the 12th the French government declared Paris an open city and moved to Bordeaux. Churchill's offer of union between Britain and France was rejected. Reynaud resigned and his successor, Marshal Pétain, accepted the German terms on 22 June.

All France north and west of a line from the Swiss frontier at Geneva, via Bourges to St Jean Pied de Port was to be occupied (**Map 4**). The French government set up its capital at Vichy in the unoccupied zone. General de Gaulle arrived in London and established the Free French forces.

Below: A German flame-thrower team in action during the capture of the Maginot Line

Below right: The fall of Paris

GREAT BRITAIN

DOVER

BELGIUM

ENGLISH CHANNEL

Army Group B

Hoth's XV Pz Corps

Pz Group Kleist

Army Group A

Somme

XIV Pz Corps

XVI Pz Corps

Second & Ninth Armies

GERMANY

CHERBOURG 18 June

ST VALÉRY
FÉCAMP

DIEPPE

ABBEVILLE

AMIENS

PÉRONNE

Pz Group Guderian

LUX.

SEDAN

XXXIX Pz Corps

XLI Pz Corps

Army Group C

LE HAVRE

Fr Tenth Army

Fr Seventh Army

ROUEN

COMPIEGNE

RETHEL

Fr Second Army

VERDUN

Maginot Line

CAEN

Oise

REIMS

Fr Sixth Army

Fr Fourth Army

CHALONS

METZ

NANCY

STRASBOURG

Channel Islands

Marne

ST DIZIER

22 June Trapped French Third, Fifth & Eighth Armies surrender

BREST 19 June

PARIS 14 June

Seine

EPINAL

ALENCON

CHARTRES

Meuse

BELFORT

RENNES 18 June

LE MANS

ORLÉANS

TROYES

BASLE

LES MANS

Loire

BRIARE 18 June

ANGERS

TOURS

Cher

VIERZON

DIJON 16 June

SWITZERLAND

BERNE

NANTES 19 June

SAUMUR 19 June

NEVERS

PONTARLIER 17 June

S

F R A N C E

Saône

BAY OF BISCAY

POITIERS

VICHY 20 June

GENEVA

ITALY

ROYAN 25 June

LIMOGES

LANSLEBOURG

TURIN

ANGOULÊME

CLERMONT FERRAND

LYONS 20 June

A

BORDEAUX

22 June 1941 Line reached by German forces at armistice

ST ETIENNE

GRENOBLE

BRIANÇON

Italy declares war 10 June 1940, attacks 21 June

Garonne

Rhône

ST JEAN DE LUZ 27 June

TOULOUSE

NICE

MENTON

MARSEILLES

TOULON

GERMAN CONTROLLED, 4 JUNE, 1941

WEYGAND LINE, 4 JUNE

FRONT LINE, 11/12 JUNE

MILES 150

PERPIGNAN

MEDITERRANEAN SEA

KILOMETRES 250

0

SPAIN

BRITAIN

BELGIUM

GERMANY

FRANCE

PARIS

(German occupied)

SWITZ

VICHY

ITALY

(Vichy)

BORDEAUX

MARSEILLES

SPAIN

④

OPERATION SEALION

The German High Command was convinced that after the fall of France Britain would sue for peace. When no peace initiative was forthcoming Hitler planned a seaborne invasion, Operation Sealion.

The Germans set aside an army of some twenty divisions for the operation, the safe arrival of which depended on the Luftwaffe rather than the small German navy. If Göring's men could destroy the RAF and drive the Royal Navy out of the English Channel, the invaders had a good chance of landing without unacceptable casualties. Once ashore, they would have had to deal with some twenty-five divisions, woefully short of modern weapons, transport, and tanks, spread out from Kent to Cromarty, with no certainty of where the enemy would land.

The Germans collected a fleet of barges and steamers in the Channel ports; many of these were hurriedly adapted for beach landings and troops were trained in the techniques which would be required. But throughout August and the beginning of September they waited at ten days' readiness to sail while the Luftwaffe fought to gain control of the skies over the Channel. By the middle of September the date of the invasion had already been postponed three times, and on 2 October the invasion troops were stood down. On 12 October, when it was obvious that the Luftwaffe had failed, the operation was postponed until 1941, and the troops began moving away from their embarkation points.

June 1940

German expansion in Europe

Above: London Home Guards on parade as Britain prepares to meet a German invasion

Opposite above: Marshal Göring and his staff look across the narrow channel at the white cliffs of Dover

Opposite below: German troops practising with assault boats for Operation Sealion

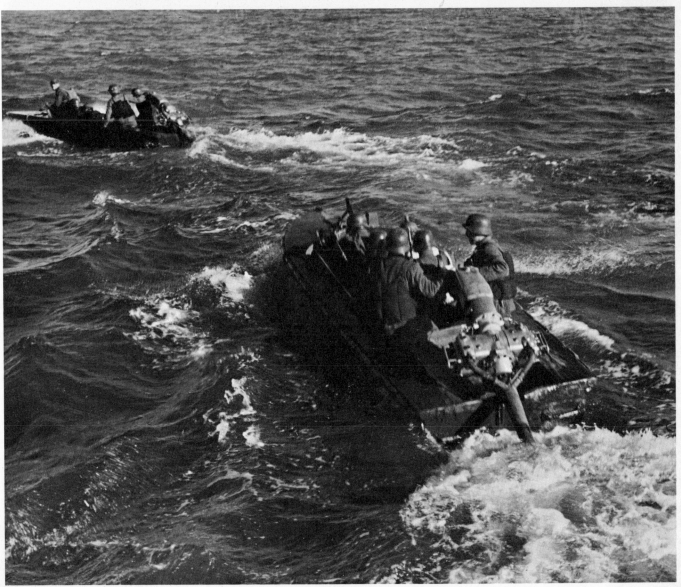

THE BATTLE OF BRITAIN

German airpower was now at its height with eleven fighter groups, two fighter-bomber groups and ten bomber groups, 2,830 planes in all flying from bases in northern France and the Low Countries. Against these forces Fighter Command had on 8 August between 6–700 fighters, organized in fifty-five operational squadrons and directed by the newly-established radar chains.

The Battle of Britain began on 10 July when German bombers attacked merchant convoys in the Channel. On 16 July Hitler issued his instructions for Operation Sealion, to be completed by the middle of August. Barges were assembled in the Channel ports and the Luftwaffe turned its attention to the airfields of south-east England. In the first ten days of their August campaign the Luftwaffe lost several times the RAF loss of 153 planes. By 5 September casualties were beginning to make the Germans lose sight of their true objective, the destruction of the RAF. Had they persevered against the airfields their greater numbers must eventually have worn down the slender reserves of Fighter Command but at the crucial moment their targets were shifted. On 7 September came the first mass attack on London and the opening of the campaign against British towns and civilian morale. German casualties continued to mount and the bombers stopped coming over in the daytime on about 5 October. On 12 October Hitler cancelled Operation Sealion. The Blitz continued by night until the Luftwaffe was sent east to Russia, but the threat of invasion had passed.

Above: A Dornier bomber shot down over southern England

Right: Air crew walking out to their Spitfires

RAF FIGHTER COMMAND
- ⓗ COMMAND HEADQUARTERS
- Ⓖ GROUP HEADQUARTERS
- ⊙ SECTOR STATION
- ● FIGHTER STATION
- ✛ LOW-LEVEL RADAR STATION
- ✛⊕ HIGH-LEVEL RADAR STATION
- ─ ─ COMMAND BOUNDARY
- TOWNS BOMBED

LUFTWAFFE BASES
- BOMBER
- STUKA (DIVE-BOMBER)
- FIGHTER (Bf109)
- ⊙ TWIN-ENGINED FIGHTER (Bf110)
- ─ ─ COMMAND BOUNDARY

MILES		100
0		
KILOMETRES		150
0		

GLASGOW

FIRTH OF FORTH

BELFAST

NEWCASTLE Ⓖ SUNDERLAND
Fighter Command 13 Group
MIDDLESBROUGH

Luftflotte 5
(from Norway and Sweden)

N O R T H   S E A

HULL

Cover of
low-level
radar (500 ft)

Cover of
high-level
radar (15,000 ft)

LIVERPOOL   MANCHESTER
SHEFFIELD

Ⓖ NOTTINGHAM
Fighter Command 12 Group

NORWICH

BIRMINGHAM
COVENTRY

Debden   IPSWICH   Martlesham

ROTTERDAM

SWANSEA
CARDIFF

Stanmore
Northolt   LONDON
Uxbridge Ⓖ   ⓗ   Hornchurch   North Weald
Croydon   Rochford
Biggin Hill   *THAMES ESTUARY*
Kenley   West   Manston
Malling   CANTERBURY
Lympne   Hawkinge

GHENT   ANTWERP

B E L G I U M

BRISTOL   Ball
BATH

Fighter Command 10 Group
EXETER

Fighter Command 11 Group
Middle Wallop

SOUTHAMPTON

Tangmere
PORTSMOUTH
VENTNOR

CALAIS

LILLE

Luftflotte 3

PLYMOUTH

E N G L I S H   C H A N N E L

AMIENS

CHERBOURG

LE HAVRE

F R A N C E

■ **PARIS**

Luftflotte 2

RENNES

31

ACTIONS IN THE FRENCH OVERSEAS EMPIRE

After the surrender of France, a major question-mark hung over the fate of her powerful and well-equipped navy. In June 1940, the French had six battleships, with one more nearing completion, and two battle-cruisers. Two of the battleships were in British ports and one was at Alexandria. Of the remainder, two battleships and the battle-cruisers were at Mers El Kebir near Oran, while the new battleship, *Richelieu*, was at Dakar. Her uncompleted sister ship, *Jean Bart*, had left her dock at St Nazaire the day before the Germans arrived and reached Casablanca safely. It was essential for the British that these ships should not fall into German hands for they would more than double German naval strength making up for her losses in the Norwegian campaign. They therefore demanded that the French ships should sail to British harbours, but when the armistice negotiations were completed it was laid down that the French fleet should be disarmed in home waters under German supervision.

Although Admiral Darlan, the French minister of marine, issued instructions that no ship should be allowed to fall intact into German hands, the British were disinclined to risk the possibility that the Germans might try to ignore the armistice regulations and seize the fleet. On 27 June 1940 it was decided that the French ships must be prevented from returning to their home ports. The next day, Vice-Admiral Sir James Somerville was given command of Force H – the battle-cruiser *Hood*, two battleships, and an aircraft-carrier – based on Gibraltar, and on 1 July he was instructed to obtain the surrender or destruction of the French naval units at Mers El Kebir.

Force H arrived off Oran on the morning of 3 July (**Map 1**), and an ultimatum was presented to the French commander, Admiral Gensoul, to join the British, demilitarize his ships, or scuttle them where they lay. He refused to reply, but radioed the message to

Darlan, prepared his ships for action, and called on all other French units for help. After the time limit for acceptance had been extended, the British opened fire at 1800 hours. Within fifteen minutes the battleship *Bretagne* had blown up, the *Provence* had been beached, and the battle-cruiser *Dunkerque* disabled. The battle-cruiser *Strasbourg* managed to escape to sea, and although the British gave chase she reached Toulon safely. No action was taken against the unarmed *Jean Bart* at Casablanca, but the *Richelieu* at Dakar was torpedoed and immobilized on 8 July by aircraft from HMS *Hermes*.

However, Vichy occupation of Dakar still seemed to pose a threat to Allied communications in the mid-Atlantic, and so it was decided to send Free French troops – Force M under General De Gaulle – to occupy Dakar and then take over the rest of the French West African territories. This sailed from England on 31 August (**Map 1**), and, after refuelling at Freetown, arrived off Dakar on 23 September. It had been hoped that the Vichy forces would not resist, but they opened fire on the British ships, and a three-day bombardment ensued in which the British battleship *Resolution* was badly damaged. When it became obvious that an unopposed landing could not be made, the operation was abandoned.

Another area still held by Vichy forces which posed a direct threat to the Allies was the French mandate territory of Syria and Lebanon. In April 1941, a nationalist revolt in Iran had led the British to intervene to protect the oilfields, and it was thought that German infiltration of neighbouring Syria might not only rekindle this but could lead to unrest in Egypt. After the fall of Greece and Crete it was decided that Vichy control in the area must be broken. On 8 June a force under General Sir Henry Maitland-Wilson consisting of 7 Australian Division, 4 Indian Brigade, and the Free French Division invaded

the area from Palestine and Trans-Jordan (**Map 2**). it was outnumbered by Vichy forces and it was only after fairly heavy fighting that Damascus was taken on 21 June (**Map 3**). As the Allied troops pushed on north further British forces from Iraq moved in to link up with them, and on 11 July an armistice was signed which placed Syria and Lebanon in Free French hands.

Opposite above: The French fleet under fire at Mers El Kebir

Opposite below: British troops crossing the Lebanese border

THE WAR IN THE MEDITERRANEAN

Opposite: An s s motorised column in
the streets of a Yugoslav town

It took the Axis powers no more than seven months to overrun the Balkans, a necessary preliminary not only to the invasion of Russia, but to the control of the Eastern Mediterranean.

Rumania and Bulgaria, so far from offering any resistance, joined the Axis camp. Greece and Yugoslavia had the courage to defend themselves, and Winston Churchill, the embodiment of pugnacity, was not slow to support them. General Sir Alan Brooke, Chief of the Imperial General Staff, was appalled by the risks the British courted by frittering away their resources. 'Are we', he asked in his diary, 'to have "Salonika supporters" as in the last war? Why will politicians never learn the simple principle of concentration of force at the vital point and the avoidance of dispersal of effort?' But Churchill's policy had powerful advocates in Anthony Eden, the war minister, and General Archibald Wavell, the Commander-in-Chief in the Middle East. The latter, with his profound interest in military history, seems to have imagined that the Balkans might prove in Hitler's day to be a theatre of war comparable with Spain and Portugal during the Peninsular War (1808–14). In such an inhospitable country even the most formidable army of modern times might lose its momentum.

On the face of it the Allies could put a substantial army of fifty-one divisions in the field: twenty-eight Yugoslav, twenty Greek, and three British. It may be recalled, for purposes of comparison, that in 1940 the Allies on the Western Front had a total of 146 divisions. That great host had been notably ill-co-ordinated, but, though they were not deployed to advantage, it had not lacked tanks. Its air cover had been thin except where it was within striking distance of England. The Allies in the Balkans had no overall headquarters, they were not well provided with either tanks or aircraft and their infantry divisions, for the most part, were armed with obsolescent

weapons and depended upon horse-drawn transport.

At sea they enjoyed some advantages. With Alexandria, Suda Bay (Crete), and Benghazi in their hands the Allies had firm strategic control of the eastern Mediterranean, and in combat with the British the Royal Italian Navy had no advantage save numbers; for in Admiral Sir Andrew Cunningham the British had a naval commander of the first rank. Only when compelled to operate within the range of shore-based German aircraft were the British warships at a disadvantage.

On 28 October 1940 Mussolini's ambassador in Athens presented an ultimatum. Without awaiting a reply the Italian army in Albania, 162,000 men in ten divisions under General Sebastiano Visconti-Prasca, was launched on the invasion of Greece. Mussolini hoped for a victory, and a cheap one at that. Generally speaking, he reasoned, a nation of forty-five million could be counted on to crush one of some seven million. Moreover, the Greek defences, the Metaxas Line, was constructed to meet an attack from Bulgaria, not Albania.

Great Britain reacted promptly with promises of support, but beyond establishing RAF bases in Crete there was little she could do to help.

November is the beginning of the rainy season in Greece, and it was scarcely prudent of Mussolini to launch his attack at that time of year. But, of course, the weather was equally inclement to both sides.

The Italian plan was to cut off the Greeks in Macedonia and in Thessaly from those in the Epirus. This they hoped to achieve by advancing up the valley of the Vijosë and the capture of Metsova. Despite initial progress it did not work. The Greek army, some 150,000 strong under General Alexander Papagos fought with real tenacity. In one action, armed with the obsolescent Boys anti-tank rifle, a weapon designed for the conditions of 1918, a consignment of which had been flown in by the RAF, the Greeks succeeded in knocking out nine tanks.

One of the better Italian divisions (3 Alpini) was trapped in the Pindus gorges and lost 5,000 men. On the Albanian front the Greeks seized the initiative and astounded the invaders by capturing Koritsa and a vast amount of sorely needed arms and equipment. By the end of December a quarter of Albania was in Greek hands, and the RAF was bombing Valona and Brindisi. Marshal Pietro Badoglio, the Italian Chief-of-Staff, resigned.

Nothing daunted Mussolini replaced Visconti-Prasca with General Ubaldo Soddu (9 November) and declared 'We'll break the backs of the Greeks, and we don't need any help'.

His friend Hitler thought otherwise and on 13 December issued Directive No. 20 for 'Undertaking Marita' in which he stated that: 'In the light of the threatening situation in Albania it is doubly important to frustrate English efforts to establish, behind the protection of a Balkan front, an air base which would threaten Italy in the first place and, incidentally, the Rumanian oilfields.'

It was his intention to concentrate some twenty-four divisions, under Field-Marshal List, in southern Rumania. When the weather improved, probably in March, this force would move across Bulgaria and overrun the northern coast of the Aegean, and if necessary the whole mainland of Greece. Airborne troops would seize English bases in the islands.

Once the British had been denied their foothold in Europe the force would be switched to 'new employment'.

By January 1941 the German X Air Corps, operating from Sicily, was attacking British naval forces in the Mediterranean. Operations to save Tripoli and Albania were planned, but though Mussolini was prepared to accept the support of the *Afrika Korps* he could not stomach the idea of being deprived of his Albanian triumph, and at a conference on 19 and 20 January

induced the Führer to modify his orders.

In March Germany compelled Bulgaria to join the Tripartite Pact, which Germany, Italy, and Japan had signed on 27 September 1940. In addition on the 24th the Yugoslavs were forced to join the Pact, but public opinion rebelled against this affront and on 26 March a *coup* led by General Simovitch overthrew the régime of Prince Paul, the young King's uncle. Britain welcomed this brave attempt with enthusiasm, while the relentless Germans resolved to fell both Greece and Yugoslavia at a blow.

On 6 April 1941 they struck and by 1 June the campaign had ended in disaster for the Allies. There are those, General Guderian among them, who thought that British intervention in Greece had the effect of delaying the German invasion of Russia (22 June). Others have argued that any delay was due to the weather. But upon reflection there really seems no reason why operations in Russia should not have been opened at least as early as 15 May, the original date set for 'Barbarossa'. If that could be proved it would follow that the British intervention, however costly, was not only justified, but decisive. On balance it seems that the pugnacity of Mr Churchill, and the optimism of Mr Eden and General Wavell, is to be commended and that General Brooke's more rigid interpretation of the principles of war was somewhat unimaginative.

Opposite above: Luftwaffe aircrew at a forward airfield in Yugoslavia

Above right: Wrecked British tanks left behind in a Greek town

Above left: A German anti-tank gun in action in Yugoslavia

Bottom left: German troops in the Greek town of Larissa

THE ITALIAN ATTACK ON GREECE

In August 1940 Mussolini demanded that Greece should renounce the guarantee of her independence which had been made by Great Britain in 1939. When this was refused, he accused her of 'un-neutral' attitudes, and began to concentrate 162,000 men in Albania on the Greek frontier. To this array the Greeks could oppose no more than 75,000 men.

On 28 October an ultimatum was presented and before it had expired, Italian troops had crossed the border. The Italian plan was to push down the valleys of the Vijosë and the Thyamis to capture Metsova and cut off the Greek forces in Thessaly and Macedonia from those in the Epirus. At first progress was rapid but the Greeks mobilized swiftly, and between 8 and 10 November they turned back 3 Alpini Division in the Pindus mountains and advanced on Koritsa which they retook on 22 November. Thereafter they pushed on until by the beginning of March the front had stabilized with almost half Albania in Greek hands.

The Germans felt obliged to come to the help of their allies but their original plan to leave Albania to the Italians and to attack Greece after persuading Bulgaria and Yugoslavia to allow free passage of troops, was thwarted by a coup in Yugoslavia which overthrew the Regency. The Germans now decided to invade both Yugoslavia and Greece, and there was some delay while the new campaign was mounted. Meanwhile a British force of 56,657 men was being landed in Greece.

Above: Italian troops landing in an Albanian harbour

Below: Italian infantry in action on the Greek border

Above: Italian artillery fighting in the mountains of Albania

Below: Italian officers captured by the Greeks are taken away for questioning

DURRËS
■ TIRANE
Ital Ninth Army
ELBASAN
PRILEP
YUGOSLAVIA
Shkumbin
L. Okhrida
MONASTIR
POGRADEC
9 Dec
L. Prespa
Devoll
BERAT
FLÓRINA
ALBANIA
MESKOPOLIS
KORCÉ
22 Nov
Macedonia
KASTORIA
Vijosë
VLORË
(VALONA)
Ital Eleventh Army
KLISURA
10 Jan
Aliakmon
TEPELENË
ERSEKË
13 Nov
Drinos
Vijosë
HIMARË
23 Dec
KORITSA
ARGYROKASTRON
SARANDE
6 Dec
Pindus Mountains
METSOVA
Corfu
Epirus
Thyamis
IOÁNNINA
TRIKKALA
PARAMITHIA
GREECE

A
D
R
I
A
T
I
C

S
E
A

▶ ITALIAN ATTACKS, 28 OCT/8 NOV 1940
◀ GREEK COUNTEROFFENSIVE
--- STABILISED FRONT, 1 MARCH 1941
✠ RAF AIRFIELDS
LAND OVER 3000 FEET

0 —————— MILES —————— 80
0 —————— KILOMETRES —————— 120

THE INVASION OF YUGOSLAVIA

On 6 April 1941, the Germans invaded Yugoslavia with 33 divisions, six of them armoured. The Yugoslavs had 28 divisions, three armoured, strung out along the border with only one in reserve. The German plan was that the Twelfth Army in Bulgaria would thrust towards Skopje and Monastir to cut off the Yugoslavs from Greek help. Two days later, von Kleist's First Panzergroup was to advance towards Nis and Belgrade, and on 12 April, Second Army from Austria and Hungary and XLI Motorised Corps from Rumania would invade towards Belgrade. The attack began with heavy bombing of Belgrade, lasting two days, and on the Yugoslav airforce which was almost totally destroyed. On the ground the advance went as planned: in the south Twelfth Army swiftly reached its objectives, and the Yugoslavs were still unready when Kleist's Panzers thrust towards Nis which was reached on the first day. By 12 April the German columns had converged on Belgrade, which surrendered that evening. The Italians had advanced into Yugoslavia on the 11th, and worked their way down the coast to Dubrovnik. Yugoslavia sued for peace on 14 April and the capitulation was signed on 17 April.

Opposite above: Armour of Kleist's First Panzergroup advancing towards Belgrade

Above: German infantry support guns in action against a Yugoslav strongpoint

Right: German tanks passing obstacles on the Yugoslav border

40

GERMANY
Austria
HUNGARY
Danube
BUDAPEST

Ger Second Army
(Weichs)

XLIX Mtn Corps
LI Corps
GRAZ

XLVI Pz Corps
Drava

Hun Third Army

SZEGED

RUMANIA

TIMISOARA

Ital Second Army
(Ambrosio)

LJUBLJANA
TRIESTE
FIUME
ZAGREB
10 Apr

Sava

NOVI SAD

XLI Motorised Corps

VENICE

ZEMUN
BELGRADE 12 Apr

TURNU-SEVERIN

FLORENCE

ZARA
(Ital)
SIBENIK
SPLIT

YUGOSLAVIA

KRAGUJEVAC
UZICE
KRUSEVAC

Danube

ITALY

SARAJEVO
16 Apr

Drina

NIS
8 Apr

Morava

XI Corps
XIV Pz Corps

First Pzgrp
(Kleist)

SOFIA
BULG.

DUBROVNIK
17 Apr

XL Pz Corps

Ger Twelfth Army (List)

Slovenia
Croatia
BELGRADE
Bosnia & Herce-govina
Serbia
Montenegro
Macedonia

ADRIATIC SEA

4 Italian divs

SKOPJE
Apr

Vardar

XXX Corps

XVIII Corps

ALBANIA
TIRANE

STRUMICA

Ital Ninth & Eleventh Armies

MONASTIR

THESSALONIKI

The states of Yugoslavia

BRINDISI

6 Apr

GREECE

GERMAN ATTACKS
ITALIAN   "
HUNGARIAN   "

0   MILES   150
0   KILOMETRES   250

THE INVASION OF GREECE

At the beginning of April 1941, the main part of the Greek army, fourteen divisions, was facing the Italians in Albania. The British force of four divisions and a Polish brigade, and four Greek divisions were deployed to cover the Aliákmon line and the Monastir Gap (see map), while three and a half Greek divisions guarded the Metaxas Line further north covering Macedonia and the Rupel Pass.

The German aim was to cut the Allies in two by piercing the centre and isolating the army in Albania. At the same time an attack through the Rupel Pass to breach the Metaxas Line would cut off Greek forces in Thrace, while another attack from Strumica round the end of the line would capture Thessaloniki from the north-east.

The German invasion began on 6 April, the same day as that of Yugoslavia. The XXX Corps moved into Thrace, three divisions attacked the Metaxas Line frontally, and 2 Panzer Division made a successful thrust to Strumica. The rapid collapse of the Yugoslavs unhinged the position of the Allied forces holding the Metaxas Line for 2 Panzer Division now advanced towards Thessaloniki which was reached on 9 April. Meanwhile, the German XL Panzer Corps had reached Monastir and was heading towards the Gap. The Allies fell back to an intermediate position on the Aliàkmon – Klissoura river line, aiming to hold the German advance on the Aliákmon–Venetikos river line. On 10 April XL Panzer Corps advanced through the Monastir Gap but was held north of the Aliákmon for two days. However, its pressure was too great, and the Allied Command prepared to defend the Servia and Olympus Passes and the coast road. The Germans were harassed as they advanced on these new positions, but their control of the air, and the speed of their armour meant that they were only temporarily delayed. Their main attacks on the Servia Pass began on 16 April and by the next day they were through and aiming for Thermopylai where the Allies were planning their last major defence line while an evacuation from the Peloponnese was begun.

The Germans were delayed by supply problems and it was not until 22 April that they began to reach the position. On the morning of 24 April the Allied evacuation got under way while the main German attack on Thermopylai was launched. This was held during the day and on the night of 24/25 April the Allied defenders were moved back through the last line at Thebes. The Germans reached this on the 26th and were halted by heavy artillery fire, but that evening the defenders fell back to Rafina and Porto Rafti where they were evacuated on 28 April.

Meanwhile, the Germans had captured the Corinth bridge by a parachute assault on 26 April. Although the bridge was subsequently blown up, their forces were soon fanning out across the Peloponnese. The British managed to evacuate some 43,000 men before the German capture of Kalamata on 28 April closed the last embarkation port. But they left behind all their heavy *matériel* and 11,000 men.

Below: British troops being evacuated from the Peloponnese

SOFIA

YUGOSLAVIA

Twelfth Army
(List)

KYUSTENDIL

PLOVDIV

Maritza

KRIVA PALANKA

DELČEVO

XL Pz Corps

B U L G A R I A

SHKODËR

Drin

SKOPJE
6 Apr

KOČANI

Vardar

NEVROKOP

ALBANIA

TIRANË

VELES
6 Apr

Struma

XVIII Corps

XXX Corps

DURRËS

PRILEP

STRUMICA

Rupel Pass

Nestos

EKHÍNOS

T h r a c e

ELBASAN

Shkumbin

L Okhrida

MONASTIR
9 Apr

DOJRAN

Beles Mts

SÉRRAI

DRÁMA

XANTHI

KOMOTINÍ

Monastir
Gap

L Prespa

Axios

KILKIS

KAVALLA

ALEXANDROÚPOLIS

Ital Ninth
Army

L Vegorritis

EDHESSA

M a c e d o n i a

Gr Second
Army

THASOS
16 Apr

Ital Eleventh
Army

FLÓRINA

AMINDAION

VÉROIA

THESSALONIKI
9 Apr

SAMOTHRACE
19 Ap

VALONA

KORCE

KLISSOÚRA

PTOLEMAÍS

Aliakmon

Piéria Óri

KATERÍNI

LÍMNOS

TEPELENË

Vijose

KOZÁNI

LESBOS
8 May

23 April

SERVIA
16 April

Mt Olympus

GJIROKASTER

Venetikos

PINDUS MOUNTAINS

'W' Force
(Wilson)

Gr First
Army

SARANDË

Mt Ossa

CORFU

IOÁNNINA
20 Apr

TRIKKALA

LÁRISA
19 Apr

Æ G E A N

Surrenders
23 April

PARAMITHIÁ

Pinios

PLAIN OF
THESSALY

VÓLOS

SKÍROS

ÁRTA

G R E E C E

S E A

KHÍOS
4 May

LEVKÁS

LAMIA

Thermopylai

MOLOS

Akheloos

BRÁLLOS

Evvoia
(Euboea)

20 April

MESOLÓNGION
26 Apr

THEBES

I O N I A N

Gulf of Corinth

ÁNDROS

KEFALLINÍA

PÁTRAI

ATHENS
27 Apr

RAFINA

PIRAEUS

PORTO RAFTI

TÍNOS

ZÁKINTHOS

CORINTH
26 Apr

PÍRGOS

Peloponnesos

NÁUPLIA

S E A

TRÍPOLIS

NÁXOS

KALAMATA
28 Apr

MONEMVASÍA

MÍLOS

C Matapan

KÍTHIRA

British evacuation
routes

CANEA

*Suda
Bay*

HERÁKLION

CRETE

STABILISED FRONT IN ALBANIA, 6 APRIL 1941
METAXAS LINE
ALIAKMON LINE
THE FRONT AT DATES SHOWN
GERMAN AIRBORNE LANDING, 26 APRIL
HEIGHT IN FEET

OVER 6000
3000–6000
1200–3000
UNDER 1200

0   MILES   100
0   KILOMETRES   160

THE ATTACK ON CRETE

Following the German invasion of Greece, Crete was of major strategic importance – from it the Allies could threaten the Balkans while the Axis could strike at shipping using the Suez Canal and at Allied bases in Egypt and Libya. On Crete the British had about 30,000 men commanded by Major-General Freyberg VC, supported by nine tanks and thirty-five aircraft. There were in addition two weak and ill-equipped Greek divisions.

Lacking naval control of the area, the Germans aimed to capture the island by airborne assault. Their airborne forces numbered 22,750 paratroops and glider-borne troops under the command of Fliegerkorps XI, and were supported by 280 bombers, 150 dive-bombers, and 180 fighters. The plan was to attack in two waves – the first, in the morning to capture Máleme airport, Caneá town, and Suda port, the second later in the day to take the towns and airports of Rétimo and Heráklion. The key to success was swift capture of an airport so that reinforcements could be flown in.

The landings began at first light on 20 May 1941: after heavy attacks, part of the assault regiment led by General Meindl landed around Máleme airfield in the 5 New Zealand Brigade area, and the remainder came down astride the Alikianou–Caneá road near Galatas to attack Caneá. Around Máleme the situation swiftly became confused and the New Zealanders were hindered in co-ordinating their defences by incessant air attacks and inadequate radio equipment. By the end of the day, despite the massive German casualties, 22 Battalion was forced to withdraw east away from the airfield towards 23 Battalion. Near Galatas the Germans had been held and the landings which took place at Rétimo and Heráklion also failed to capture their airfields.

However, the next day the Germans succeeded in clearing Máleme airfield

and were not immediately counter-attacked. When this did take place, it met very heavy opposition and failed to retake the airfield. The New Zealanders were withdrawn towards Platanias and the two German forces began to co-ordinate their attacks towards Caneá. The second phase of the battle was the Allied attempt to hold on to Suda Bay, while the Germans tried to outflank their positions. On 25 May Galatas was occupied, and on the 27th Freyberg realized that the Allied position was untenable and began to withdraw to the south. Meanwhile the Germans occupied Caneá and Suda and pressed on to relieve their forces at Rétimo and Heráklion. During 29–30 May a bridgehead was maintained around Sfakia to allow evacuation, but the Rétimo garrison was forced to surrender. The next day the last evacuations took place and the Germans entered Sfakia. Nearly 15,000 Allied troops had been saved, but 18,000 remained behind. The Germans suffered some 7,000 killed – nearly one-third their landing force – and were never again to mount an airborne operation on such a scale.

Right: German assault troops move away from their dropping zone

Opposite above: Paratroops advance through a village

Opposite below: Suda Bay with shipping burning after a Luftwarfe attack

German airborne and paratroop landings, 20 May

Night, 31 May, Final Commonwealth forces evacuated from Crete

CRETE

COMMONWEALTH/GREEK DISPOSITIONS, MORNING 20 MAY

GERMAN AIRBORNE & PARATROOP LANDINGS, 20 MAY

DIRECTION OF GERMAN ADVANCE

THE NORTH AFRICAN CAMPAIGN

The war in the desert presented conditions and problems all its own, for none of the combatants on either side were really prepared for desert warfare. Scorching days and bitter nights; lack of cover and tactical features which meant that places at which defensive positions could be prepared were few and far apart; navigational difficulties; unaccustomed ailments – all these contributed to the problems which each side were compelled to face. The Italians, although more or less accustomed to the climate had rearmed first of all the European powers and their weapons were already obsolescent in 1940. The British for their part were more or less acclimatized thanks to the fact that numbers of their regulars, officers and men, had seen a good deal of service in India, Palestine, and Egypt. Quite apart from the fact that they were used to the hot sun, there were eccentrics among them who had actually made long trips into the desert and had devised navigational aids. These flashes of private initiative were to be of great advantage when places like the Siwa Oasis, and units like the Long Range Desert Group, began to be of tactical importance. It was greatly to the credit of the methodical Germans that, with little previous experience of conditions in the Middle East, they were able to produce at short notice their admirable Afrika Korps.

However, the greatest of all the problems in the desert war, and the one which was eventually to prove crucial, was the age-old military essential of supply. The distance between the main Axis supply base at Tripoli, and the Allied bases around Alexandria was 1,500 miles of largely waterless and roadless desert with very few intermediate harbours at which new depots could be established. All essentials, petrol, water, ammunition, and food, had to be brought up along rough and highly vulnerable lines of communication.

This accentuated the basic military axiom that an advancing army becomes increasingly vulnerable as its supply lines stretch, and a retreating one becomes correspondingly stronger in proportion as it falls back on its basis. Twice the Axis and twice the Allied forces found that after huge advances they were so overextended that an enemy counterattack meant not a limited withdrawal to a defensive position, but a precipitate retreat across the bulge of Cyrenaica where every possible defensive position was vulnerable to outflanking moves.

Ultimately, the victor in the desert war would be the side which got the most and best supplies in the shortest time. On both occasions that Rommel began his great advances Axis domination of the centre of the Mediterranean had meant that his forces had received adequate fuel and equipment. But by the time the Afrika Korps reached El Alamein Eighth Army had never been better placed despite its apparently perilous position. Its supply lines were only 70 miles long and it was receiving petrol and equipment in unprecedented quantities. Rommel was now 370 miles from even his most forward base at Tobruk, and Allied domination of the sea and air meant that few supplies were even getting across the Mediterranean let alone forward to his troops.

Also, Rommel had an additional problem in that the enormous demands of the German armies fighting in Russia meant that little new material could be spared for what many at Supreme Headquarters increasingly saw as a sideshow – a successful but nonetheless basically peripheral campaign far away from the truly vital fronts. In contrast, the Western Allies had now accepted that their first major thrust against the Axis must come from the Mediterranean, and Eighth Army, as the means of clearing the North African shore, was receiving the pick of the new equipment available.

When the Allies broke through at El

Alamein it was inevitable that Rommel would have to fall back at least as far as El Agheila where Eighth Army had twice been halted. But the Allied landings in Algeria and their advance into Tunisia introduced a new factor – not just Rommel's lines of communication but his very bases were directly threatened. He had to fall right back to protect them, and it is a measure of the supply difficulties that they encountered that Eighth's Army's pursuit was so slow and tentative.

The war in North Africa fell into three distinct phases. In the first Wavell, though against desperately long odds, had very much the better of the Italians. Major-General O'Connor's brilliant offensive, the first series of Allied victories, had a very important moral effect.

The second phase was the Rommel era, whose opening coincided with Wavell's ill-starred, but unavoidable campaign in Greece. It was a phase when the British had important successes, but when, on the whole, the Axis succeeded in baffling their opponents, and delivering telling blows such as the capture of Tobruk. British generals of real distinction, Wavell, Cunningham, and Auchinleck were unable to master the redoubtable Rommel.

Rommel was a very stylish corps

commander with splendid qualities of leadership. Of Bir Hacheim he writes: 'I frequently took over command of the assault forces myself and seldom in Africa was I given such a hard-fought struggle.' The fact is that he was still the ardent platoon and company commander who had so greatly distinguished himself in the First World War. In most armies a corps commander who exposed himself in such fashion would be roundly condemned by the pundits.

In phase three, with Alexander as commander-in-chief in the Middle East and Montgomery in command of Eighth Army, the tide quickly changed against the Axis. The defensive battle of Alam Halfa, followed, when he was ready, by the battle from which Viscount Montgomery took his title, marked the turn of the tide. As Winston Churchill put it – not without a measure of exaggeration – 'Before Alamein we never had a victory. After Alamein we never had a defeat.' But the end in Africa did not come quickly. Despite the landings in North Africa, Operation Torch, which began only four days after the successful conclusion of El Alamein, the Germans and Italians succeeded in holding out until May 1943.

Once Montgomery had taken over, Eighth Army changed its style

completely. Its new commander was swift to detect its strengths and weaknesses, and was severely critical of its state of training. 'Most commanders,' he thought, 'had come to the fore by skill in fighting and because no better were available: many were above their ceiling, and few were good trainers . . . The Eighth Army had suffered some eighty thousand casualties since it was formed, and little time had been spent in training the replacements.' When one recalls that O'Connor had begun his offensive with but 30,000 men one can appreciate the magnitude of the problem. Battle experience is in itself a form of training, and Eighth Army had seen plenty of fighting. On the other hand no battle is like the one before, and soldiers are all too prone to draw general tactical rules from their own particular experiences. That can be a dangerous snare for the unwary, for the truth is that every military problem whether strategical, or logistical, must be treated on its own merits, the factors analysed, and the plan made regardless of preconcieved ideas and prejudices.

Compared with Rommel Montgomery, was altogether less of a paladin: more the professional. General Eisenhower, who knew him better than most wrote: 'General Montgomery had no superior in two most important characteristics. He quickly develops among British enlisted men an intense devotion and admiration – the greatest personal asset a commander can possess. Montgomery's other outstanding characteristic is his tactical ability in what might be called the "prepared" battle . . . He is careful, meticulous and certain.' The British soldiers who fought under Montgomery soon came to believe that, whilst they served under him, they simply could not be beaten. It was not that they considered themselves supermen. It was just that they credited him with knowing everything, caring for their welfare, and, thanks to expert co-ordination of the various arms

and services, reducing their casualties to the minimum.

In July 1943 Hitler gave it as his opinion that the protracted defence of Tunisia postponed the invasion of Europe by six months and kept Italy in the Axis. It cost the Axis 250,415 men, counting only prisoners of war. It was Hitler's view that, without the prolonged resistance in North Africa, the Allies would have been able to land in Italy unopposed and push forward to the Brenner, at a time when Germany as a result of Stalingrad 'would not have had a single man available to put there'. His argument is totally unconvincing. The men and tanks he lost in Tunisia could have been deployed to very much greater advantage for the defence of Sicily and Italy.

The campaign in North Africa ended in a triumph for the Allies, and not least for the Americans who emerged with an army greatly improved in tactical efficiency. By fighting in North Africa, where they could not deploy anything like their full strength, the Germans presented the Allies with a substantial victory, at a time when they were building up their forces for the invasion of Europe. Beyond question the experience won in North Africa was a pearl of great price for the British and for the Americans. To have attempted the invasion of Italy or Normandy in the teeth of the Wehrmacht, with inexperienced troops and commanders whose latest campaign – if any – had been Dunkirk, would have been to court disaster. The Allied armies which invaded Europe in 1943 or 1944 would have been raw indeed without the veterans of Africa.

Opposite above: Men of the Afrika Korps at El Agheila

Centre: A 25-pounder in action during the Battle of El Alamein

Above: German armour heads towards Mersa Bregha

WAVELL'S OPENING OFFENSIVE

In June 1940, the Italian forces in North Africa consisted of nine regular divisions, three 'Blackshirt' divisions, and two native divisions, a total of 250,000 men commanded by Marshal Graziani. Facing them the British had 36,000 men in Egypt and 27,000 in Palestine, under the overall command of General Sir Archibald Wavell. The force on the Egyptian border named Western Desert Force, consisted of 7 Armoured Division, 4 Indian Division, and the New Zealand Division, and was commanded by Major-General Richard O'Connor. As soon as war was declared, Western Desert Force began a series of raids which led the Italians to overestimate grossly the force facing them.

In September they moved cautiously over the border and occupied Sidi Barrani, but instead of continuing their advance they began to build a series of fortified camps south of the town (**Map 1**). The British plans for a counterattack were aided by the arrival of a major convoy with more than fifty infantry tanks. Wavell and General Wilson who commanded the forces in Egypt aimed for a limited attack to recapture Sidi Barrani. If successful, this could be extended to capture Tobruk and then to advance deeper into Libya.

The two fronts were separated by some 70 miles, and Western Desert Force began its approach on the night of 6 December, laagered in the desert on the 7th, and on the afternoon of the 8th reached 'Piccadilly'. The 7 Armoured Division then swung behind the Italian camps to cut the coast road at Buq Buq, while 4 Indian Division and 7 Royal Tank Regiment attacked Nibeiwa camp early on 9 December. This fell swiftly and by the evening Tummar West had also been taken. Meanwhile an independent column, Selby Force, had advanced along the coast road towards Sidi Barrani, and this was attacked and taken on the 10th with 38,000 Italian prisoners. Wavell now had to withdraw 4 Indian Division for service in the Sudan, and there was a delay while it was replaced by 6 Australian Division. This division began the next stage of the advance by capturing Bardia and another 38,000 Italians on 3 January 1941 (**Map 2**). The Italians had now lost almost eight divisions and were in full retreat, but the British supply lines were becoming over-stretched, and Wavell was being warned that he would soon have to withdraw troops to be sent to Greece However, Tobruk was taken on 22 January, Derna was abandoned by the Italians on the 29th and occupied the next day, and by 9 February the British reached El Agheila where they were halted. Despite the fact that there was no apparent resistance further west, forces now had to be withdrawn to Greece, and a thin covering force was left to guard the new territories.

Below: Italians surrendering during the capture of Tobruk

Opposite: A British tank passes destroyed Italian aircraft at El Adem

① SIDI BARRANI
10 Dec
Naval bombardment
BUQ BUQ
MAKTILA
9 Dec
TUMMAR W   TUMMAR E
NIBEIWA
9 Dec
7 Armd
Div
7 RTR & 4 Indian Div
RABIA
SOFAFI
'Piccadilly'
7/8 December 1940,
O'Connor's force
from Mersa Matruh
■ ITALIAN FORTIFIED CAMPS
0   MILES   20
0 KILOMETRES   30

② MEDITERRANEAN SEA
0   MILES   100
0 KILOMETRES   150
DERNA 30 Jan
BARCE
BENGHAZI   Jebel Akhdar   GAZALA
TOBRUK 22 Jan
BARDIA 3 Jan 1941
MECHILI   SOLLUM
BUQ BUQ
SIDI BARRANI 10 Dec 1940
GHEMINES   SOLUQ   EL ADEM   MERSA
FORT CAPUZZO   MATRUH
MSUS 4 Feb   BIR HACHEIM
BEDA FOMM   BIR EL RABIA
6/7 Feb   Cyrenaica   ABAR EL
AGEDABIA   KANAYSIS
EL AGHEILA   LIBYA   JARABUB   Qattara
9 Feb   EGYPT   Depression

THE ETHIOPIAN CAMPAIGN

With France out of the war, it seemed possible that Mussolini would use his African armies to expel Britain from her African territories and achieve complete control over the Mediterranean and Suez route to the Far East (**Map 1**). On paper his forces were impressive: in addition to the army in Libya there were 350,000 men in Ethiopia faced by 9,000 British in the Sudan, 8,500 in Kenya, 2,500 in Aden, and 1,500 in British Somaliland, a total of but 21,500. The campaigns in East Africa began with the conquest of British and French Somaliland (**Map 2**), which enabled the Italians to tighten their control of the southern entrance to the Red Sea. The small British garrison was swiftly overwhelmed, its survivors being evacuated from Berbera on 19 August On 2 December, General Wavell assigned the task of retaking Ethiopia to Lieutenant-Generals Sir William Platt, commanding the forces in the Sudan, and Sir Alan Cunningham, commanding those in Kenya. The Italians had overestimated British strength in the Sudan and failed to move against Khartoum. Border raids induced them to evacuate Kassala, and General Platt's offensive began earlier than planned on 19 January 1941 with an advance into Eritrea which forced the Italians back to the well-nigh impregnable fortress of Keren. This eventually fell on 27 March after severe fighting in which the British lost 4,000 men and the Italians 3,000. This defeat broke Italian resistance in Eritrea, and Asmara and Massawa were swiftly occupied.

Meanwhile Cunningham had begun his advance on 10 February, crossing the Juba river to occupy Kismaya on 16 February. The 275-mile advance to Mogadishu was made in less than three days against negligible resistance, and Cunningham asked for permission to advance on Harar via Jijiga – 774 miles overland. He moved off on 1 March and made his first contact with the Italians midway between Gorrahei and Jijiga before capturing the latter on 17 March. A small force from Aden retook Berbera on 16 March and pushed forward to link up with the main force. Addis Ababa was abandoned by the Italians on 4 April, and the British now thrust north-west towards Dessie to link up with an advance south from Eritrea. The remnants of the Italian army were entrenched at Amba Alagi and after two weeks of stubborn resistance the Duke of Aosta surrendered with the honours of war. The final operations were expeditions towards Jimma and Ghimbi south and west of Addis Ababa, and towards Gondar where the last Italian resistance ended on 27 November.

ITALIAN TERRITORIES
BRITISH TERRITORIES

Below: Abyssinian guerrillas firing on an Italian fort

Opposite above: South African troops cross the Juba river

Map 2 — 3 August 1940, Italians attack

GULF OF ADEN

ADEN

FR SOMALILAND

DJIBOUTI
ZEILA
5 Aug

ERIGAVO

BERBERA
19 Aug

BURAO

Tug Argan Pass

HARGEISA
5 Aug

BURAO

BRITISH SOMALILAND

HARAR

ABYSSINIA

ITALIAN SOMALILAND

3 August 1940, Italians attack

| 0 | MILES | 200 |
| 0 | KILOMETRES | 300 |

| 0 | MILES | 200 | 400 |
| 0 | KILOMETRES | 300 | 600 |

RED SEA

KARORA

19 January 1941,
Gen Platt's force
(4 and 5 Ind Divs
and Sudan Defence
Force) invades

KEREN 27 Mar

MASSAWA
8 Apr

SANA

ADEN PROTECTORATE

YEMEN

KHARTOUM

KASSALA

KERU

AGORDAT

BARENTU

ASMARA
1 Apr

ERITREA

27 November 1941,
Italian resistance
ends

ANGLO-
EGYPTIAN
SUDAN

GALLABAT

CHILGA

Takazze

Amba Alagi
16 May

ASSAB

ADEN

GULF OF ADEN

GONDAR

Lake Tana

DEBRA TABOR

FRENCH
SOMALILAND

DJIBOUTI
ZEILA

BERBERA
16 Mar

ERIGAVO

J Belaia

DESSIE
18 Apr

White Nile

Blue Nile

DEBRA MARKOS

ADDIS
DERRA

Awash

DIREDAWA 29 Mar

JIJIGA

HARGEISA
20 Mar

BRITISH
SOMALILAND

ADDIS ABABA
6 Apr

HARAR
17 Mar

Awash

GHIMBI

A B Y S S I N I A

JIMMA
21 June

SHASHAMANNA

GORRAHEI

Webbe Shibeli

ITALIAN
SOMALILAND

OBBIA

Omo

Bottego

SODDU

L Abaya

NEGELLI
21 Mar

Ganale Dorya

BELET UEN

YABELO

MEGA

L Rudolf

MOYALE

EL UACH

Juba

MOGADISHU
25 Feb

MARSABIT

WAJIR

UGANDA

Victoria
Nile

K E N Y A

10 February 1941,
Gen Cunningham's force
(11 and 12 African Divs
and 1 S African Div)
invades

KISMAYU

INDIAN OCEAN

Lake Victoria

ROMMEL'S FIRST OFFENSIVE

General Erwin Rommel arrived in Tripoli on 12 February 1941, and the first German troops began landing on 14 February. At the end of the month their patrols were clashing with the British near Sirte, and by the middle of March, Rommel had realized that not only had the British no further plans for attack, but that they were actually depleting their forces. All O'Connor's forces had been withdrawn and General Philip Neame vc was left to hold Libya with a two-brigade, 2 Armoured Division, 9 Australian Division, and an Indian motorised brigade at El Adem. Although a concerted attack by the Germans was not expected he had orders to fall back if necessary as no reinforcements were available.

Rommel struck on 24 March (**Map 1**) capturing El Agheila with almost no resistance. His 5 Light Division went on to attack the British 2 Armoured Division at Mersa Brega, and after fierce fighting was halted. But the British failed to counterattack and were then forced to pull back. By 2 April the Germans were at Agedabia with the choice of going north to Benghazi, north-east to Msus and Mechili, or east to Tengeder to threaten British supply lines. Wavell had first taken over direct command himself, and then brought in O'Connor to act as Neame's adviser.

Above: General Rommel meets his Italian opposite number General Gariboldi

On 4 April Rommel attacked in all three directions meeting little resistance since 2 Armoured Division had fallen back. The swiftest Axis formation was that in the south which reached Tengeder on 5 April and Mechili the next day although it was too weak to attack 3 Indian Brigade which had moved forward to occupy the place. The appearance of this German force threatened to cut the British supply lines, and 9 Australian Division began to withdraw from Derna to which it had already retreated from Benghazi. On 8 April the remnant of 2 Armoured Division, which had lost most of its tanks through mechanical failure, and 3 Indian Brigade were overwhelmed at Mechili.

Meanwhile the British were reinforcing Tobruk with the 7 Australian Division. The first German units arrived piecemeal on 10/11 April and an improvised attack on the 11th was driven off. It was not until 14 April that 5 Light Division made a major assault from the south (**Map 2**) but their initial penetration ran into heavy artillery fire and counterattacks and by the afternoon the Germans were forced to retreat. The situation now stabilized with Italians replacing the German units which were preparing to cross the Egyptian frontier. On 25 April the Germans struck at Halfaya Pass and by the next day had pushed the British back to the line Buq-Buq/Sofafi. On 30 April Rommel made a full-scale attempt to capture Tobruk, but though a salient was pushed into the western sector, after four days fighting it was contained.

Below: Armoured cars of the Afrika Korps during the swift German advance through Libya

Above: A British patrol moves through the barbed wire of the Tobruk perimeter

OPERATION BREVITY

After the occupation of Halfaya Pass by the Germans on 25 April, the situation stabilized while both sides concentrated on building up their forces. Wavell knew that without Halfaya he could not hope to mount any major operations to relieve Tobruk, and when he learned that a large convoy, 'Tiger', was bringing him additional tanks and aircraft, he gave Brigadier Gott the task of mounting an operation, 'Brevity', to recapture Halfaya. The attack was launched on 15 May against three points: the pass itself; Sollum and Fort Capuzzo; and the left flank. Halfaya Pass was swiftly taken and Fort Capuzzo seized after heavy fighting. Rommel thought that Brevity was the beginning of a major advance and sent in an immediate counterattack which recaptured Capuzzo, but when the Germans probed forward to find 7 Armoured Brigade they discovered that the British had withdrawn to Halfaya. Ten days later 8 Panzer Division recaptured Halfaya Pass by outflanking the British positions and compelling their defenders to fall back.

Below: German infantry advance through the sand dunes

Right: Italian artillery bombarding Tobruk, the eventual goal of Operation Brevity

OPERATION BATTLEAXE

Despite the abandonment of 'Brevity', the arrival of the 'Tiger' convoy with 238 tanks on 12 May, enabled Wavell to mount another offensive. On the German side a new Panzer division – 15 – had begun to arrive. The British plan was to attack Halfaya frontally while 4 Armoured Brigade and part of 4 Indian Division swung round the desert flank of Capuzzo and Sollum, and 7 Armoured Brigade moved forward to occupy Hafid Ridge. Rommel, forbidden by the Axis Supreme Command to attack and lacking sufficient strength due to supply problems, had dug his troops in behind the 88-mm anti-aircraft guns – which were to prove fatal to tanks – and fortified Points 206 and 208 (on Hafid Ridge) to protect Capuzzo. The 15 Panzer Division was in reserve south of Bardia. The British attack began on 15 June and attempts to break through at Halfaya were soon halted by artillery. In the centre, Point 206 was taken by the evening and Capuzzo captured by 4 Armoured Brigade shortly after midday, and 22 Guards Brigade dug itself in. The 7 Armoured Division was heavily engaged on Hafid Ridge but had established a foothold by the evening. Rommel allowed his defensive positions to break up the British attacks and moved 5 Light Division around the west of Hafid Ridge towards Sidi Omar in an attempt to outflank the whole British force. Throughout 16 June they were fought by 7 Armoured Brigade which lost almost all its tanks through battle damage or mechanical failure. Meanwhile 4 Armoured Brigade was withdrawing south to link up with 7 Armoured and protect the left flank. But this was upset early on the 17th when 8 Panzer Regiment disengaged from Capuzzo and swung south and east to join 5 Light Division in a major attack towards Halfaya. The British then had to retreat swiftly so that by the afternoon Rommel had relieved the defenders of Halfaya Pass.

Below: The German 88-mm anti-aircraft gun which proved lethal to British armour during Operation Battleaxe

THE CRUSADER BATTLES

After the failure of Battleaxe, Wavell was removed from command and replaced by General Auchinleck with General Cunningham commanding Eighth Army. Both sides were short of supplies but Churchill pressed Auchinleck to mount an immediate offensive. The tactical concept behind Operation Crusader was that XIII Corps should contain Halfaya Pass and outflank it to strike towards Capuzzo while XXX Corps advanced to Gabr Saleh and engaged the enemy armour. The attack began well on 18 November with 7 Armoured Brigade reaching Gabr Saleh virtually unopposed (**Map 1**). The next day it continued its advance on Sidi Rezegh, but on the flanks 22 Armoured Brigade met unexpectedly heavy resistance at Bir El Gubi from the Ariete Division, and 4 Armoured Brigade moving north to protect the XIII Corps flank was heavily attacked by a group from 21 Panzer Division (the renamed 5 Light Division). Rommel had mistaken the British attack for a reconnaissance, and it was General Cruewell commanding Afrika Korps (the two German Panzer divisions) who made the first countermoves (**Map 2**), striking east to Sidi Azeiz on 19 April under the false impression that a major British force had reached that area. Realizing his error he turned southwest and on 20 November attacked 4 Armoured Brigade. To meet the threat 22 Armoured Brigade was moved from Bir El Gubi to Gabr Saleh. Rommel now ordered Cruewell to strike towards Sidi Rezegh on the morning of 21 November. He was followed by 4 and 22 Armoured Brigades, while the Tobruk garrison began its breakout to meet up with 7 Armoured. But since this had to turn to face Cruewell's attack the attempt was halted and 7 Armoured Brigade in fighting off the Panzer attack lost 113 of its 141 tanks. On the right, the New Zealand Division struck past the German frontier positions and moved up to Sidi Azeiz. On 22 November the fighting continued around Sidi Rezegh with 5 South African Brigade and 21 Panzer Division both suffering heavy losses. During the night 15 Panzer Division making a wide encircling movement to support 21 Panzer ran into 4 Armoured Brigade and virtually destroyed it.

Confused fighting in the Bir El Gubi/Sidi Rezegh area continued on 23 November with the British suffering such losses that Rommel became convinced that their tank strength must now be totally eroded. This idea led him to take the Afrika Korps on a dash for the frontier, designed to relieve the Halfaya garrison and cut off Eighth Army (**Map 3**). But the New Zealanders continued their advance towards Tobruk and Rommel had to turn north and then west on 28 November to follow them. There was a shortlived relief of Tobruk but by 1 December the Germans had cut the link. Rommel was now being threatened from the Bir El Gubi area by XXX Corps which had been recovering there: his deteriorating supply situation and the exhaustion of his troops induced him to pull back first to Gazala (**Map 4**), and then, unwilling to risk being cut off in the Benghazi bulge,

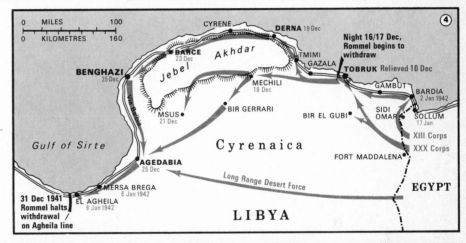

to El Agheila. In the battle the Axis forces had suffered about 38,000 casualties as against the British 18,000 and lost 300 tanks against 278.

Opposite: German prisoners being taken near Bardia

Below: Advancing British infantry take cover during a German bombardment

ROMMEL'S DRIVE TO GAZALA

When the British had followed Rommel back to the El Agheila area, they estimated that he would be unable to react for some time, and dispersed their units in order to refit. In reality, heavy air attacks on Malta had eased the Axis supply lines across the Mediterranean, and his forces were quickly rebuilt. Rommel decided not to await Eighth Army's next move, and on 21 January 1942 his forces advanced, pushing Eighth Army back towards Agedabia (**Map 1**). When DAK found Agedabia only lightly held, with the British obviously surprised by their advance, Rommel pushed on to Antelat, and then to Msus. After a short halt there for supplies, 90 Light Division and Italian XX Corps struck north towards Benghazi, while a DAK task force moved to Er Regima to cut British communications. The threat of encirclement forced the British out of Benghazi and for the next eight days they were continually in retreat until the Axis forces halted close to the Gazala defensive position behind which Eighth Army had retired. The Gazala line consisted of minefields running south to Bir Hacheim with a series of fortified 'keeps' each containing a brigade group from XIII Corps (**Map 2**). These were designed to break up an Axis attack while the armour of XXX Corps intercepted any outflanking move and counterattacked. Rommel indeed aimed to outflank the line around Bir Hacheim – and to strike north towards Achoma. He hoped to open supply lines down Trigh Capuzzo and Trigh El Abd, but had failed to identify 150 Brigade's keep which lay astride these. The British had 849 tanks to the Axis 560, but only 320 aircraft against 704.

Holding attacks by Force Cruewell began in the afternoon of 26 May, and by night the main Axis force swung round Bir Hacheim. Trieste Division got lost and blundered into 150 Brigade, but by the morning of the 27th, 4 Indian Motor Brigade, 7 Motor Brigade, and 4 Armoured Brigade had been pushed back. However, as the Germans moved north across Sidra Ridge, they were attacked on both flanks, had lost about one-third of their armour, and were running short of water and fuel. For two days DAK was

Below: A German 88 in action against British armour

Above: A Stuka banks over advancing German tanks

②

Group Cruewell, early afternoon, 26 May

15 Lt Inf Bde

GAZALA

Via Balbia

Eighth Army (Ritchie) HQ at Gambut
(5 Ind Div and 10 Ind Bde in reserve)

3 S Afr Bde

Seacol

2 S Afr Bde

6 S Afr Bde (less one bn)

TOBRUK

2 S African Div

BIR TEMRAD

Sabratha Div

1 S Afr Bde

1 S Afr Div

Commonwealth Keep ▲209

32 Army Tank Bde

28 May

Solaro Escarpment

ACROMA

4 S Afr Bde

9 Ind Inf Bde (less one bn at El Adem)

SIDI BREGHISC

ALEM HAMZA

Trento Div

ELUET ET TAMAR

Stopcol

To Gambut, 16 miles

Italian X and XXI Corps

151 Bde

69 Bde (less one bn)

Brescia Div

Tobruk perimeter

Pavia Div

Trigh el Abd

1 Army Tank Bde

50 Div

Rigel Ridge

Sidra Ridge

201 Gds Bde

Batruna Ridge

2 Armd Bde

Axis By-pass

BELHAMED

ROTONDA SEGNALI

ROTONDA MTEIFEL

Trigh Capuzzo

SIDI MUFTAH

Knightsbridge

EL ADEM

BIR LEFA

XIII Corps

EL DUDA

Trigh Capuzzo

SIDI REZEGH

150 Bde

The Cauldron

31 May/1 June, 150 Bde destroyed

22 Armd Bde

BIR EL HARMAT

1 June To 'Bridgehead'

1 Armd Div

27 May

Rommel, 2100 hrs, 26 May

Trieste Div (in error)

Italian XX Corps

90 Lt Div

15 and 21 Pz Divs (DAK)

Ariete Div

Trigh Bir Hacheim

21 Pz Div

XXX Corps

4 Armd Bde

7 Armd Div

BIR BEUID

29 Ind Bde

BIR EL GUBI

1 Free French Bde
BIR HACHEIM

3 Ind Mot Bde

15 Pz Div

7 Mot Bde

RETMA

Trigh el Abd

0600 hrs, 27 May

90 Lt Div

AXIS

→ INITIAL ATTACKS

⇐ ROMMEL WITHDRAWS ARMOUR INTO 'BRIDGEHEAD' ('THE CAULDRON') 30 MAY/1 JUNE

0 MILES 15
0 KILOMETRES 25

EIGHTH ARMY – POSITIONS ON 26 MAY
CORPS HEADQUARTERS
DIVISIONAL HEADQUARTERS
BRIGADE HEADQUARTERS
MINEFIELDS
AIRFIELDS AND LANDING FIELDS

held up, unable to push a supply line through the British minefields, until on 30 May Rommel abandoned his move north, and moved all his armour into the 'Cauldron' with its back to the British minefield to await Eighth Army's counterattack.

In the next four days, 150 Brigade was overwhelmed, and at last a supply line was opened through to DAK. Inexplicably the British attack did not come until 5/6 June and was easily beaten off with heavy losses. On the night of 10/11 June after fierce fighting the defenders of Bir Hacheim were forced to retreat, and the next day DAK burst out of the Cauldron (**Map 3**) swinging south and east. Piecemeal British counterattacks were beaten off by superior firepower and Eighth Army was forced to abandon the Gazala position and fall back to Tobruk and beyond. By 18 June the Axis forces had surrounded Tobruk

③

2 S Afr Bde

6 S Afr Bde (less one bn)

TOBRUK

XIII Corps

1 S Afr Bde

1 S Afr Div

2 S African Div

ALEM HAMZA

32 Army Tank Bde

Solaro Escarpment

▲209

ACROMA

4 S Afr Bde

151 Bde

69 Bde

50 Div

ELUET ET TAMAR

One bn + two coys (1 S Afr Div)

11 Ind Bde

Trento Div

Rigel Ridge

1 Armd Div

Tobruk perimeter

Brescia Div

Sidra Ridge

22 Armd Bde

Axis By-pass

Ital X Corps

Pavia Div.

Trigh Capuzzo

Knightsbridge

201 Gds Bde

EL ADEM

BIR LEFA

7 Armd Div

21 Pz Div

DAK HQ

SIDI MUFTAH

Ariete Div

(5/6 June 9 & 10 Ind Bdes, 22 Armd Bde)

2 Armd Bde

ROTONDA MTEIFEL

Trigh el Abd

The Cauldron

15 Pz Div

4 Armd Bde

29 Ind Bde (less one bn)

11 June, Axis forces breakout from 'The Cauldron'

BIR EL HARMAT

Night 10/11 June
1 Free French Bde withdraws

Trigh Bir Hacheim

Trieste Div

BIR BEUID

EIGHTH ARMY
POSITIONS AT 11 JUNE
◄ MAIN COUNTERATTACKS DURING 1/10 JUNE
◁ MOVEMENTS, PM 11 JUNE
MINEFIELDS

1 Free French Bde
BIR HACHEIM

11 June

90 Lt Div

4 S Afr Armd Car Regt

7 Mot Bde

BIR EL GUBI

0 MILES 10
0 KILOMETRES 15

THE FALL OF TOBRUK

Rommel's attack on Tobruk began at first light on 20 June 1942 in the same south-eastern sector that O'Connor had selected in 1941. After heavy dive-bomber attacks, DAK pushed through the perimeter defences and by mid-morning had reached the minefields. At 1600 hours the airfields had been overrun, and three hours later, 21 Panzer Division moved into Tobruk. Isolated fighting continued during the night, but at 0800 hours on 21 June, General Klopper, the South African commander of the garrison, surrendered and during the rest of the day all remaining resistance was overcome.

Below: German troops in the main square of Tobruk

62

THE GERMAN ADVANCE TO EL ALAMEIN

As Tobruk fell, Eighth Army was attempting to re-form on the Egyptian frontier, and on 23 June it was authorized to withdraw to Matruh. Over 50,000 men had been lost as against 3,360 Germans, and the armour of XXX Corps was almost totally destroyed. On 25 June Auchinleck sent General Ritchie on leave, took over personal command of Eighth Army, and prepared to hold the Matruh position. Ritchie had intended to hold the area between Sidi Hamza and the sea with X Corps while striking at any outflanking attacks with the remains of XXX Corps, but Auchinleck saw that both corps were widely dispersed with an alarming gap south of 'Charing Cross', and so he decided that Eighth Army should withdraw as the enemy advanced to the more easily defensible El Alamein position. On 26 June although still weak (DAK had only sixty tanks left running and about 1,500 infantry), the Axis forces attacked astride the southern escarpment (**Map 1**). By the afternoon of the 27th, 90 Light Division had reached a position from which it could strike towards the coast, and 21 Panzer and 2 New Zealand Divisions were heavily engaged while 1 Armoured was holding 15 Panzer. But during the evening XXX Corps Headquarters ordered its divisions to fall back, and 90 Light Division cut the

coast road. The X Corps was now surrounded and the next day its units broke out of Mersa Matruh in small parties while Eighth Army fell back on El Alamein (**Map 2**).

Right: A German supply column during the advance to El Alamein

THE FIRST BATTLE AT EL ALAMEIN

Above: British units under artillery bombardment near El Alamein

Below: A German patrol returns from probing the British positions

With only two fully operational infantry divisions and a still-unorganized armoured division Auchinleck set about holding the El Alamein position. He aimed to rely on a fluid defence south of El Alamein based on the Ruweisat Ridge and Bab el Qattara. Although DAK was still seriously understrength, Rommel was confident that he could break through, bypass and surround El Alamein, and strike for the Delta. His forces moved off on 1 July, with 90 Light Division moving along the El Alamein perimeter closely behind the retiring 4 Armoured Brigade until halted near Alam el Onsol. DAK overran Deir el Shein, but was held near Point 64 on the Ruweisat Ridge. For two days, fighting continued here without the Germans making any headway while a southward move by the Ariete Division was shattered by 2 New Zealand Division. The Axis forces were now held in an arc from the sea to south of the Ruweisat Ridge, and Auchinleck decided to pull XIII Corps back northwards while preparing a counterattack by XXX Corps in the north against the Italians who were covering from the sea to the ridge. When he learned of XIII Corps withdrawal, Rommel was convinced that he had achieved a breakthrough and prepared to exploit it. But an attack by 9 Australian Division on Tell el Eisa during the night of 10/11 July compelled him to send his last reserves north to bolster the collapsing Sabratha Division, and two British attacks along the Ruweisat Ridge on 14/15 July and 21/22 July caused DAK such losses that Rommel had to abandon the operation and regroup. Auchinleck was determined to concentrate on building up his forces and his refusal to consider a further attack before mid-September caused Churchill to replace him by General Harold Alexander as Commander-in-Chief, Near East, and General Bernard Montgomery as commander of Eighth Army.

Above: Units of the Afrika Korps preparing
to attack El Alamein

EIGHTH ARMY

■ CORPS HEADQUARTERS

⚑ DIVISIONAL HEADQUARTERS

⚑ BRIGADE HEADQUARTERS

(POSITIONS ARE THOSE ON MORNING OF 1 JULY)

MILES 0 — 10

KILOMETRES 0 — 16

10/11 July,
Auchinleck's newly arrived
9 Australian Div recovers
Tell el Eisa

Tell el Eisa

Italian XXI Corps

*Tell el
Makh Khad*

DAK

90 Lt Div

TELL EL AQQAQIR

Italian XX Corps

Italian X Corps

15 Pz Div

21 Pz Div

Miteirya Ridge

3 S Afr Bde

EL ALAMEIN

El Alamein
perimeter

1 July,
4 Armd Bde arrives
just ahead of 90 Lt Div

4 Armd Bde

1 S Afr Div

ALAM EL ONSOL

2 S Afr Bde Col

1800 hrs,
1 July

Deir el Abyad

Deir el Shein

18 Ind Bde

Pt 63

Ruweisat Ridge

1 S Afr Bde Col

22 Armd Bde

El Mreir

Pt 64

1 Armd Div

XXX Corps

Ariete Div

3 July

Alam el Halfa Ridge

Deir el Hima

2/4 July,
Rommel's attacks
twice repulsed

6 NZ Bde

Bab el Qattara

NZ Artillery

NZ Infantry

Alam Nayil

XIII Corps

NZ Div

Deir el Munassib

7 Motor Bde

9 Ind Bde

*Nagb Abu
Dweis*

5 Ind Div

El Taqa Plateau

7 Armd Div

Barrel Track

Qaret el Himeimat

Qattara Depression

To Alexandria, 55 miles

To Cairo, 130 miles

65

THE BATTLE OF ALAM HALFA

Above: Italian troops advancing for a diversionary attack

Within seventeen days of his arrival, Montgomery had to face Rommel's last attempt to break through the El Alamein position. His defensive plan, broadly inherited from Auchinleck, was to defend the Alam Halfa Ridge and threaten any German offensive in the south with 7 Armoured Division. Rommel tried the tactics which had served him so well in the past – covering attacks in the north with his main attack swinging south of the British positions to come round east of Alam Halfa and surround Eighth Army. But in the event, the threat of 7 Armoured Division on the right flank forced Rommel to swing north earlier than he had intended; DAK was unable to break through the Alam Halfa position, and shortage of fuel forced it to halt. An attempt by 15 Panzer Division to outflank 22 Armoured Brigade on 1 September was prevented and on the 2nd Rommel ordered his forces to pull back to the line El Taqa/Bab el Qattara. On the night of 3/4 September, 2 New Zealand Division attacked south-west but was withdrawn after two days of heavy fighting.

The Axis forces now dug in and began to prepare a defensive position of great depth between the sea and the Qattara Depression. Rommel realized that if they were driven out of this line, they would be overwhelmed for lack of vehicles and the fuel to withdraw or fight a mobile battle. Thus he planned to hold each piece of ground at all costs halting each British attack with an immediate counterattack.

Right: German artillery bombards the British positions

66

Above: A British fieldgun in action against German vehicles

GERMAN   ITALIAN
→ ⇢ ROMMEL'S INTENDED ADVANCE
→ ⇢ ROMMEL'S ACTUAL ADVANCE
        EASTERN EDGE OF AXIS MINEFIELDS
        MAIN ALIGNMENT OF
        EIGHTH ARMY'S MINEFIELDS

0   MILES   10
0   KILOMETRES   16

164 Div

20 Aust Bde
Tell el Eisa
24 Aust Bde

Trento Div

1 S Afr Div
EL ALAMEIN
9 Australian Div
XXX Corps
26 Aust Bde

Diversionary attacks

3 S Afr Bde

1 S Afr Bde

2 S Afr Bde

Secondary attacks

161 Ind Bde

5 Ind Div 5 Ind Bde

44 Div

131 Bde

Bologna Div

9 Ind Bde
Ruweisat Ridge

23 Armd Bde

Alam Halfa Ridge
10 Armd Div
133 Bde
XIII Corps

132 Bde

NZ Div

6 NZ Bde

Alam Nayil

22 Armd Bde

15 Pz Div
1 Sept

Bab el Qattara

5 NZ Bde

8 Armd Bde

Main attacks,
2300 hrs,
30 August
1942

90 Lt Div

7 Mot Bde

21 Pz Div

Deir el Munassib

Ital Motorised Corps

Ariete Div

Littorio Div

15 and 21 Pz Divs

Folgore Div

Recce Group

7 Armd Div

El Taqa Plateau

4 Lt Armd Bde

Samaket
Gaballa

▲ Qaret el
Himeimat

THE BATTLE OF EL ALAMEIN

Montgomery was determined not to attack until he had massive superiority, particularly in the air and in armour (see diagram). The Sherman tank was at last proving a match for the German Mark IV. Montgomery was faced with a heavily defended position whose flanks resting on the sea and the Qattara Depression could not be turned. His plan (**Map 1**) was to attack north of the Miteirya Ridge, with the infantry of XXX Corps pushing forward to the line 'Oxalic' and opening corridors in the minefields through which the armour of X Corps would pass. The XXX Corps would then form a screen at 'Pierson' while the infantry broke down the enemy defences before the final move to 'Skinflint' destroyed the Axis armour. The Germans had split their tanks to cover north and south of the line while the Italians provided the main static defences. Rommel was in hospital in Germany, leaving General Stumme in command, and did not return until 25 October.

Above left: British troops advance through a smoke screen

Left: A German sentry observes British positions before the battle

Military strength at El Alamein

Axis · British

Men		Tanks		Guns		Aircraft	
104,000	195,000	489	1029	1219	2311	675	750
German: 50,000		German: 211 Italian: 278		German: 644 Italian: 575		German: 275 (150 serviceable) Italian: 400 (200 serviceable)	(530 serviceable)

↑ =2000 men ↑ =50 tanks ↑ =100 guns ↑ =50 aircraft

AXIS MINEFIELDS

'OPERATION LIGHTFOOT'

– · – · – 'OXALIC'; XXX CORPS' FINAL OBJECTIVE (0310 HRS, 24 OCT)
• • • • • 'PIERSON'; X CORPS' FIRST OBJECTIVE (DAWN, 24 OCT)
– – – – 'SKINFLINT'; X CORPS' FINAL OBJECTIVE

| 0 | MILES | 10 |
| 0 | KILOMETRES | 16 |

SIDI ABD EL RAHMAN
90 Lt Div
164 Div
Littorio Division
Tell el Aqqaqir
Tell el Eisa
9 Aust Div
1 Armd Div corridor
Kidney Ridge
51 (H) Div
NZ Div
15 Panzer Division
10 Armd Div corridor
S Afr Div
Miteirya Ridge
Rahman Track
XXX
X Corps
Corps

The battle began at 2130 hours on 24 October with a massive artillery bombardment, and at 2200 hours XXX Corps began its advance while XIII Corps mounted divisionary attacks in the south (**Map 2**). By dawn most units of XXX Corps had reached their 'Oxalic' positions but the armour of X Corps had not been able to clear the minefields. Axis reaction was hesitant, not knowing which was the main attack, and General Stumme died of a heart attack during the afternoon. By the evening 1 Armoured Division had got some units out, but 10 Armoured Division was still held up in its corridor. The XIII Corps was holding 21 Panzer Division in the south. Early in the morning of 25 October, congestion in the southern corridor reached a dangerous level, but Montgomery confirmed that the attempt to break through must continue. The New Zealand Division cleared the minefield and began to attack south-west, fighting off counterattacks by 15 Panzer Division. At midday Montgomery decided to switch the axis of attack sending 9 Australian Division to strike north covered by 1 Armoured Division. This attack began on 26 October, and compelled the Germans to commit their reserves in the north. Montgomery now decided to regroup, pulling out 2 New Zealand Division and moving 1 South African and 4 Indian Divisions north.

By this stage the Axis fuel problem was acute for two tankers had been sunk in Tobruk harbour. Rommel ordered 21 Panzer Division north and on the 27th DAK launched a series of unsuccessful attacks on 1 Armoured Division. On the evening of the 28th further attacks by 9 Australian Division had almost reached the coast road, and Montgomery began to prepare for a final breakout using X Corps. His first intention to attack in the far north was amended because German 90 Light Division had moved forward, and at 0200 on 2 November infantry assaulted the Italian positions further south and the armour began to break through. Although at the outset the attacks were contained by German counterattacks, by the evening Rommel had decided to pull back. This was delayed for twenty-four hours because Hitler forbade any withdrawal, but on the 4th, the British armour finally reached open ground.

Right: British troops pinned down by Axis fire during the fighting in the corridors

OPERATION TORCH

On 8 November 1942, four days after Rommel started to retreat from El Alamein, American and British forces began landing in French North Africa (**Map 1**). The Western and Centre Task forces were American and the Eastern British. It had been hoped to arrange that French forces would not resist, but there was sporadic opposition – landing difficulties delayed the attacks on Casablanca and Mehdia, there was considerable fighting at Oran, and two destroyers were lost at Algiers. A ceasefire was arranged on 9 November. The weak point of the Allied plan was that Tunisia could not be occupied in the first landings; German troops began to arrive there on 9 November in order to protect Rommel's rear, and pushed out to form a defensive perimeter. The British made seaborne landings at Bougie on 11 November while airborne troops occupied Bône on the 12th only minutes ahead of German paratroops. The Allies now began to push forward overland towards Tunisia and fresh parachute drops were made on 15 November by the Americans at Youks les Bains, and British at Souk el Arba on the 16th (**Map 2**). The British force had advanced to Beja by the evening, and the next day pushed forward to Sidi Nsir. On 18 November they made contact with the first German patrols. Heavy fighting developed in an attempt to seize Medjez el Bab, but on the 26th the Germans withdrew. The advance of First Army was now being held by a series of German strongpoints in the hilly terrain, and an attack on Djedeida was repulsed after the town had been occupied for a short time. The British 2 Parachute Battalion landed at Depienne and marched on Oudna, but ground forces were unable to break through to it, and it had to retire. The Germans now began to edge forward to meet the Allies until a front was established running from Bou Arada through Medjez and west of Sedjenane.

Above: American paratroops after their landing at Youks les Bains

Opposite above: British troops coming ashore east of Algiers

ALLIES
ALLIED AIRBORNE LANDINGS
GERMAN
BRITISH V CORPS FRONT, 1 JANUARY 1943

MILES 20
KILOMETRES 30

HEIGHT IN FEET
OVER 7000
5000-7000
1000-5000
UNDER 1000

BIZERTA

Sidi Ahmed

9 November,
German advance
parties land

Lake of
Bizerta

Garaet Achkel

Tindja

C Serrat

26 Nov,
36 Bde
TAMERA

30 Nov,
36 Bde repulsed Dj Azzag
SEDJENANE ▲

Dj Ajred ▲

MATEUR

Gulf of Tunis

18 Nov,
German attack
repulsed

10 November,
Germans establish
bridgehead

DJEBEL ABIOD

16 Nov, Hart Force
17 Nov, 36 Bde

18 Nov,
1 Para Bn

27 Nov,
1 Para Bn

26 Nov,
Allies attack
airfield

DJEDEIDA

El Aouina

TABARKA

SIDI NSIR
17 Nov

TEBOURBA

27/29 Nov,
5 Northampton Regt
1 E Surrey Regt

TUNIS

Hart Force
36 Bde

T U N I S I A

ST CYPRIEN

26/27 Nov,
Bn, 11 Bde

Longstop ▲
Medjerda

First Army
(Anderson)

BÉJA

25 Nov,
11 Bde

MEDJEZ EL BAB

1 Dec,
2 Para Bn retires

Oudna
1 Dec

30 Nov

SOUK EL KHEMIS

25 Nov

SLOUGHIA

29 Nov,
German road block

29 Nov, 2 Para Bn
Depienne

SOUK EL ARBA

16 Nov, 1 Para Bn
18 Nov, Blade Force

Blade Force

TEBOURSOUK 23 Nov

To Le Kef 40 miles

56 Recce Regt

PONT DU FAHS

BOU ARADA

THE ADVANCE OF EIGHTH ARMY

For the first three weeks of its advance from El Alamein, although hampered by heavy rains which had fallen on 6 November, Eighth Army met little opposition, for Rommel's forces were too disorganized to counterattack. Temporary defence lines at Fuka and Mersah Matruh were abandoned as soon as pressure built up, and news of the 'Torch' landings convinced Rommel that Halfaya could not be held. His main objective was to gain time in which to prepare defences at El Agheila and in this he was aided by the weather which had delayed Eighth Army's pursuit and supply problems which permitted Montgomery to keep only three divisions forward. By 23 November Eighth Army had reached Agedabia where it halted to reorganize, so that it was not until 12 December that Mersa Brega was attacked. The place was evacuated the next day and Eighth Army closed up to the El Agheila defences. On 14 December Montgomery sent 2 New Zealand Division deep into the desert to outflank the line and by the 16th it was threatening Axis supply lines so that Rommel had to complete his evacuation of El Agheila. The Germans left a delaying force at Sirte, while they fell back to Buerat. This line was both attacked frontally and outflanked on 15 January, and the second Axis position, Homs-Tarhuna, was swiftly breached and Tunis occupied on 23 January. Here supply problems again forced Eighth Army to halt, and it was not until 4 February that the first units crossed into Tunisia. The capture of Medenine on the 16th brought Eighth Army up towards the Mareth Line which was reached on 24 February.

Left: Axis prisoners outside Bardia

Opposite: Armour of Eighth Army entering Ben Gardane

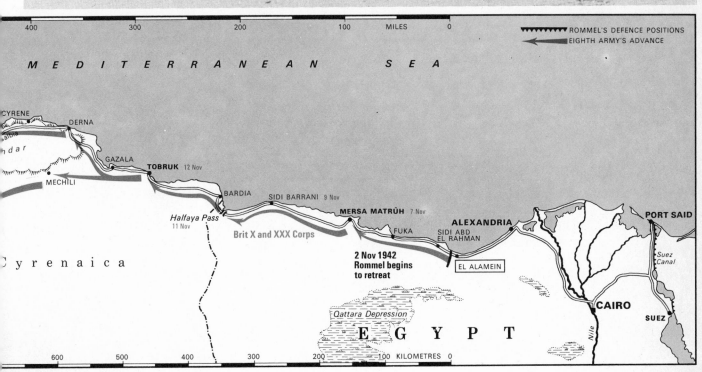

400   300   200   100   MILES   0

▼▼▼▼▼▼▼▼▼ ROMMEL'S DEFENCE POSITIONS
◀━━━━━ EIGHTH ARMY'S ADVANCE

M E D I T E R R A N E A N   S E A

CYRENE

DERNA

albia

ndar

GAZALA

TOBRUK   12 Nov

MECHILI

BARDIA

SIDI BARRANI   9 Nov

Halfaya Pass
11 Nov

MERSA MATRŪH   7 Nov

ALEXANDRIA

PORT SAID

Brit X and XXX Corps

FUKA

SIDI ABD
EL RAHMAN

*Suez
Canal*

C y r e n a i c a

**2 Nov 1942
Rommel begins
to retreat**

EL ALAMEIN

CAIRO

SUEZ

Qattara Depression

Nile

E G Y P T

600   500   400   300   200   100   KILOMETRES   0

THE BATTLE OF KASSERINE

By the beginning of February 1943, with the bulk of Rommel's forces back behind the Mareth Line, and the Eighth Army so stretched as to pose no immediate threat, the Axis Supreme Command in North Africa accepted Rommel's proposal that a determined assault should be made on the Allied First Army so as to relieve pressure on Tunisia. The Allies were now lying along the Eastern Dorsale (**Map 2**) and had been pushed back from their most forward positions by limited counterattacks launched during January by General von Arnim. Rommel's plan (**Map 1**) was to strike between the American and French sectors towards Kasserine and Tebéssa and if the Allies began to fall back, to push towards Bône and Constantine. The major flaw in Axis planning was that although parts of von Arnim's and Rommel's forces were to be involved, neither had overall command. Von Arnim was more concerned with limited improvements in the Axis defensive positions than any spectacular breakthrough. General Anderson commanding the Allied First Army knew that his forward positions were still too weak, and had instructed his commanders to fall back where necessary to the Western Dorsale.

The Axis attack began at 0400 on 14 February, with twin thrusts which captured Sidi Bou Zid, and isolated the US forces on Djebels Lessouda and Ksaira. A counterattack by US 1 Armoured Division on 15 February failed to recapture Sidi Bou Zid, while a second Axis thrust captured Gafsa. During the night the US troops on Djebel Lessouda withdrew successfully, and the next day Axis troops began thrusting towards Fériana and Sbeitla. By 18 February both were in Axis hands and their forces were pressing up to Kasserine. Rommel was now urging an immediate thrust towards Tebéssa, but at the same time von Arnim was pulling 10 Panzer Division out of Sbeitla to move into a defensive position further north.

Below: Allied Shermans during the return to Kasserine

However, Rommel was now authorized to attack towards Le Kef, and this he did on 19 February with attacks towards Sbiba by 21 Panzer Division and towards Thala by 10 Panzer Division which had been recalled. A diversionary thrust by DAK units towards Tebéssa was held by US 1 Armoured Division.

Meanwhile, General Alexander, who had taken command of the Allied armies, ordered that there should be no further retreat from the Western Dorsale, and began sending units of British 6 Armoured Division down to buttress the defences at Thala and Sbiba. These they reached just as Axis pressure was threatening a breakthrough. By the afternoon of 22 February Rommel had decided to call off the attacks and pull back. The Allies retook Kasserine on 25 February. They had suffered 10,000 casualties, 6,500 from US II Corps, as against only 2,000 Axis troops.

Below: American troops lifting mines after the recapture of Gafsa

BREAKING THE MARETH LINE

With the ending of the Kasserine battle, Rommel turned back to face Eighth Army which was now preparing to assault the Mareth Line. As soon as 15 and 21 Panzer Divisions were spotted moving south again, Montgomery reinforced his units in the forward positions around Medenine, and dug in his troops behind minefields and strong anti-tank defences. His tactical method was to break up any German attacks with artillery and not to involve his armour unless there was actual danger of a breakthrough. On 6 March Rommel put in attacks on a wide front, the main pressure being in the centre where the line was held by the British 131 Lorried Infantry Brigade and 201 Guards Brigade (**Map 1**). Both this and 10 Panzer Division's attack further south were successfully halted by anti-tank fire and by mid-morning the Axis units had pulled back. A second assault in the afternoon was equally unsuccessful, and the Germans fell back with the loss of 50 of their 150 tanks.

Montgomery's plan for breaking the Mareth Line was to send 2 New Zealand Division and 8 Armoured Brigade (now called New Zealand Corps) deep around the left flank through the Matmata Hills and north to the Tebaga Gap from which they could menace the El Hamma plain. The XXX Corps would then attack the Mareth Line frontally and form a bridgehead through which X Corps' armour could strike towards Gafsa and Sfax. The hazardous New Zealand Corps' move was made successfully, and by evening on 20 February it had closed up to the Tebaga Gap while German 164 Light Division began to pull back from the Mareth Line to ward off the threat (**Map 3**). During the night of the 20th, 50 Division supported by a tremendous barrage, launched the main attack and although a foothold had been formed by morning it was thrown back on the 22nd (**Map 2**). The German 21 Panzer and 164 Light Divisions were holding

the New Zealanders at the Tebaga Gap, and on 22 February 15 Panzer Division launched a major counter-attack on the bridgehead which severely mauled 50 Division.

Montgomery now altered his original plan completely by sending 1 Armoured Division and X Corps headquarters (General Horrocks) round via the Tebaga Gap, while 4 Indian Division made a short hook around the Mareth Line. Traffic congestion delayed the moves, but by 26 February 1 Armoured Division had reached Tebaga, and the next day it burst through the Gap, rolling up the Axis defences. However the Germans

improvised a defence line at El Hamma, and due to Horrocks' determination to destroy this before moving on to Gabes they were able to pull back most of their forces to the Wadi Akarit. This was assaulted by Eighth Army during the night of 5/6 April. By morning 4 Indian Division had captured Point 275 and Djebel Mjerda and turned the Line. But there was no attempt to exploit this breakthrough, and, after counterattacks, the Axis forces were again able to disengage and retreat north. The fighting between these two experienced armies had been extremely severe. None the less Mareth must be regarded as one of Montgomery's most skilful tactical battles. This was Rommel's last battle in Africa, for he was ordered home to Germany a few days later.

Above: A British 17-pounder in action against German armour at Medenine

Right: Italian troops digging defences at Wadi Akarit

Below: Units of the New Zealand Corps during the advance to the Tebaga Gap

AXIS FRONT, 21 MARCH

0   MILES   20

0   KM   30

HEIGHT IN FEET

OVER 1200
900–1200
300–900
UNDER 300

To Gafsa

To Sfax

W Akarit

Chott el Fedjadj

EL HAMMA

GABES

Djerba

22 March, 21 Pz Div

El Hamma Plain

28 March

27 March, Outflanked Axis forces escape

26/27 March, NZ Corps and 1 Armd Div break through Tebaga Gap

Djebel Tebaga

Tebaga Gap

Night, 21/22 March
Ital Saharan Group

22 March, 164 Lt Div

MARETH

Mareth Line

20/22 March, 50 Div held at Bridgehead

MATMATA

BENI ZELTEN

28 March

20 March, NZ Corps

TOUJANE

25 March, 1 Armd Div

4 Ind Div

D a h a r

24/25 March, 5 Ind Bde

MEDENINE

BIR SOLTANE

KSAR EL HALLOUF

M A T M A T A   H I L L S

23 March, X Corps (incl 1 Armd Div) moves up to Tebaga Gap

To Ben Gardane

7 Ind Bde

NZ Corps (incl 8 Armd Bde)

KSAR RHILANE

FOUM TATAHOUINE

Night, 19/20 March

12/19 March, NZ Corps assembly area

Wilder's Gap

THE END IN AFRICA

By the middle of April 1943, the Axis forces had been pressed into a tight perimeter based on the last hills before the coastal plain around Bizerta and Tunis (**Map 2**). Determined defence of these hills had halted the Allied First Army, but Eighth Army had now pushed up to a position just south of Enfidaville. The nineteen Allied divisions had some 1,200 tanks and 1,500 guns, against thirteen understrength Axis divisions with 500 guns but only 130 tanks. Allied airpower was now predominant. Alexander gave Eighth Army the first attempt to break through in the south, but their attack was contained and made little progress (**Map 1**). A German assault between Goubellat and Medjez el Bab on 20/21 April was also held, and on 22 April the First Army launched a series of assaults designed to capture the main remaining hills – particularly Hill 609 which dominated the valley which had been nicknamed the 'Mousetrap' through which the Americans could reach the plain, and those hills around 'Longstop' and 'Peter's Corner' which commanded the Medjerda Valley. By 29 April, US II Corps had made progress towards controlling the Mousetrap, but the other attacks had been halted. Alexander decided to regroup, and

transferred 4 Indian Division and 6 and 7 Armoured Divisions north from Eighth Army to IX Corps. He intended that once V Corps had captured Djebel Bou Aoukaz and opened the Medjerda Valley, IX Corps (now commanded by Lieutenant General Horrocks in place of Lieutenant-General Crocker who had been injured) would burst through. While this was taking place, US 9 Division had broken through in the north, and on 1 May was threatening Mateur and the German positions around the Mousetrap. On the same day, Hill 609 was taken, but US 1 Armoured Division's progress was held until the 3rd when it broke through to Mateur where the Germans had formed a new defence line and were still fighting with determination. On the evening of 5 May, Djebel Bou Aoukaz was taken, and early on the 6th, 6 and 7 Armoured Divisions supported by very heavy bombing pushed through into the plain. Their advance was enterprising for though the Axis communications had broken down, their forces were more or less intact. Tunis fell on 7 May, by which time US II Corps had broken through in the north and taken Bizerta. The coastal strip and Cap Bon were occupied, and by

Below: British infantry moving up for an attack on Longstop Hill

11 May all resistance had
ceased.

The Italian, Marshal Messe,
surrendered on 13 May. The
moonlight advance of 6 Armoured
Division from Hamman Lif to
Hammamet (8 May) was one of the
strangest, yet most impressive
operations of the war. Without
stopping to mop up they drove to the
heart of the Axis position, stampeding
the enemy into wholesale surrender.
This exploit was the brain-child of
General Alexander. By 12 May
250,415 German and Italian troops
laid down their arms.

OPERATION BARBAROSSA

'When Barbarossa begins, the world
will hold its breath.'
Adolf Hitler

Opposite: A Panzer column moves at night
past burning buildings during the opening
days of Barbarossa

Whatever the rest of the world may have felt when on 22 June 1941 Hitler's armies invaded Russia, the general opinion in Britain was that his final defeat was now inevitable. The British had never felt that they would lose the war, but so far it had not been exactly easy to see how they were going to win it. Now, like Charles XII of Sweden and Napoleon I, Hitler seemed doomed. Churchill, with his sure instinct for the mood of the moment, lost no time in declaring Britain's full and loyal support for the somewhat unlikely ally now thrust upon him.

But though the invasion of Russia unquestionably raised British morale there was in fact no solid ground for this optimism. The German onslaught had been carefully planned, wrought immense havoc, and came within an ace of capturing Moscow itself. The Russian army which had not shown to much advantage in Finland had been gravely weakened by Stalin's purges of the officer corps in 1937. At the outset Russian strategy was inept. By trying to hold too far forward all along the frontier they contrived, despite their enormous numbers, to be weak everywhere. The Russian soldier was courageous, robust, and frugal and he showed a remarkable skill at digging himself in. But lacking education he also lacked initiative, and from the first, being deployed to little advantage, suffered cruel losses in killed and wounded and staggering numbers of prisoners. Only time, it seemed, was against the Wehrmacht and for this Wavell's abortive Balkan campaign may perhaps be accorded some credit.

Hitler's attack on Russia was no sudden inspiration. It was part of his political philosophy to give the German people *Lebensraum*. The black-soil region of south Russia and east Europe had long figured on his map of the Greater Germany: his grand design. Nevertheless it seems that early in 1941 Hitler had come to recognize that he could not defeat England, and that he must, therefore, change his line of operations. In Berlin on 14 June 1941 the Führer explained this concept to an assembly of his generals, including Guderian, the great armoured warfare expert, who is our authority for what Hitler said. Under the circumstances only a decisive victory on the Continent could bring the war to a successful conclusion. To ensure Germany's position the defeat of Russia was essential. Most of his audience knew enough military history to depart with heavy hearts. As for Guderian himself his opinion was clear: 'So long as the war in the West was still undecided, any new undertaking must result in a war on two fronts; and Adolf Hitler's Germany was even less capable of fighting such a war than had been the Germany of 1914.' Even so Adolf Hitler could dispose of 205 divisions: 145 of them on the Eastern Front. Of these last, nineteen were armoured and twelve motorized, but the rest like Napoleon's *Grande Armée* before them depended for their transport, their mobility, upon the horse. It is difficult a generation later to realize that of the great armies of the Second World War only the British and the American were genuinely motorized throughout. Nevertheless it is a factor that goes far to explain their eventual triumph.

Despite the lessons of history, Hitler, sustained by the opinions of his experts, was confident of a swift victory in Russia. General Halder (Chief of the Army General Staff) reckoned that eight to ten weeks would suffice. The Luftwaffe and the *Waffen-SS* prudently provided winter clothing for their men, but it was not until the end of August that the army recognized that it might be useful – yet 1812 was part of the folk memory of the European peoples and not least of the Germans who had formed at least a third of Napoleon's polyglot host.

Had Hitler not been supremely confident he could easily have built up his 'Russian' army by another ten divisions drawn from the thirty-eight in the West and the twelve in Norway. But on 22 June 1941 it seemed to him quite unnecessary to add to the mighty host that was about to pass the Niemen – the river that Napoleon had crossed exactly 129 years ago. Hitler was superstitious, but since 22 June was the first anniversary of the Armistice he had imposed on the French in the Forest of Compiègne, he could afford to ignore Napoleonic memories.

In the summer of 1941 Stalin was very far from wishing to antagonize the Germans. He had honoured the agreement of January 1941 and delivered both food and raw materials to the Germans. He had ignored numerous violations of Soviet air space. and, it seems, had managed to persuade himself that there was nothing sinister about them.

It is not easy to say with any real exactitude how strong the Russians were in 1941. It may be that she had as many as 12,000,000 men under arms, including reserves. She had perhaps 160 infantry and 30 cavalry divisions, with, in addition, 35 armoured or motorized brigades. This mighty host had relatively little motor transport and was not trained for the *Blitzkrieg*. Traditional Russian assets were what they depended upon: plenty of room for manoeuvre – that is to say withdrawal; scorched earth; guerillas or partisans to operate in the enemy's rear; unmetalled roads; and those two celebrated generals Janvier and Février. It may be that the Russians had 7,500 aircraft, but they were quite outclassed by the Luftwaffe. They had no proper network of airfields and were seriously short of trained pilots. The Germans claimed that they destroyed 3,000 aircraft in the first week of the campaign. However that may be, Lieutenant-General Kopels of the Russian Military Air Power committed suicide on the second day, when he had already lost 600 planes and could not claim more than a dozen Germans shot down.

The Russians may have had as many

Far left: Soviet anti-tank guns in action

Left: Soviet cavalry advancing during the winter counteroffensive

Right: Gas holders are carried through Leningrad during the siege

as 20,000 tanks, but of this formidable number many were obsolescent. The KV and T-34s were only just coming into production. The Germans for their part, although they were now producing 1,000 tanks a year, were reduced to using French tanks in their new tanks division. The Panzer IV was neither as heavy nor as effective as the Russian T-34, which first went into action in July 1941. The German Army Ordnance Office had had the temerity to ignore Hitler's personal order to provide the Panzer III with a 50-mm cannon!

The first weeks of the campaign were weeks of triumph for the Germans. The spoils included 1,200 tanks, 600 guns, and 150,000 prisoners. By 10 July the Germans, having covered 400 miles in eighteen days, were before Smolensk. Moscow lay but 200 miles ahead. But now at last Russian resistance began to stiffen. A few more modern aircraft began to put in an appearance; the celebrated Katyusha mortar came into service (15 July); and generals alleged to have failed, like G. D. Pavlov, commander of the Western Front, were court-martialled and condemned to death.

Thus far the Germans had done pretty well – so well indeed that the Führer felt the time was ripe for a display of his skill as a commander. He informed his generals that events in France had proved that large-scale envelopments were not justified. According to Guderian Hitler 'preferred an alternative plan by which small enemy forces were to be encircled and destroyed piecemeal and the enemy thus bled to death.' In the opinion of his officers 'these manoeuvres on our part simply gave the Russians time to set up new formations and to use their inexhaustible man-power for the creation of fresh defensive lines in the rear area; even more important, we were sure that this strategy would not result in the urgently necessary, rapid conclusion of the campaign.'

As late as 4 August Hitler was still uncertain as to his objectives. On that day he held a conference at Novy Borissov, the HQ of Army Group Centre, and gave the industrial area round Leningrad as his first objective. He had not yet quite made up his mind whether to strike after that at Moscow or the Ukraine, but for various reasons the latter seemed to him the more favourable. Army Group South seemed to be poised for victory there; Germany needed the resources of the area and Hitler saw in the Crimea 'a Soviet aircraft-carrier operating against the Rumanian oil-fields . . .' In any case he hoped to have Moscow and Kharkov before winter.

By 21 August when he gave out his orders for the capture of Kiev Hitler had decided that: 'Of primary importance before the outbreak of winter is not the capture of Moscow but rather the occupation of the Crimea, of the industrial and coalmining area of the Donetz basin, the cutting of the Russian supply routes from the Caucasian oilfields, and, in the north, the investment of Leningrad and the establishment of contact with the Finns. . . . The capture of the Crimean peninsula is of extreme importance for safeguarding our oil supplies from Rumania.' It was a strategy of dispersal, but nevertheless in the short term it brought a dazzling success. On 18 September Kiev fell and by the 26th the Russians had lost 665,000 prisoners in the battle.

Early in October the Germans began their final advance on Moscow. 'Today', declared Hitler on 2 October, 'begins the last great decisive battle of the year!' At first all went well, and three weeks later von Bock's armour was within 30 miles of the capital. Meanwhile von Rundstedt had overrun the Crimea where only Sevastopol held out. The Soviet government and the *corps diplomatique* departed to Kubyshev, but Stalin stayed on in the Kremlin where on 7 November he galvanized his countrymen with his Holy Russia speech, in which he inspired them with the examples of their heroic ancestors, Alexander Nevsky, Dimitri Donskoi, Minin, and Pozharsky, Alexander Suvorov, Michael Kutuzov, and Lenin. Nor did he fail to mention the material aid, aircraft, tanks, and dollars, which Mr Harriman and Lord Beaverbrook had promised during the recent Moscow Conference. 'All this shows that the coalition between the three countries is a very real thing which will go on growing in the common cause of liberation.'

By mid-October, as in 1812, the weather broke. The 'Napoleon weather' which had broken the morale of the *Grande Armée* now brought the Germans to a standstill. First it was the mud, and then bitter cold. But Hitler had not finished, and it was as late as 15 November that he compelled his frost-bitten host to make another great offensive towards Moscow. It carried them into the suburbs, but by 6 December it had run out of steam. By that time their successes had cost the Germans 750,000 casualties on the Russian Front, including 8,000 officers and nearly 200,000 men killed. 'I would never have believed,' wrote Guderian, 'that a really brilliant military position could be so b . . . . d up in two months.' The story of the Russian campaign, with its occasional triumphs and its frequent disasters, would henceforth be influenced at every turn by the strategic inspirations and the will-power of Adolf Hitler. Halted before Moscow in the bitter cold his generals urged withdrawal. But Hitler insisted that they hang on. When in February the great Russian winter counteroffensive lost its momentum, and German Army Group Centre, despite dire sufferings, was saved, he could boast that it was thanks to his rejecting the advice of his staff-trained generals. From this time the Führer was his own commander-in-chief. Despite his occasional flashes of strategic insight and tactical skill, this was to prove very much to the advantage of the Allies.

THE MILITARY BALANCE ON THE EASTERN FRONT

Hitler ordered the preparation of an attack on Russia as early as 21 July 1940. The first plans of OKH (*Oberkommando des Heeres*/Army High Command) envisaged two major thrusts to Moscow and Kiev with a covering thrust in the north (**Map 1**). This was altered after war games, to include a major attack in the north, the main objective still being Moscow (**Map 2**). However, at planning conferences early in December Hitler directed that Leningrad was the most urgent target, and that part of the central thrust might be diverted after the capture of Smolensk to support this plan (**Map 3**). It was on this general idea that 'Barbarossa', the final plan was drawn up. The Germans aimed for a rapid campaign with deep armoured penetrations to surround and smash the Red Army well before winter. They had allotted 138 divisions, including 48 Panzer divisions, to the task. They estimated Russian strength at about 155 divisions. This proved an underestimate, for, of a total of some 230 divisions, the Red Army had 170 within operational distance of its Western front: but in no other way was it ready for war in 1941. The leadership had not recovered from the 1937 purges; a major reorganization and re-equipment programme put in hand after the Finnish War was not yet completed; units in the west were far too close to the frontiers; and the building up of a strong reserve to meet any deep penetrations had only just begun.

The front was divided into two separate halves by the Pripet marshes, and the bulk of German strength lay in the north (**Map 4**). Von Leeb's Army Group North with Leningrad as its objective was faced by an almost equal number of Russian divisions but these were deployed so far forward that they were vulnerable to being pushed back against the coast by a deep thrust towards Riga and beyond. Von Bock's Army Group Centre, with two Panzer armies, was the strongest. The Red Army West Front facing it was not only considerably weaker, but had a complete army lying invitingly in the salient around Bialystock. This the Germans planned to surround by striking from both flanks – the Panzer armies aiming to meet at Minsk while the infantry closed in to the east of Bialystok. The bulk of the Red Army lay south of the Pripet marshes defending the agricultural and industrial wealth of the Ukraine. Once again the Red Army's dispositions made it vulnerable to a south-easterly thrust by the bulk of von Rundstedt's Army Group South.

The massive German build-up had, of course, been observed by the Russians, but Stalin was so determined not to give Hitler any excuse to attack that in June 1941 the Red Army was still on a peacetime footing with most units widely scattered for summer training.

Below: A sentry guarding the Channel coast after Axis interest had moved east

Map labels:

BALTIC SEA

Latvia — RIGA

North Front (Popov)

MEMEL

EAST PRUSSIA

Lithuania

DANZIG

Eighth Army (Sobennikov)

North-West Front (F.I. Kuznetsov, then Sobennikov) 24 divisions (inc 4 tank divs)

Army Group North (Leeb) 26 divisions (inc 3 panzer divs) Luftflotte I

reserve

added later for security operations

Eighteenth Army (Küchler)

KÖNIGSBERG

Fourth Panzergruppe (Hoeppner)

Sixteenth Army (Busch)

Eleventh Army (Morosov) — KAUNAS

Third Panzergruppe (Hoth)

SUWALKI

Ninth Army (Strauss)

Third Army (V.I. Kuznetsov)

West Front (Pavlov, then Timoshenko) 38 divisions (inc 8 tank divs)

Vistula

BIALYSTOK

Tenth Army (Golubev)

MINSK

Army Group Centre (Bock) 51 divisions (inc 9 panzer divs) Luftflotte II

reserve

WARSAW

Fourth Army (Kluge)

Bug

Thirteenth Army (Filatov) Front reserve at Minsk

Fourth Army (Korobkov)

Belorussia

POLAND

Second Panzergruppe (Guderian)

BREST LITOVSK

PINSK

Sixth Army (Reichenau) — KRAKOW

LUBLIN

Pripet Marshes — Pripet

Fifth Army (Potapov)

First Panzergruppe (Kleist)

Seventeenth Army (Stülpnagel)

Slovakia

PRZEMYSL

ROVNO

LVOV

Sixth Army (Muzychenko)

Pre-war Polish boundary

South-West Front (Kirponos, then Budenny) 56 divisions (inc 16 tank divs)

reserve

Twenty-sixth Army (Kostenko)

HUNGARY

Hungarian divs

Ukraine

Army Group South (Rundstedt) 59 divisions (inc 5 panzer divs, 14 Rumanian divs & 2 Hungarian divs) Luftflotte IV

reserve

CHERNOVTSY

Twelfth Army (Ponedelin)

Carpathian Mts

Rum Third Army (Dumitrescu)

Eighteenth Army (Smirnov)

Eleventh Army (Schobert)

JASSY

Moldavia

South Front (Tyulenev) 16 divisions (inc 4 tank divs)

Prut

Rum Fourth Army (Ciuperca)

Ninth Army (Cherevichenko)

ODESSA

RUMANIA

GALATI

Danube

BLACK SEA

ARMOURED DIVISIONS

OTHER DIVISIONS, including motorised infantry (in Panzergruppen) and cavalry

0 — MILES — 150

0 — KILOMETRES — 200

THE GERMAN ASSAULT

German forces invaded Soviet territory at 0300 hours on 22 June 1941, achieving almost total tactical surprise. In the north Fourth Panzergroup took Daugavpils by 26 June and began establishing bridgeheads across the River Dvina. Ostrov was reached by 4 July, and the Luga river by the 14th.

Army Group Centre began sealing off the Russian forces facing it around Bialystok and Gorodishche, and Second and Third Panzergroups met west of Minsk on 29 June. By 9 July all resistance in the pockets had ended with the Red Army losing some 300,000 prisoners and 2,500 tanks. Meanwhile the Panzers had pushed on across the Berezina on 1 July. On 3 July the two groups were merged into Fourth Panzer Army and the units of Fourth Army were renamed Second Army. Fourth Panzer was given the task of breaking through to Smolensk, and its units began crossing the rivers Dvina and Dniepr on 9 July. Smolensk was reached on 16 July but Russian counterattacks halted any further advance and prevented the Soviet forces near the city from being completely surrounded.

Army Group South had experienced the toughest resistance. A successful initial breakthrough by First Panzergroup was counterattacked on 10 July from the north near Korosten by the Russian Fifth Army and from the south near Kazatin. These were fought off but though the Panzers had pushed on to within ten miles of Kiev by 11 July they were unable to assault the city. The Soviet Fifth Army pulled back but continued to threaten the northern flank of the German advance.

It was now that Hitler began to envisage halting Army Group Centre and concentrating on capturing the Ukraine. On 19 July OKW (*Oberkommando der Wehrmacht*/Supreme High Command) directed that after the destruction of the Russian forces near Smolensk, Second Panzergroup and Second Army should swing south to destroy the Russian Fifth Army and surrounded Kiev by linking up with units from First Panzergroup which would strike north.

Guderian, commanding Second Panzergroup, objected strongly to abandoning the Moscow offensive, but used the opportunity to strike southeast on 1 August to break up Russian forces strengthening his flank from Roslavl. The ring around the Russian forces at Smolensk had been closed on 27 July, and by 5 August these had been destroyed. Meanwhile First Panzergroup had struck towards Pervomaisk on 30 July linking up with units of Seventeenth Army on 3 August. Russian resistance in the pocket near Uman ended on 8 August, and Army Group South pushed on to reach Dnepropetrovsk and form a bridgehead at Kremenchug.

On 23 August Second Panzergroup and Second Army began moving south through Gomel and Starodub. The Russians had been reinforcing their South-West Front and on 30 August they launched a counteroffensive north of Gomel which was turned back, however, without halting the German advance. On 12 September First Panzergroup struck north from Kremenchug, and on the 15th the two pincers met at Lokhvitsa. During the next two days the Russian Fifth and Thirty-Seventh Armies were totally destroyed and about 500,000 men lost.

In the north, Army Group North had reached Novgorod by 16 August, and was poised to close in on Leningrad.

Above right: German motorized units pursue the Russians

Right: Engineers repairing a bridge over the Dniepr

THE FINNISH ATTACKS

Finland's defeat by the Red Army in 1939/40 meant that Hitler had a ready ally for 'Barbarossa'. A co-ordinated attack by German troops from Norway in the far north and the Finnish army under Marshal Mannerheim in Karelia was planned to link up with Army Group North. The attacks began on 29 June, but by the beginning of September the three northern attacks had been halted. Further south Mannerheim's attacks north of Lake Ladoga had begun well with a breakthrough which reached the lake east of Sortavala on 16 July. But the Russians withdrew their outflanked forces by water, and fell back steadily so that by 1 September the Finns had reached a stop-line, close to the 1939 frontier. On the Isthmus an attack through Vuosalmi to outflank Viipuri began on 31 July and reached Vuosalmi on 16 August. But a chance to cut off the Russian forces at Viipuri was narrowly missed, and they were able to withdraw. By 1 September the Finns had reached the pre-1939 defences of Leningrad. Here they halted, for Mannerheim, having regained the territory lost in 1939–40, was reluctant to become more deeply involved in the attack on Russia.

The second stage of the offensive attacks north of Lake Ladoga to capture Petrozavodsk and cut the Murmansk railway began on 3 September and by the 8th the line had been cut at Lodeynoye Pele. Russian resistance was steadily increasing and Petrozavodsk was not taken until 1 October. For the next two months attacks continued in the area but once Medvezhegorsk was taken on 6 December the Finns went over to the defensive.

Below: Finnish troops advance through a ruined town in eastern Karelia

Map legend

— · — 1939 RUSSO-FINNISH BOUNDARY
DISPOSITION OF DIVISIONS, 10 JULY 1941
✝ FINNISH 卐 GERMAN ★ RUSSIAN
▪▪▪▪ MANNERHEIM'S STOP LINE, 1 SEPTEMBER 1941
▪▪▪▪ FINAL FRONT LINE DECEMBER 1941

0 — MILES — 200
0 — KILOMETRES — 300

ARCTIC OCEAN

NORWAY (Occupied by Germany)

PETSAMO
Rybachiy Peninsula
Gebirgskorps (Mountain Corps)
Litsa
MURMANSK
Fourteenth Army

AOK Norwegen (Falkenhorst)

Kola Peninsula
Murmansk railway
KANDALAKSHA

SWEDEN

XXXVI Corps
KEMIJÄRVI
SALLA
ROVANIEMI

KUUSAMO
KESTENGA
LOUKHI
White Sea

Fin III Corps

Gulf of Bothnia
FINLAND
OULU
UKHTA R U S S I A
KEM

Seventh Army
BELOMORSK

New relief railway

Soviet Karelia
L Seg
L Vyg

Finnish Army Group (Mannerheim)

MEDVEZHEGORSK 6 Dec
POVENETS

Fin VI Corps

Fin Karelian Army

Fin VII Corps

L Onega

Fin II Corps
SORTAVALA 16 July
PETROZAVODSK 1 Oct

Fin S-East Army
VIDLITSA

Fin IV Corps
OLONETS 6 Sept
Svir

VUOSALMI 11 Aug
L Ladoga 1 Sept
LODEYNOYE POLE 8 Sept

HELSINKI

VIIPURI
Twenty-third Army

Gulf of Finland
HANKO (USSR) 3 Dec
LENINGRAD
SCHLÜSSELBURG (Petrokrepost)
1 Sept

Estonia
Army Group North

88

THE ATTACK ON LENINGRAD

On 1 September 1941 the forces of
Army Group North were close enough
to begin the artillery bombardment of
Leningrad. The Germans who had
decided against storming the city
strove to surround it and starve it into
surrender. On 15 September, with the
capture of Schlüsselburg, the city was
completely cut off from overland
communication with the rest of Russia.
The food remaining in the city was
sufficient, heavily rationed, for about
one month, and starvation began to set
in during October and November with
11,000 people dying in the latter
month. A supply route from Tikhvin to
Lednevo had been used to get some
food across the lake in barges, but on
9 November the Germans took Tikhvin
and in the middle of the month, ice
on the lake – not yet thick enough to
stand the weight of trucks – made
navigation impossible. A new road
from Zaborie via Karpino to Lednevo
was opened on 6 December, but what
with the weather and the difficult
terrain trucks could scarcely do twenty
miles a day on it. However, on
9 December, as part of the Red Army's
great winter counteroffensive,
Tikhvin was recaptured and the
Germans were pushed back to the
Volkhov river. The railway was
repaired and an ice road opened
across the lake allowing a proper
supply line to the city. But the supply
situation remained precarious; on
25 December, the day when it proved
possible to increase the bread ration,
3,700 people died of starvation.

Right: A policeman looks at the corpses of
civilians who had died of starvation
in Leningrad

THE BATTLE FOR MOSCOW 1

With the ending of the Kiev battle, the Germans redeployed their forces for the assault on Moscow. Hoth's Third Panzergroup, brought down from Army Group North, and Fourth Panzergroup were to strike towards Vyazma while Guderian's Panzergroup further south aimed at Orel and Bryansk. The Germans had forty-four infantry divisions, eight motorized divisions, and fourteen Panzer divisions for the assault with a 2:1 superiority in men and tanks and about 3:1 in the air. Because of the greater distance to be covered Guderian's attack began on 30 September and the other on 2 October (**Map 1**). By 7 October large pockets of Russian troops had been cut off around Vyazma and Bryansk. But the next day heavy rains began and mud started to hinder the German mobile units which were now pushing towards Tula and Kaluga in the south and Rzhev and Kalinin in the north. The pocket at Vyazma was destroyed on 14 October and that at Bryansk on 20 October. However, increasingly stubborn Russian resistance along the Mozhaysk defence line and the weather meant that by 30 October the German attacks had halted between 45 and 75 miles short of Moscow. Now the freeze began to harden the roads again and the Germans prepared for the final thrusts to reach the Volga canal north of Moscow and the Moskva river to the south before undertaking the close encirclement of the city. The Germans had now virtually lost their superiority in men and tanks, and were finding it difficult to adapt to the extreme cold. The assault began on 15 November and by 27 November units of Third Panzergroup had reached the Volga canal within 19 miles of the centre of Moscow, while on the 25th units of Second Panzer Army reached Kashira but had to fall back for lack of support. The Germans were now unable to make any further progress and on 5 December it was decided to

pull Third Panzergroup back to the Istra/Klin line and Second Panzergroup back to the Don/Ulla line and to go over to the defensive.

Meanwhile, Army Group South had launched attacks to capture Kharkov and secure the Ukraine (**Map 2**). Von Kleist's First Panzergroup burst across the Dniepr and Samara on 30 September, swinging south behind the Russian Eighteenth and Ninth Armies to reach Berdyansk on 6 October. More than 100,000 prisoners were captured in this pocket, but rain and mud were now slowing the German advance, and the Russians were no longer trying to hold the Germans with linear defences but were pulling back gradually towards the Donets while building up a new army – the Thirty-seventh – in the Krasnodon area to threaten the flank of any attack on Rostov. Kharkov was occupied by the Germans on 24 October and on 1 November First

Panzergroup began its thrust towards Rostov. This reached the Tuslov river on 14 November, but the threat of Thirty-seventh Army on the flank forced the Germans to abandon plans to outflank Rostov, and the city was taken by frontal attack on 20 November. On 29 November Thirty-seventh Army and part of Second Army put in a counterattack which threatened to cut off the German units in the city. Von Rundstedt therefore ordered his forces to pull back to the Mius river, and resigned when Hitler tried to countermand the order.

Below: As the first snows arrive, German troops struggle to release an assault gun trapped by mud

①

RUSSIAN
▲▲▲ VYAZMA DEFENCE LINE
△△△ MOZHAYSK DEFENCE LINE
▬ ▬ MOSCOW DEFENCE LINES
▨ TRAPPED POCKETS

MILES 0 — 100
KILOMETRES 0 — 160

North-West Front

Kalinin Front

West Front

Reserve Front

West Front

Bryansk Front

South-West Front

Army Group North

Ninth Army

Third Panzergruppe (Hoth)

Fourth Army

Fourth Panzergruppe (Hoeppner)

Army Group Centre (Bock)

Second Army

Second Panzer Army ('Panzergruppe Guderian')

Army Group South

Twenty-second Army
Twenty-ninth Army
Thirtieth Army
Nineteeth Army
Sixteenth Army
Thirty-first Army
Forty-ninth Army
Thirty-second Army
Twentieth Army
Twenty-fourth Army
Forty-third Army
Fiftieth Army
Third Army
Thirteenth Army
Fortieth Army

DEMYANSK
VISHNI VOLOCHEK
Lake Seliger
OSTASHKOV
SELIZHAROVO
KALININ
Volga Reservoir
Volga
DMITROV
ALEKSANDROV
VLADIMIR
TOROPETS
OLENINO
STARITSA
YAKHROMA
KLIN
KRASNAYA POLYANA
RZHEV
BELYY
SYCHEVKA
VOLOKOLAMSK
SOLNECH-NOGORSK
KHIMKI
ISTRA
MOSCOW
Klyazma
DUKHOVSHCHINA
GZHATSK
BORODINO
NARO-FORMINSK
PODOLSK
Moskva
YARTSEVO
VYAZMA
MOZHAYSK
BOROVSK
MALOYAROSLAVETS
Moscow Highway
MEDYN
SMOLENSK
Dniepr
YELNYA
YUKHNOV
Ugra
KALUGA
SERPUKHOV
KASHIRA
Oka
RYAZAN
ALEKSIN
VENEV
MIKHAYLOV
SUKHINICHI
TULA
KIROV
STALINOGORSK
ROSLAVL
BELEV
Upa
TEPLOYE
GORLOVO
BOLKHOV
DANKOV
MTSENSK
YEFREMOV
POCHEP
BRYANSK
Oka
OREL
NOVOSÍL
STARODUB
YELETS
LIVNY
Sosna
NOVGOROD SEVERSKI
SEVSK
DMITRIEV–LGOVSKIY
Don
CHERNIGOV
Desna
KURSK
VORONEZH
KONOTOP
OBOYAN
TIM
Second Panzer Army begins offensive 30 September. All other armies attack 2 October
SUMY
PRILUKI
BELGOROD
Kharkov 30 miles

GERMAN
▬▬▬ FRONT LINE, 30 SEPTEMBER 1941
➤ OFFENSIVE, 30 SEPT/30 OCT
▬·▬· FRONT LINE, 10 OCTOBER
▬ ▬ FRONT LINE, 30 OCT/15 NOV
➤ OFFENSIVE 15 NOV/5 DEC
▬▬▬ FRONT LINE, 5 DECEMBER
×××× ARMY GROUP COMMAND BOUNDARY

THE BATTLE FOR MOSCOW 2

On 5/6 December just as the Germans had decided to go over to the defensive, the Russian Kalinin, West, and South-West Fronts launched a counteroffensive. *Stavka* (The Soviet Supreme Command) had been bringing up fresh divisions from Siberia and had been planning the attacks from the last week in November. The main thrusts, spearheaded by First Shock Army to the north of Moscow and Tenth Army to the south, aimed to push back the Germans from their nearest penetrations to the city, and to threaten their supply lines from the south. The first week brought spectacular successes as disorganized German troops fell back swiftly and Stalin began to envisage a massive counteroffensive all along the front, which would relieve Leningrad and regain the Donbas region of the Ukraine, as well as cutting off the German Army Group Centre. *Stavka* and particularly General Zhukov, commanding West Front, advised against any widening of objectives which would weaken the existing thrusts and bring the Red Army up against prepared positions, but Stalin was insistent. Orders went out on

5 January and the new offensives began on the 7th.

In the north, Third Shock Army and Thirty-fourth Army struck west against Army Group North, while Fourth Shock Army thrust south towards Vitebsk aiming to cut the main supply lines of Army Group Centre. Kalinin Front pushed forward towards Rzhev, while Bryansk Front tried to cut behind the German Fourth Army and reach Bryansk. By late January the scale of the offensive had used up all Russian reserves and the Germans were beginning to counterattack. In the north seven divisions of German

II Corps, surrounded near Demyansk, could not be destroyed and were eventually relieved. The southern attacks on Vyazma were being counterattacked from the flanks, and Twenty-ninth Army which had almost reached Vyazma from the north had its line of retreat cut south of Rzhev. For the next two months fighting continued, but the Germans, despite large-scale partisan activity behind their lines, were able to stabilize their front, holding on to the Rzhev/Gzhatsk/Vyazma triangle.

Above: Russian troops, well-equipped to withstand the extreme conditions, assault a German position

Below: Soviet tanks in attack. The Germans were shocked by the scale of the Russian operations

THE
JAPANESE
OFFENSIVE

Opposite: Japanese light tanks crossing a
bridge near Manila in the Philippines

On 7 December, without awaiting the declaration of war, the Japanese attacked the US Pacific Fleet in Pearl Harbor, taking it by surprise and inflicting heavy casualties. Many an Axis victory still lay ahead, but beyond question no event in the whole war equalled in importance the act which brought in the United States, with their wealth of resources, squarely on the Allied side. For Great Britain it was a turning point even more significant than the day nearly six months earlier, when the Germans invaded Russia.

No good American thought it possible that Japanese intentions could have been suspected in Washington, and when President Roosevelt denounced 7 December as 'a date which will live in infamy' his people readily accepted his declaration that the war was a single whole, comprising German and Italian enemies as well as Japanese. This too was of great advantage to the British, especially after it was agreed that the European war should take priority.

The Axis leaders were not unduly perturbed when their Japanese allies pushed the United States into the war, though Count Ciano, the Italian Foreign Minister, unlike his jubilant German counterpart, von Ribbentrop, had the wit to see that America would now enter the European conflict, which would be so long that she would be able to bring all her potential forces to bear. In this he proved absolutely right.

Japan had already been at war since 1937: against China. Like Hitler she was bent on obtaining *Lebensraum*, the so-called 'Greater East Asia Co-Prosperity Sphere'. In July 1941 the French government of Marshal Pétain, unable to protect Indo-China, had agreed to its occupation by Japan. Roosevelt, who had been financing and supplying the Chinese, immediately froze Japanese assets in the USA. Great Britain and the Netherlands followed suit. Major-General J. F. C. Fuller saw this as 'a declaration of economic war', and it may be that the Japanese were

persuaded that they had now to choose between war and economic ruin.

It is hard to conceive that General Tojo's government, which came to power in October 1941, can have hoped for complete victory over two such great maritime and industrial powers, as the USA and Great Britain, whose homelands were, practically speaking, beyond their reach. Rather the Japanese hoped by a swift onslaught to seize and consolidate a controlling position in the Pacific before the balance of forces should swing against them. In the short term they were in a strong position, whilst many Allied possessions were extremely vulnerable. Japan's main strength lay in her ten fast modern carriers, each of which carried some seventy-five aircraft. Japanese pilots were extremely well-trained and to a great extent Japan owed her initial successes to superiority at sea and in the air. In Malaya and the Philippines the Japanese did not owe their victory to any vast superiority in the strength of her land forces. The most important factor was that they had a balanced force, and the backing of numbers of efficient, modern aircraft. Their forces were, moreover, well-versed in the techniques of amphibious warfare. Their morale was excellent, and even at the end of the war it was rare indeed for them to lose more than a handful of prisoners. The men were hardy, frugal, and, it must be said, bloodthirsty. Tactically they were enterprising, never afraid to operate at night or in jungle, or to cut loose from their lines of communications. They had, moreover, four years of recent battle experience behind them.

A factor of some importance was that for the most part the indigenous inhabitants were not unduly disturbed at seeing their white rulers, however benevolent, ejected. And they had not all been benevolent.

It was ironical that by knocking out the American battleships at Pearl Harbor the Japanese had altered the nature of sea warfare, and practically

deprived their own numerous and expensive battleships of their *raison d'être*. In the decisive battles of the Pacific, battles between carriers, no ship on either side was to see an opposing capital ship. And as it turned out the Americans were rather quicker to master the new techniques of maritime warfare.

The first six months of the land fighting in the Far East was a period of practically unrelieved gloom. The splendid resistance of Major James Deveraux and his 500 United States Marines on Wake Island, and Lieutenant-General Jonathan Wainwright's dogged defence of Corregidor were practically the only bright spots, though General Douglas MacArthur emerged as a leader of real quality, and one who had prepared his command for war. In Malaya Lieutenant-General A. E. Percival had had only seven months in which to make ready, and what with the prevailing attitude of the white population and the lamentable state of training of his troops the task proved too much for him. Only one battalion, 2 Argyll and Sutherland Highlanders, is thought to have made any serious attempt to train for jungle warfare. Perceval still had some 85,000 British, Australian, and Indian troops when he surrendered – by far the biggest surrender in the annals of the British army. In Burma the British though gravely outnumbered, deployed too far forward and suffered a nasty setback in the Battle of the Sittang River, which led to the longest retreat any British force has ever made. Had it not been for the arrival of General Alexander and Lieutenant-General Slim Burma Corps might well have disintegrated. As it was the survivors lived to form the cadre of the Fourteenth Army, which was one day to reconquer the country.

Opposite above: A Japanese photograph of the US fleet under attack at Pearl Harbor

Above: Japanese troops advancing into Singapore under cover of a tank

Right: An Australian anti-tank gun in action outside Singapore

R U S S I A

Kamchatka

ULAN BATOR ·

MONGOLIA

MANCHURIA
(MANCHUKUO)
HARBIN ·

MUKDEN ·

VLADIVOSTOK

Sakhalin

Kurile Is

ETOROFU
Tankan Bay

26 Nov 1941
Nagumo's fleet
sails

4 D
Re
po

Hokkaido

SEA OF
JAPAN

C H I N A

PEKING ·

KOREA
SEOUL ·

Honshu

TOKYO ■
JAPAN

Hwang Ho

NANKING
HANKOW

Shikoku

7 Dec 1941

16 Dec
Part of fleet
to Wake I. i
support of a

CHUNGKING ·

Yangtse kiang

CHANGSHA ·

NAGASAKI ·
KAGOSHIMA ·
SHANGHAI

Kyushu

BONIN IS

Burma Road

KUNMING ·

Ryukyu Is

IWO JIMA

P A C I

8 Dec
Wake I. attack
23 Dec
surrendered

DELHI ■

NEPAL

Ganges

IMPHAL ·

LASHIO ·

PESCADORES
IS ·

CANTON ·

Formosa
(Taiwan)

WAKE (USA)

KARACHI ·

CALCUTTA ·

MANDALAY ·

HONG KONG
(Brit.)

Luzon

Marianas
Islands

SAIPAN ·

I N D I A

BURMA

HANOI ·

HAINAN

MANILA ·

PHILIPPINE
ISLANDS

O C E

GUAM (USA)

ENIWETOK ·

BOMBAY ·

RANGOON ■

THAI-
LAND

FRENCH
INDO-CHINA

Mindanao

YAP ·

KWAJALEIN ·

Marsh
Island

MADRAS ·

BANGKOK ■

SAIGON ·

DAVAO ·

PALAU IS

TRUK ·

MAJU

ANDAMAN
IS

SOUTH CHINA
SEA

MAK

BAY OF
BENGAL

TRINCOMALEE ·

NICOBAR
IS

KHOTA BHARU ·

N BORNEO

HALMAHERA

Caroline Islands

TARAWA ·

Gil
Is

COLOMBO ■

Ceylon

SARAWAK

NAURU ·

OCEAN I

Maldive
Is

Equator

SINGAPORE ■

MALAYA

Borneo

Sumatra

Celebes

DUTCH EAST INDIES

New Guinea

NEW
IRELAND

NEW
BRITAIN

RABAUL

NANUMEA

BATAVIA ■

Java

FLORES

PAPUA

BOUGAINVILLE

Solomon Is

Ellice
Is

I N D I A N

TIMOR

ARAFURA SEA

NEW
GEORGIA

GUADALCANAL ·

O C E A N

TIMOR SEA

PORT
MORESBY

SANTA
CRUZ IS

CORAL SEA

ESPIRITU-SANT

DARWIN ·

CAIRNS ·

New
Hebrides

F
Is

EFATE ·

Northern
Territory

Queensland

New
Caledonia

A U S T R A L I A

ROCKHAMPTON ·

NOUMEA ·

Western
Australia

South
Australia

BRISBANE ■

NORFOLK ·

PERTH ·

New South
Wales

ADELAIDE ·

SYDNEY ■
CANBERRA ■

Victoria

TASMAN

AUCKLAND

MELBOURNE ■

SEA

WELLINGTON
NEW ZEALAND

CHRISTCHURCH ·

JAPANESE EMPIRE, 1933
OCCUPIED BY JAPAN, JULY 1937/DECEMBER 1941
MILITARY BASES ESTABLISHED BY JAPAN, SEPTEMBER 1940
ABDA (American, British, Dutch, and Australian) COMMAND
MERCATOR'S PROJECTION

The map on the left shows the Pacific with labels.

ATKA

Aleutian Islands

Japanese carrier
strike force

MIDWAY

0600 hrs, 7 Dec 1941
Air strike on
Pearl Harbor launched

P A C

Hawaiian Is
OAHU
PEARL HARBOR

I F I C

N

PALMYRA

CHRISTMAS

JARVIS

Phoenix Is   MALDEN

VICTORIA

Tokelau Is   CAROLINE

Samoa Is   SUVOROV

TAHITI

Cook Is   Society Is

Tonga Is
RAROTONGA   TUBUAI

KERMADEC IS

International date line (Monday)
(Sunday)

THE SITUATION IN THE PACIFIC

Japan had invaded China in 1937, and by 1941 had occupied about one-third of the country. But Chinese resistance was being bolstered financially by the United States and she was receiving supplies via the Burma Road and through the ports of French Indo-China. In August 1940 Japan persuaded the French to allow her airforce units to operate from northern Indo-China, and in July 1941 she presented an ultimatum demanding the use of bases throughout the country. America which had diplomatically opposed the steady growth of Japanese expansion, now reacted by freezing her assets and thus effectively cutting off her oil supplies.

It now seemed essential to the Japanese government that if Japan was to remain able to realize her long-term aim of ousting the colonial powers as the controllers of the Far East, she must strike decisively to seize the oil-rich Dutch East Indies and the British,

French, and American colonies astride the sea routes, before her supplies ran out. War plans were drawn up which envisaged first the invasions of Malaya and the Philippines and then the capture of the Dutch East Indies and Burma. The Japanese forces available were relatively modest – only eleven of the total fifty-one divisions could be spared from China and Manchuria – and they would be outnumbered in each theatre during the initial attacks. But they were well-supported in the air and had been trained in jungle warfare. The British and Dutch forces were depleted by two years of warfare elsewhere and the Americans had only just begun to build up the defences of the Philippines. At sea the Japanese fleet with six large and four smaller carriers, as well as eight battleships, outnumbered the US Pacific Fleet which had only four carriers and nine First World War battleships. The Japanese knew that they could not hope to win a long war but they were confident that they would achieve their aims within six months.

The attack was to begin with the destruction of the American fleet by a carrier-borne raid on Pearl Harbor at dawn on 7 December. Landings in Malaya would begin the same day and those on the Philippines two days later. Indo-China and Thailand would also be occupied during the first phase of the operation.

Below: Australian troops in the Malayan jungle before the Japanese attacks

PEARL HARBOR

The Japanese strike force to attack Pearl Harbor sailed on 26 November. It consisted of six fleet carriers escorted by two battleships and two heavy cruisers. It refuelled on 4 December and turned south-east on 6 December (see map on previous page) to reach the launch position at daybreak on the 7th. American monitoring of increased Japanese radio traffic during November had made it clear that some operation was planned and all forces in the Pacific had been alerted. But as the Japanese approached Pearl Harbor, the forces there were still on a peacetime – and weekend – footing: aircraft undispersed, ships anchored in lines with many of their crews ashore, and no extra reconnaissance flights being flown. The two carriers *Lexington* and *Saratoga* were away taking supplies to Wake Island, but eight battleships lay at anchor.

The Japanese strike force began launching its aircraft at 0600 hours.

The attack was to be made in two waves. The first wave was spotted at 0700 hours by a radar station; but its report was ignored. At 0740 the aircraft reached the north coast of Oahu and swung west around the island. A few minutes before 0800 the torpedo bombers went in to attack the harbour while fighters began to strafe the airfields. In the first attack five battleships – *West Virginia, Arizona, Nevada, Oklahoma, California,* and the target ship *Utah* were hit, and only *Maryland* and *Tennessee*, which were on inside berths, and *Pennsylvania*, which was in dock, were not struck by torpedoes. The dive bombers and high-level bombers then joined in so that by 0835 *West Virginia* was sinking, *Arizona* had settled on the bottom, *Oklahoma* and *Utah* had capsized, *Tennessee* was badly on fire, and *Oklahoma* mortally damaged. *Nevada* was under way for the harbour entrance, while almost all the US aircraft had been destroyed.

The second Japanese wave attacking a few minutes later damaged *Pennsylvania* and forced *Nevada* to beach herself. The Americans had reacted with remarkable speed and this wave was met with a more effective defence. The Japanese withdrew at 0945 hours, having lost only nine fighters, fifteen dive bombers, and five torpedo bombers, but their commander Vice-Admiral Nagumo refused to launch another attack which might have caught the aircraft carriers and completed destruction of the port facilities. The strike force withdrew, despatching some units to assist in

the subjection of Wake Island. This came under steady air and sea bombardment on 8 December. The US Marine Corps garrison succeeded in sinking two Japanese destroyers, and it was not until 23 December that the Japanese landed and overwhelmed it after a heroic defence.

Opposite above: The crew cheers as Japanese aircraft take off for the attack on Pearl Harbor

Opposite below: US sailors attempting to douse the flames on uss *West Virginia*

THE INVASION OF MALAYA

The invasion of Malaya had been assigned to the Japanese Twenty-fifth Army commanded by Lieutenant-General Yamashita. This consisted of three divisions – 5, 18, and Imperial Guards – supported by 600 aircraft. Against it Lieutenant-General A.E. Percival had two divisions supported by about 150 aircraft. Transports carrying Twenty-fifth Army left Indo-Chinese ports on 4 December, and at dawn on the 8th, while Fifteenth Army began the occupation of French Indo-China and Thailand, the 5 and 18 Divisions began landing at Singora and Patani on the Kra Peninsula just north of the Malay border, and 'Takumi Force', a regimental group, landed at Khota Baru (**Map 1**). The northern landings were unopposed, but Takumi Force had to fight its way ashore and was not secure until the evening. Meanwhile air attacks on RAF bases had reduced its strength to about fifty aircraft.

The Japanese 5 Division now led a double advance south, and the forward British force – 11 Indian Division – sited around Jitra was attacked on 11 December. After a series of Japanese breakthroughs it fell back in disorder to Alor Star on 12 December. Japanese momentum built up, and with the Guards Division keeping to the coast and 5 and 18 Divisions moving inland, they pushed back 11 Division, outflanking any attempts at defence. A defence line at Kampar was outflanked by sea, and the Slim River line forced by frontal attack. Kuala Lumpur was taken on 11 January by the Japanese 5 Division. The British had now brought forward the Australian 8 Division and 91 Indian Division to hold the Muar River line, but this again was outflanked by a seaborne operation and on 20 January the British forces began to withdraw to Singapore Island, the last units reaching there on 31 January. On 7 February the Japanese Guards Division launched a feint landing on Pulau Ubin (**Map 2**) and the next evening 5 and 18 Divisions crossed in the north-west. By the evening of 9 February they had taken Tengah airfield, and on the 15th the British surrendered.

Opposite above: Japanese troops storm into Kuala Lumpur

Opposite below: General Percival and his staff on their way to surrender Singapore

Below: Australian forces training before the disaster

THE FALL OF HONG KONG

Hong Kong also was invaded on 8 December. Here the Japanese had a massive superiority over the defenders and had pushed them back to the Gindrinkers Line by the evening of 9 December. Once this had been breached by the capture of Shing Mun Redoubt the mainland had to be evacuated and this operation was completed on 13 December. On 18/19 December the Japanese crossed on a wide front and by evening they had captured more than half the island. Fierce fighting continued, but by 22 December most of the reservoirs had been taken and on 25 December the garrison surrendered.

Above right: Japanese officers parade through Hong Kong after the fall of the city

Opposite: HMS *Prince of Wales* in harbour at Singapore shortly before her last voyage

Opposite below: Survivors scramble from HMS *Prince of Wales* to an attendant destroyer

THE SINKING OF FORCE Z

As the likelihood of a Japanese attack on Malaya had increased, Churchill had despatched Force z – the battleship *Prince of Wales* and the battle-cruiser *Repulse* to Singapore, which they reached on 2 December. When Japanese landings were reported on the 8th, the force sailed to intercept the convoys, but was sighted on the afternoon of the next day and turned back to Singapore. Reported Japanese landings at Kuantan made the force head there and *en route* it was sighted by Japanese submarines. Finding nothing at Kuantan the force turned again for Singapore but was attacked by Japanese bombers at 1100 hours: by 1320 both ships were sunk.

THE FALL OF THE PHILIPPINES

In July 1941 the Philippines army was brought into the service of the United States, and General Douglas MacArthur became commander of US Forces in the Far East (USAFFE). He had some ten divisions consisting of 19,000 American troops and 160,000 Filipinos with about 200 aircraft. The bulk of his troops were underequipped and undertrained and the Japanese were confident that their Fourteenth Army with only two divisions supported by 500 aircraft could successfully conquer the islands.

The Japanese launched heavy air attacks on US air bases on 8 December (the same day as the attack on Pearl Harbor but dated one day later because of the International Date Line). Warned by Pearl Harbor, the USAFFE had flown its bombers off Clark Field in the morning, but by midday, when the Japanese attacked, they were back on the ground with their escorting fighters. More than fifty fighters and seventeen B-17s were destroyed and the attacks continued for the next two days so that US air power had ceased to exist when the Japanese made their first landings in the north of Luzon to capture the airfields at Vigan, Laoag, and Tuguegarao, and in the south to capture Legaspi as a base from which to threaten US seaborne reinforcements The airfields were captured with little resistance, while two other landings were made on Mindanao and Jolo, islands in the south of the Philippines group. The Japanese in the north then began moving south to meet the main landings which took place in Lingayen Bay on 22 December. There was little resistance and after delays due to rough seas a firm beachhead was formed by the 24th. The Japanese began to move out of this the next day (see inset map). Despite a determined stand by 26 Cavalry Regiment near Binalonan they were able to push down the major roads to Manila with little trouble. Realizing that his troops were unable to put up an effective resistance, MacArthur had announced his plan to withdraw to Bataan on 23 December, and on the 27th he declared Manila an open city.

By 2 January the Japanese had entered Manila, and come up to the Porac Line at the top of the Bataan peninsula. This they attempted to rush on 2 January but were halted by heavy artillery fire. The defenders then pulled back further along the peninsula.

Below: Japanese light tanks and infantry advance north of Manila

Legend (top left)

xxx	US ARMY COMMAND BOUNDARIES
	AIRFIELDS
*	UNDER FOURTEENTH ARMY COMMAND

Fourteenth Army
(Homma)

Special Task Force
from Formosa

BATAN
8 Dec

10 Dec
Tanaka Detachment
from Pescadores Is.

10 Dec
Kanno Detachment
from Pescadores Is.

CAMIGUIN
10 Dec

**Main Japanese
landings**
22 December 1941
48 Division
(Tsuchibashi)
from Pescadores Is.

APARRI

GONZAGA

LAOAG

Kanno and
Tanaka Dets

VIGAN

TUGUEGARAO
12 Dec

Cordillera Central

Sierra Madre

Cagayan

ILAGAN

BONTOC

L u z o n

BAYOMBONG

SAN FERNANDO
BAUANG

BAGUIO
24 Dec
AGOO
ROSARIO
DAMORTIS

Lingayen G.

Zambales Mts

Agno

TAYUG
CARMEN

SAN JOSE

LINGAYEN

IBA

TARLAC
30 Dec

CABANATUAN
GAPAN
30 Dec

Clark Field
PORAC
Del Carmen Field
SAN FERNANDO
CALUMPIT 2 Jan

DINALUPIHAN
OLONGAPO

23 Dec
MacArthur withdraws
HQ to Bataan

27 Dec
Manila declared
an open city

Bataan
Peninsula

Manila
Bay

MANILA
2 Jan
Nielson & Nichols Fields

CAVITE

CORREGIDOR

Laguna de Bay

MAUBAN

ATIMONAN

Lamon Bay

TIAONG
29 Dec
BATANGAS

SIAIN

DAET

Bicol Peninsula

NAGA

CATANDUANES

24 Dec
16 Division part * (Morioka)
from Amami Oshima (Ryukyu Is.)

South Luzon Force (Parker)
2 infantry divs

North Luzon Force (Wainwright)
4 infantry divs
1 cavalry rgt

Reserve Force (Moore)
1 infantry div near Manila

BOAC

M i n d o r o

SAN JOSE

BURIAS

12 Dec
Kimura Detachment
(33 Rgt, part)
from Palau Is.

LEGASPI

IROSIN

Visayan-Mindanao Force (Sharp)
3 infantry divs

S i b u y a n
S e a

0	MILES 100
0	KILOMETRES 150

Inset map (top right)

BAUANG
NAGUILAN

9 Regt

48 Div
+ 2 tank
regts

BAGUIO
24 Dec

CABA
AGOO
DAMORTIS
ROSARIO

Lingayen Gulf

Caraballo Mts

26 Cav Regt

DAGUPAN
BINALONAN

LINGAYEN
71 Div
TAYUG

11 Div
SAN CARLOS
21 Div
① 24 Dec

91 Div
CARMEN
48 Div

Agno
② 25 Dec
MONCADA

1 Regt
SAN JOSE

BONGABON

③ 27 Dec
PANIQUI

Zaragoza

TARLAC
9 Regt
④ 28 Dec
SANTA ROSA

CABANATUAN
29 Dec

GAPAN
Tank
Dets

DAMBAN
⑤ 31 Dec
Clark Field

Zambales Mts

PORAC

21 Div
Del Carmen Field
2 Jan

SAN FERNANDO
91 Div 71 Div

11 Div
BALIUAG
CALUMPIT 2 Jan
PLARIDEL

DINALUPIHAN

OLONGAPO

Bataan
Peninsula

Manila Bay

Pampanga

MANILA
2 Jan 1942

▲▲▲▲▲	NORTH LUZON FORCE'S (NLF) DELAYING
⑤ 31 Dec	POSITIONS AS PLANNED AND DATES TAKEN UP
	NLF POSITION OF 1/4 JANUARY 1942
→	ROUTE OF SLF INTO BATAAN

THE CONQUEST OF BATAAN

MacArthur's main defence line on Bataan ran down the sides of Mount Santa Rosa. This was taken up on 7 January as the defenders were forced back on to the peninsula. There were now about 80,000 troops and 26,000 civilians in the area. The Japanese began their attack on the main battle position on 9 January with a frontal assault following a heavy bombardment (**Map 1**). This was held after severe fighting, and an attempt on 11 January to outflank the line was thwarted after minor infiltration. But by 23 January, Japanese pressure on the eastern sector of the American line and the threat of an outflanking move forced II Corps to pull back to the reserve battle positions, swiftly followed by I Corps. The Japanese were now suffering from disease and the continual fighting and were unable to make any significant headway during the next two months. Meanwhile MacArthur was flown out on 12 March and Lieutenant-General Jonathan Wainwright took over command. Various attempts to establish seaborne beachheads behind the US lines were defeated and it was not until 3 April that the Japanese, reinforced with a fresh division, began their final offensive with a five-hour air and artillery bombardment. By the morning of 7 April a deep penetration had been achieved in the US II Corps sector and US I Corps was forced to fall back as well. During the next two days the Japanese pushed forward until on 9 April the decision was made to surrender.

The last US forces held out on Corregidor Island which had been under heavy bombardment since the beginning of January. By the end of April most of the defenders' artillery had been knocked out and on 5 May the Japanese launched their assault (**Map 2**). Their troops were to land in the Malinta Tunnel area, but strong tides swept them down to Cavalry Point. They were met by heavy fire, but were able to establish a beachhead.

By 1030 on 6 May the US defences in the Malinta Tunnel area had been breached, and soon afterwards the island was compelled to surrender.

Below: Japanese troops coming ashore on Corregidor

Corregidor

2330 hrs, 5 May 1942
Japanese establish beach-head

North Pt

Cavalry Pt

Kindley landing field

Battery Pt

Malinta Tunnel

BOTTOM-
SIDE

Rock Pt

Monkey Pt

SAN JOSE

0130 hrs, 6 May

MIDDLE-
SIDE

Hospital

TOPSIDE

Barracks

1030 hrs, 6 May
Japanese occupy last
US defence line,
Americans surrender

Hooker Pt

Golf
course

Geary Pt

⚲ GUN BATTERY   ⊥ AA BATTERY

0   MILE   1

0   KILOMETRE   1

Below: The artillery of Corregidor firing in
support of the defenders of Bataan

THE FALL OF DUTCH EAST INDIES

By the beginning of 1942, with their campaigns in Malaya and the Philippines proceeding well, the Japanese could set about the occupation of the Dutch East Indies. This was to be undertaken by a three-pronged attack: Western Force from Indo-China and Sarawak, which had been taken during December 1941, would attack southern Sumatra, western Java, and North Borneo; Central Force from Davao would attack Borneo; and Eastern Force, also from Davao, would take the Celebes, Amboina, and then Timor, Bali, and eastern Java. The Allies in the South-West Pacific had set up a combined command – (ABDA:

American, British, Dutch, and Australian) – under General Sir Archibald Wavell, but this had few forces except a six-cruiser naval flotilla under the Dutch Rear-Admiral, Karel Doorman.

The first Japanese landings, by Central Force at Tarakan and Eastern Force at Manado and Kema, were made on 11 January. By the 13th all three places had been firmly occupied. The next attacks were at Balikpapan, where four US destroyers sank three Japanese transports before withdrawing, and Kendari, where an important airbase was swiftly captured. By 10 February the Japanese had complete control north of the Java and Flores Seas. On 14 February Western Force began landings on Sumatra and parachute landings were made at Palembang on the 16th. Both were successful, and on 20 February the Japanese landed on Timor and Bali. The invasion force for the latter was attacked in the Lombok Straits by the Allied naval force on the night of 18/19 February but managed to beat it off.

The final Japanese move was against western Java with units from Western and Eastern Forces. Once again the Allies sighted Eastern Force and Admiral Doorman attacked the convoy on the evening of 27 February. In the

Battle of the Java Sea both Dutch cruisers were sunk before they could damage the Japanese transports and in the aftermath HMS *Exeter* was also destroyed. The next day, HMAS *Perth* and USS *Houston* came upon the Japanese Western Force and were sunk after causing it considerable damage. Once the Japanese were ashore, there was little to stop them and hostilities ended on 8 March.

Right: Netherlands East Indies troops training

Opposite below: Japanese troops storm ashore during a landing in the Dutch East Indies

THE FALL OF BURMA

The Japanese invasion of Burma began on 15 January 1942 when a detachment of Fifteenth Army occupied Victoria Point before moving north to take Tavoy on 19 January. British defences in Burma had been seriously neglected and only one brigade of 17 Indian Division and a Burmese division under Lieutenant-General T. J. Hutton were available. The main Japanese advance began on 20 January, thrusting towards Moulmein. The British attempted to hold the town but were forced to retreat and fell back with the Japanese continually threatening to outflank them. Delaying actions were fought at the Salween and the Bilin rivers, and a stand was made on the Sittang. Once this had been forced on 21 February the Japanese pushed forward to Rangoon which they occupied on 8 March, only just missing cutting off the British garrison which pulled out hurriedly. General Hutton was now replaced by General Sir Harold Alexander, the British ground forces being placed under Lieutenant-General W. Slim.

Meanwhile the Chinese Fifth and Sixth Armies began to advance into Burma towards Taunggyi where they were attacked by the Japanese on 24 March. When this fell on 30 March the British at Prome had to fall back for fear of being outflanked. The Japanese then continued to pursue the British and Chinese northwards until by 15 May they had completed the conquest of Burma.

Opposite above: Japanese troops take cover while their aircraft bombard a Burmese town

Above: Equipment ablaze at the oilfield of Yenangyuang as the British prepare to retreat

Right: Japanese light tanks crossing an improvised bridge

BHUTAN

TEZPUR   *Brahmaputra*

A s s a m

DINAPUR

I N D I A

SYLHET

KOHIMA

IMPHAL

COMILLA

KALEMYO

KALEWA

SHWEGYIN

CHITTAGONG

YEU

BUDALIN

MONYWA
1 May

MYINGYAN

B U R M A

PAGAN

CHAUK

MAUNGDAW

YENANGYAUNG

MAGWE

AKYAB

MINHLA

33 Div

PYINMANA

Part
55 Div

ALLANMYO

TAUNGUP

B A Y   O F

B E N G A L

Arakan Yoma

PROME
2 Apr

SHWEDAUNG
PAUNGDE

OKPO

Burma Army
(Hutton, Alexander later)

BASSEIN

RANGOON
8 Mar

SADIYA

LEDO

FORT HERTZ

Patkai Mts

SUMPRABUM

TALIFU

*Kachin
Hills*

MYITKYINA
8 May

C H I N A

Burma Road

WANTING

INDAW

WANTHO

KATHA
8 May

BHAMO

MIENNING

S h a n

KUNLONG

LASHIO
29 Apr

Ch Sixty-
sixth Army

SHWEBO

MANDALAY
1 May

AVA

KEHSI MANSAM
28 Apr

S t a t e s

56 Div

KENGTUNG

MEIKTILA

HOPONG

HEHO

NAMSANG

TAUNGGYI

18 Div

TAUNGDWINGYI

Ch Fifth
Army

Ch Sixth
Army

LOIKAW

Karen Hills

BAWLAKE

Salween

CHIENG MAI

TOUNGOO
30 Mar

MAUCHI

Sittang

PAPUN

Mae Nam Ping

UTTARADIT

PEGU

SITTANG

MOKPALIN
BILIN

THATON

PA-AN

KAWKAREIK

RAHENG

20 January 1942
Jap. Fifteenth Army (Iida)
launches main attack

MARTABAN

MOULMEIN
30 Jan

18 and
56 Divs

*Three Pagodas
Pass*

YE

NAKHON SAWAN

T H A I L A N D

AYUTTHAYA

A N D A M A N

S E A

TAVOY

Andaman
Islands

MERGUI

TENASSERIM

Gulf of

Southern Army
(Detachment of
Jap.Fifteenth Army)

CHUMPHON   *Siam*

VICTORIA POINT
15 Jan

Isthmus of Kra

✈ AIRFIELDS

HEIGHT IN FEET

	OVER 10000
	6000 – 10000
	3000 – 6000
	1500 – 3000
	500 – 1500
	UNDER 500

0   MILES   200

0   KILOMETRES   300

NAKHON

THE ITALIAN CAMPAIGN

The paramount task before us is, . . .
using the bases on the African shore,
to strike at the underbelly of the
Axis in effective strength and in the
shortest time.

Winston S. Churchill, January 1943

Opposite: Allied forces passing the Colosseum
after the capture of Rome

With the collapse of the Tunisian bridgehead (12 May 1943) Italy found herself in the front line. Her main ally, inextricably engaged in Russia, was not exactly forthcoming with offers of assistance. 'Can our country resist an invasion?' demanded General Guiseppe Castellano. 'The Italians do not lack patrotism, but it cannot be claimed that they will endure beyond a certain limit when their hopes of a final victory are fading day by day.' Already in March there had been serious strikes in the industrial towns of north Italy, and Mussolini had sacked his chief of police and the secretary of the Fascist party for failing to suppress this discontent. In a meeting with Hitler near Salzburg on 7 April Mussolini had utterly failed to persuade the Führer to patch up a truce with Russia and concentrate on the defence of the Mediterranean – a policy which had the support not only of Rumania and Hungary but of Japan.

The time was not yet ripe for an Allied invasion of northern France, but an assault on Sicily and Italy was calculated to bring about the disintegration of the Axis.

The invasion was not exactly a surprise to the Italian High Command or to their German colleagues in Rome. Strategic bombing – especially that of Pantelleria – and the concentration of shipping in North African ports, clearly indicated what lay ahead. But the Germans, deeply involved with the planning of Operation Citadel, the ill-fated battle of Kursk, had few troops to spare. At the same time they had few illusions as to the state of Italian morale. As General von Rintelen reported to Hitler on 5 May an Allied landing was likely to be followed by 'most unpleasant consequences' . . . 'in view of the prevailing atmosphere of fatalism'. He proved a true prophet. The Sicily landings (10 July) met with far less resistance than had been expected, and some Italian units surrendered *en masse*. Even so General Montgomery's rush to

take Catania failed, and the Axis forces, with the German General Hube virtually in command, reacted very creditably, ensconcing themselves in a formidable position around Mount Etna.

Hitler was furious at the poor performance of his allies in defence of their own soil. General Vittorio Ambrosio, Chief of the Italian General Staff, for his part had the hardihood to blame the Germans, and to point out that it was up to them to put things right. His memorandum of 4 July made it clear to Mussolini that they now faced the prospect of a Second Front on Italian soil. Italy herself lacked the land and air forces to meet such a situation. The Germans must remedy it even if that meant suspending operations in Russia. 'If we cannot prevent the setting up of such a front', he wrote, 'it will be up to the highest political authorities to consider whether it would not be more expedient to spare the country further horror and ruin, and to anticipate the end of the struggle, seeing the final result will undoubtedly be worse in one or more years.' Mussolini, now a sick man, did not contradict Ambrosio. On the other hand he did not dare to put his views to Hitler, though he did consider it. Instead on 21 July he assured von Rintelen that he was resolved to defend Sicily to the last man.

By this time the defeatism of the Italians had aroused the suspicions of Hitler's advisors. A conference at Feltre (19 July) between the two dictators was not a success. Hitler had been briefed by Warlimont to demand a unified command; Mussolini by Ambrosio to tell the Führer frankly that Italy could not go on with the war. Neither spoke to their brief, indeed Mussolini hardly spoke at all, except to read out, in a shaken voice, an announcement that Allied aircraft had just attacked Rome for the first time. Ambrosio was furious at the negative results of the conference, and soon afterwards was drawn into the

Above: Sherman tanks advancing near Cassino

Opposite above: Allied artillery bombarding Cassino

Below: An American anti-tank gun in action at Anzio

plot by which Marshal Badoglio and members of the Royal family were contriving to get rid of Mussolini, who, by his lack of moral courage at Feltre, had let slip his last chance to save himself. On 24 July the Fascist Grand Council, led by Count Grandi voted for the Crown to assume more power, and next day Mussolini was arrested, on Ambrosio's orders, as he emerged from an audience with the King. He was spirited away to the island of Ponza.

The news threw Hitler and his advisors into a turmoil of planning from which emerged Operation *Achse* (Axis) the first orders for which went out on 28 July. A new Army Group B, consisting of eight divisions mostly drawn from France, began to assemble under Rommel whose headquarters were at Munich. Kesselring, the German commander-in-chief in Italy was to conduct his relations with the Italian High Command in such a way that the penetration of German divisions into northern Italy would be unhindered. The Germans had to tread delicately for, whilst doing nothing to provoke Italian hostility or hasten her collapse, they had to be ready to deal with either.

On the very day (28 July) that the first orders for Operation Axis went out the Badoglio government decided to make overtures to the Allies and sent envoys to Lisbon and Tangier.

The Allies did not take the fullest advantage of this situation. For this there were various reasons. The chief was American insistence on Unconditional Surrender. Mr Roosevelt in a speech delivered on 28 July voiced this viewpoint. 'Our terms for Italy are still the same as our terms for Germany and Japan – Unconditional Surrender. We will have no truck with Fascism in any way, shape or manner. We will permit no vestige of Fascism to remain.' It was stirring stuff, but not very realistic at a time when patriotic senior officers like Ambrosio and Castellano had come to loathe their German allies. At a time when it was essential to enlist

Italian cooperation in support of the Salerno landing, it was not very sensible to offer the Italians no hope at all. It should not have been beyond the wit of man to foresee the collapse of Italy. It behoved the Allies, and especially the staff of their Foreign Offices, to work out and agree well in advance the terms upon which Italy should be allowed to withdraw from the – or change sides.

As it was the Italian surrender was arranged in such a way that chaos ensued. The royal family and most of the key figures of the High Command and the government managed to escape to Brindisi. But they left no orders, and the Italian army, not knowing how to behave under the circumstances, permitted itself to be disarmed practically without a shot. General Carboni made an attempt to organize the defence of Rome but in vain. The Germans, who had been planning for two months for just such a situation, were able to meet the Salerno landing practically undistracted by their luckless former allies.

Until the invasion of Normandy the campaign in Italy was, of course, the most important being waged by the Anglo-American Allies in Europe. It tied down, as it was to do until the end, a rather larger number of German divisions – about twenty-five – than the Allies themselves deployed there. By the capture of the Foggia airfields it brought heavy bombers within striking distance of targets in southern Germany. The advance up the Adriatic coast and the occupation of Vis enabled the Allies to support and encourage the partisans groups in the Balkans, and especially Yugoslavia, who themselves managed to occupy the attentions of a number of German divisions. But, after the battle of the Sangro, troops and landing-craft began to be drawn away to England in preparation for the Second Front: General Alexander's campaign now took second priority in the eyes of the Allied strategists. Still the very presence

of Allied troops in the peninsula was a continuing threat not only to Germany's position in the Balkans, but to her southern frontier. The long slog up Italy could have been immeasurably less lengthy and less costly had the Allies been more amply provided with landing-craft, for operations similar to the Termoli landing of 1943, might have 'unlocked' the successive river lines which the Germans held during the course of their long rearguard action.

In the opinion of the late Major-General J. F. C. Fuller the Italian campaign was one 'which for lack of strategic sense and tactical imagination is unique in military history'. He failed to take into account the extent to which the Allied commanders were handicapped by the continual withdrawals of divisions and of landing-craft, not only for Normandy, but for Operation Dragoon, the landing in the south of France – an operation of very doubtful value. The defence of Italy cost the Germans 556,000 casualties, and the Allies 312,000 killed and wounded. The twenty-one Allied divisions contained a total of something like fifty-five German divisions in the Mediterranean area, troops which might well have tipped the balance against the Allies in Russia or in France in the campaigns of 1944.

THE INVASION OF SICILY

With the surrender of the final Axis forces in Tunisia on 13 May, the whole of North Africa was in Allied hands. Where should these victorious Allied troops next be used? As there was still no possibility of a Second Front in north-west Europe, it was considered that the Mediterranean offered further opportunity, but where? Two major strategic opportunities were immediately apparent (**Map 1**): a 'left hook' through Sardinia into northern Italy and southern France, and a 'right hook' into Sicily and southern Italy. The latter alternative was adopted as it offered safer sea communications and allowed the western Allies to draw German forces further away from their supply bases in Germany and from the front in Russia. Moreover parts of Sicily were within range of fighter cover, based on Malta.

The Italian island fortress of Pantelleria lay between Tunis and Sicily, and had to be neutralized before the invasion went in. After an

Below: Unloading stores on the beach at Syracuse

②

TYRRHENIAN SEA

1015 hrs, 17 August
US 3 Div enters Messina

Cape S Vito
TRAPANI
CASTELLAMMARE
PALERMO
22 July
TERMINI IMERESE
23 July
CEFALU
US landings outflank German rearguards
C Orlando
11 Aug
8 Aug
15 Aug
MESSINA
BARCELLONA
SCALETTA
PATTI
SANT' AGATA
Strait of Messina
REGGIO
ALCAMO
Aosta Div
US 2 Armd Div
US 82 Abn Div
Part 15 Pz Gr Div
SALEMI
CORLEONE
US 45 Div
US 3 Div
31 July
SAN STEFANO
RANDAZZO
LINGUAGLOSSA
16 Aug
MARSALA
Assietta Div
PRIZZI
PETRALIA
US 1 and 9 Divs
NICOSIA
TROINA
BRONTE
Mt Etna
GIARRE
ACIREALE
MENFI
SCIACCA
RIBERA
Belice
HQ Ital Sixth Army (Guzzoni)
ENNA
US 1 Div
LEONFORTE
AGIRA
Salso
REGALBUTO
CENTURIPE
Group Schmalz
ADRANO
78 Div
PATERNO
CATANIA
5 Aug
US II Corps
US Provisional Corps
CALTANISSETTA
18 July
Platani
VALGUARNERA
RADDUSA
231 Bde
Gornalunga
GERBINI
Simeto
Primasole Bridge
Night 13 July Airborne troops and commandos land to take bridges
AGRIGENTO
CAMPOBELLO
207 Coastal Div
PORTO EMPEDOCLE
Part 15 Pz Gr Div
Livorno Div
US 45 Div
MAZZARINO
Salso
PIAZZA ARMERINA
Hermann Göring Pz Div
51 (H) Div
FRANCOFONTE
LENTINI
AUGUSTA
13 July
PALMA DI MONTECHIARO
CALTAGIRONE
PONTE OLIVO
NISCEMI
VIZZINI
Napoli Div
PRIOLO
PALAZZOLO
SYRACUSE
10 July
LICATA
GELA
18 Coastal Bde
PIANO LUPO
PONTE DIRILLO
BISCARI
CHIARAMONTE GULFI
COMISO
CASSIBILE
Gulf of Gela
VITTORIA
RAGUSA
NOTO
206 Coastal Div
AVOLA
5 Div and Commandos
SCOGLITTI
SANTA CROCE CAMERINA
MODICA
POZZALLO
50 Div and Cmdos
PACHINO
231 Bde
51 (H) Div
1 Cdn Div and Cmdos
US 3 Div; CC'A', 2 Armd Div and Rangers
US 1 Div and Rangers
US 45 Div

HEIGHT IN FEET
OVER 6000
3000-6000
1000-3000
UNDER 1000

Napoli Div — POSITION OF AXIS FORCES, AM 9 JULY 1943 (COASTAL DEFENCE UNITS OTHER THAN THOSE SHOWN WERE SITUATED ALONG THE COAST)
o—o—o—o US SEVENTH ARMY'S FIRST OBJECTIVE ('YELLOW LINE')
FRONT LINE, 18 JULY
" " 3 AUG
AIRBORNE LANDINGS, NIGHT 9 JULY
AIRFIELDS AND AIRSTRIPS

0 MILES 40
0 KILOMETRES 60

US II Corps (Bradley)

'HUSKY', 10 July 1943
15 Army Group
(Alexander)

Br XXX Corps (Leese)

Br XIII Corps (Dempsey)

US Seventh Army (Patton)
Parts US 1 Div and 2 Armd Div as floating reserve

Eighth Army (Montgomery)
78 Div in reserve in N Africa

aerial bombardment lasting a week, the garrison surrendered on 11 June as an assault force was approaching the island. The way was now open for the invasion fleet for Sicily. Meanwhile, Allied air forces operating from North Africa continued their bombardment of Axis airfields and communications in Sicily, Sardinia, and southern Italy. This aerial bombardment was prosecuted with great vigour for a whole month up to the time of the actual invasion. The land forces for this comprised General George S. Patton's US Seventh Army and Montgomery's British Eighth Army, both from Alexander's 15 Army Group, and were transported to Sicily in some 3,000 vessels. The Axis defence was entrusted to General Alfredo Guzzoni's Italian Sixth Army, a mainly Italian force with powerful German strengthening.

The assault went in on 10 July, the Americans landing in the Gulf of Gela and the British in the Gulf of Syracuse (**Map 2**). Allied airborne landings, intended to secure a preliminary beachhead and coastal communications, were not particularly successful as a result of rough weather and inexperience in this type of operation. The poor weather did, however, have one good effect, in that the Italians did not expect a landing and were therefore taken by surprise. Allied naval gunfire in support of the landings was particularly effective.

The landings were effected with little difficulty, though the Americans had to face vigorous counterattacks by German divisions on 11 and 12 July. Thereafter the forces of the two Allies advanced evenly against strengthening Axis resistance until 18 August, when Montgomery's progress was checked in front of Catania. Patton's forces, however, continued to sweep forward towards the north-west until they reached the north coast and turned east towards Messina. Western Sicily

had been cleared by 23 July. Resistance was now becoming more and more a German matter, and battlefield command was being exercised by a German, Colonel-General Hube. But with the aid of small amphibious operations along the north coast, Patton continued to advance on Messina, while Montgomery was able to speed up his progress again after 5 August. The Italians evacuated the island in some disorder between 3 and 16 August, leaving the Germans to fight an excellent rearguard campaign up to the 17th, when Patton occupied Messina.

119

THE LANDINGS IN ITALY

With the overthrow of Mussolini on 24 July and his replacement as head of government by Marshal Ugo Cavallero, secret talks were started with the Allies for an armistice for Italy. Hitler was ignorant of this, but, naturally suspicious, he started to send reinforcements into northern Italy to safeguard German communications. Meanwhile Field-Marshal Albert Kesselring, the German supreme commander in the south, reckoned that the Allied conquest of Sicily would soon be followed by a landing in Italy, in all probability on the Gulf of Salerno, just south of Naples.

The armistice with Italy, which was to be published and made effective on 8 September, was signed on 3 September, the day that the British Eighth Army made a landing on the toe of Italy, at Reggio di Calabria

Below: British troops come ashore from an American landing ship at Salerno

XIV Pz Corps

LIMIT OF FIFTH ARMY'S BEACH-HEADS,
NIGHT 9 SEPTEMBER
FRONT LINE, AM 12 SEPTEMBER
GERMAN COUNTERATTACKS, 12/14 SEPT
FRONT LINE, 14 SEPTEMBER

NAPLES

▲ Mt Vesuvius

Hermann Göring
Pz Div

3 Pz Div

TORRE DEL
GRECO

Pompei

NOCERA INF

15 Pz Gr Div

TORRE ANNUNZIATA

Gulf of Naples

CASTELLAMMARE

Chiunzi Pass

Molina Pass

SALERNO

MONTECORVINO

Tenth Army
(Vietinghoff)

SORRENTO

MAIORI
AMALFI

VIETRI

Montecorvino
Airfield

26 Pz Div

BATTIPAGLIA
EBOLI

CONTURSI

CAPRI

US Rangers

Commandos

46 Div

56 Div

Ponte Sele

PERSANO

16 Pz Div
Hill 424

Gulf of Salerno

Tobacco
Factory

ALTAVILLA

29 Pz Gr Div

Br X Corps
(McCreery)

Northern attack force
Southern attack force

Hill 140

ALBANELLA

0330 hrs, 9 Sept 1943
US Fifth Army (Clark)

13/14 Sept
US 82 Abn Div

ROCCADASPIDE

36 Div

Paestum

CAPACCIO

US VI Corps
(Dawley)

45 Div
(floating reserve)
lands 10 Sept

AGROPOLI

Calore

HEIGHT IN FEET
OVER 3000
1500–3000
500–1500
UNDER 500

MILES   0   15
KILOMETRES   0   25

LXXVI Pz Corps

CASTELLABATE

(**Map 1**). This was in fact a diversionary attack, designed to draw German reinforcements down from the Salerno area. Kesselring still thought that the main landing would be at Salerno, and so sent only minor forces to slow the British advance in the south.

The main landing in southern Italy was indeed to be at Salerno. Here, on 9 August, after the publication of the Italian armistice, landed General Mark Clark's US Fifth Army (**Map 2**). This was composed of the British X and the US VI Corps. The German defence was ready, however, and by nightfall the Allies had only secured four small beachheads. Further south, Montgomery was advancing through Calabria, and a British division had landed further east at Taranto.

At Salerno, the position was desperate. The Germans shelled the beachheads with great accuracy from the hills surrounding the gulf, and a powerful German attack on 12 September nearly cut the Allies in two. US artillery just managed to save the situation on the 13th. The Allies managed to hold on during the 14th, during which reinforcements reached them, and by 18 September had consolidated the beachhead. On the 16th Montgomery's advance units made contact with Fifth Army, and Kesselring began to withdraw cautiously north to his main defensive position, the Gustav Line running along the rivers Garigliano and Sangro.

The Allies pursued, Americans in the west and British in the east. By 8 October the Volturno/Termoli line had been reached, and here the Allies halted for four days to rest before assaulting the Gustav Line. The Americans resumed their advance in appalling conditions of weather and terrain on the 12th and the British on the 22nd.

Right: US troops beginning to move off the beachhead at Salerno

GERMAN DEFENCE POSITIONS
∨∨∨∨∨ BARBARA LINE
↑↑↑↑↑ BERNHARD(REINHARD) LINE
▼▼▼▼▼ GUSTAV LINE

FRONT LINES
━━━ 12 OCTOBER 1943
╸╸╸ 15 JANUARY 1944

0   MILES   15
0   KILOMETRES   25

Gran Sasso d'Italia

PENNE

PESCARA

90 Pz Gr Div

CHIETI   TOLLO
                VILLA GRANDE
                ROGATTI
L'AQUILA   SAN VITO
        ARIELLI
        POGGIOFIORITO   1 Cdn Div   78 Div
        ORSOGNA   FOSSACESIA
                                               30 Nov
GUARDIAGRELE   LANCIANO   20 Nov 1943
                              5 Div MOZZOGROGNA   Eighth Army
                    2 NZ Div   28 Nov   crosses the Sangro
M Sirente   65 Div
                              CASOLI   8 Ind Div
                                       PERANO
Rome Line   M Amaro   1 Para Div   Adriatic Sea
POPOLI   VASTO
CELANO   TORNARECCIO   2 NZ Div   5 Nov
SULMONA   ARCHI   SAN SALVO
                                CASALANGUIDA   TERMOLI
                    29 Pz Gr Div   16 Pz Div
AVEZZANO   PALENA   1 Para Div   78 Div
To Rome   PALMOLI
Tenth Army   5 Nov
(Vietinghoff)   26 Pz Div   TORREBRUNA
                    ROCCARASO   CASTIGLIONE MONTEFALCONE   Br V Corps
BALSORANO   10 Nov   (Allfrey,
M Enerci   M Arazecca   VAGNONE   TRIVENTO   Keightley later)
                    CASTEL DI SANGRO   SERRACAPRIOLA
SORA   ALFEDENA   5 Div   8 Ind Div   LARINO
        S. DONATO   1 Cdn Div   CASACALENDA
ARPINO   VAL DI COMINO   5 Div
ARCE   ATINA   CAMPOBASSO   Br XIII Corps
        5 Mtn Div   26 Pz Div   Fr Exp Corps   VINCHIATURO   (Leese)
                    2 Mor Div   COLLI   RICCIA
44 Div   3 Alg Div ISERNIA   29 Pz Gr Div   Eighth Army
Monte   5 Nov   (Montgomery)
Cassino   US 34 Div   504   CANTALUPO   SAN BARTOLOMEO
CASSINO   305 Div   Para Bn   29 Oct   IN GALDO
Route 6   3 Pz Gr Div M Sammucro   1 Cdn Div
XIV Pz Corps SAN PIETRO VENAFRO   Monti del Matese
(Hube)   M Lungo   M Rotundo 2 Nov US 45 Div
          M Maggiore MIGNANO M Cesima
SANT'AMBROGIO   PRESENZANO
15 Pz Gr Div   M Camino   PIEDIMONTE D'ALIFE   S. MARCO DEI CAVOTI
FONDI   M Petrella   M la Difensa US 3 Div
        94 Div   56 Div M Sta US 36 Div DRAGONI 26 Pz Div
MINTURNO Garigliano Croce   M Acero
                46 Div   AMOROSI   US 45 Div
GAETA   TEANO   Adriatic Sea
Raid by   SESSA   US 3 Div
commandos   AURUNCA   CAIAZZO   SCHILLE   BENEVENTO
Dec 1943   7 Armd Div   Triflisco 3 Pz Gr Calore
        M Massico SPARANISE Ridge   Div
                Hermann
MONDRAGONE   Göring   US 3 Div US 34 Div   US VI Corps
        15 Pz   Pz Div CAPUA CASERTA   (Lucas)
        Gr Div GRAZZANISE
Tyrrhenian Sea 7 Armd Div 56 Div
        13 Oct 1943   CASTEL VOLTURNO   Br X Corps   US Fifth Army
        US Fifth Army 46 Div   (McCreery)   (Clark)
        crosses the Volturno

HEIGHT IN FEET
OVER 6000
3000-6000
1500-3000
600-1500
UNDER 600

NAPLES

Mt Vesuvius

To Salerno

To Foggia

To Frosinone & Rome

THE DRIVE TO THE GUSTAV LINE

The major obstacle facing the US Fifth Army when it resumed its offensive on 12 October 1943 was the Volturno river, which was in spate with the autumn rain, and whose bridges the Germans had demolished. Clark managed to get both his corps across by the 15th, but then made appallingly slow progress over the roadless mountains north of the river.

On the other side of Italy, Montgomery's regrouped Eighth Army resumed the advance on 22 October and forced a passage over the Trigno river. On both sides of the central mountains, however, the Germans continued to slow the Allied advance with skilful delaying actions. On 15 November Alexander decided that his forces had had enough and halted the offensive. Kesselring, meanwhile, had been using the time won for him by his men to complete the Gustav Line. This magnificent defensive line, in places ten miles wide, ran along the line of the Garigliano and Rapido rivers, over the central mountains and then just north of the Sangro river to the Adriatic. The line was held by the German Tenth Army under General Heinrich von Vietinghoff. On the western end, the Gustav Line was particularly strong, backed up as it was by the mountains on either side of the Liri and by Cassino.

It was against this sector of the line that the US Fifth Army attacked on 20 November. Progress was made, but at enormous cost. At the end of the year, the Fifth Army had been brought to a halt in arctic conditions some five miles south of the Rapido. In the east the British had slightly better fortunes – switching two divisions from his left wing, Montgomery formed a powerful right and forced the Sangro on 15 November. The Eighth Army then broke through the Gustav Line east of Lanciano and took Ortona on 27 December.

Above: US artillery advancing
Below: Supplies being brought forward

THE CASSINO BATTLES

At the beginning of 1943, US Fifth Army had reached the Gustav Line along the Garigliano, but was still held in front of the Bernhard Line along the Rapido section of the Gustav Line. Alexander then ordered a head-on offensive which, coupled with the Anzio landings about to take place, would force Kesselring to evacuate the Gustav Line. The US VI Corps, aided by the French Expeditionary Corps, finally reached the Rapido and the frontal assault went in on 17 January (**Map 1**).

The British X Corps managed to secure a bridgehead across the Garigliano, while the US II Corps, which had replaced VI Corps, had mixed fortunes. Its 36 Division was repulsed with heavy losses, while 34 Division made slightly better progress and crossed the Rapido. The French Expeditionary Corps also made limited advances but suffered extremely heavy casualties. Further attacks, by the New Zealand Corps, were also unsuccessful between 15 and 18 February. Attempts to take Cassino by storm having failed, Alexander halted the offensive to rest and regroup. At Cassino there had been a six-week interval after the failure of the February offensive. During this period the Allies were considerably regrouped and reinforced for the next attempt, which started on 11 May 1944 (**Map 2**).

The renewed offensive was launched along a 20-mile front running from east of Cassino to the sea. The British managed to push over the Rapido, but the Germans succeeded in containing this attack. On the coast the Americans broke through the Gustav Line but were then held at Santa Maria Infante. On the Americans' right, however, the French Expeditionary Corps stormed over the Garigliano and advanced to cut the German communications. Kesselring realized that the position was lost and ordered a withdrawal on 17 May. Next day the Poles had the final honour of taking Cassino, or what remained of it after the bombing and shelling.

At Anzio (see next page), VI Corps had been reinforced and broke out of its beachhead on 23 May. On the 25th advance units of the US II and VI Corps established contact.

Although the Anzio landing had been designed to lift pressure from Cassino, it was in fact the Allied success at Cassino that allowed the US VI Corps to break out of its beachhead. A point worth noting is that the Allied success at Cassino would not have been possible without the starvation of the German garrison of many essential supplies by Allied bombers and fighter bombers. This was a factor that was to become increasingly important as the Italian campaign progressed.

Right: A German paratrooper amid the ruins of the abbey at Monte Cassino

125

ANZIO AND THE DRIVE TO ROME

The plan behind the Anzio landing was for the US VI Corps under Major-General John Lucas to land behind the German lines at the same time that the frontal assault on Cassino was being launched in January 1944 (**Map 1**). Advancing rapidly inland,

VI Corps was to cut German communications between Rome and Cassino, and either isolate the German Tenth Army or compel it to abandon the western end of the Gustav Line. Whatever happened, the Allies would soon find themselves across the Rapido and in possession of Cassino. Meanwhile, Eighth Army would continue its advance up the east coast.

The operation was a failure. The first landings took place on 22 January, most of the 50,000 troops were ashore within the next two days (**Map 2**). But instead of pressing inland Lucas decided to wait for his heavy artillery and tanks, and meanwhile dig in to consolidate the beachhead. Not so much as a reconnaissance in force did he venture.

The Germans, as usual, reacted swiftly, improvising the Fourteenth Army under General Hans Georg von Mackensen. This soon pinned down VI Corps in its beachhead until

Below: Supplies coming ashore at Anzio

Mackensen had massed forces for a major counterattack. This went in on 16 February and had considerable initial success until halted on 19 February. Lucas was replaced by Major-General Lucius Truscott on the 23rd, but the position was past immediate redemption. Both sides then settled down to a siege, which lasted well into May.

With the final breaking of the Gustav Line at Cassino, the Allies could once more resume their advance northwards (**Map 3**). But instead of swinging his Fifth Army eastward, which would in all probability have trapped the German Tenth Army, Clark decided on the capture of Rome, which now had little strategic, but great propaganda, value. The Germans, yet again fighting skilful rearguard actions, checked the Americans at Velletri and Valmontone long enough to allow the complete escape of all the German forces in the area. Rome was entered on 4 June – two days before the Normandy landings.

Right: American troops advancing under cover of a Sherman tank into the suburbs of Rome

THE PACIFIC WAR

Success went to the heads of the Japanese. Imperial General Headquarters were now afflicted by what, after the war, one of their own admirals was to describe as 'Victory Disease'. It was understandable enough, but it led the Japanese to look farther afield than they had originally intended. They now planned to capture Tulagi in the Solomons and Port Moresby in Papua, in order to give their air force control of the Coral Sea. They would then follow this up by seeking out the US Pacific Fleet. A victory by their main fleet would, they hoped, give them Midway and the Western Aleutians. They saw, correctly, the importance of fighting the US Pacific Fleet before American war production could build it up. The Japanese strategists intended to follow up this operation by taking New Caledonia, Fiji, and Samoa, which would, in all probability, deprive Australia of American support.

By mid-April American Intelligence, thanks to breaking of the Japanese naval code, knew that they were planning a battle for the Coral Sea, and Admiral Chester W. Nimitz (CINCPAC) sent Rear-Admiral Fletcher there with Force 17, which included the carriers *Lexington* and *Yorktown*. A curious battle ensued, the first in which the main units on either side were carriers and in which no ship made visual contact with the enemy. Both sides were learning a new technique as the fighting developed.

The two forces were fairly evenly matched with the Japanese having two fleet and one light carriers with about 150 aircraft, and the Americans two fleet carriers with 122 aircraft. By the end of the battle one of the US carriers, the *Lexington*, had been sunk, and the other, *Yorktown*, was damaged. The Japanese had lost their light carrier, and one of the others had been damaged. In terms of losses inflicted, the battle was very even, but in reality the Japanese had suffered a major strategic defeat for the projected attack on Port Moresby, the key to New Guinea, was abandoned.

Both sides, not surprisingly in a battle of a kind the world had not previously seen, made serious blunders at every level particularly with regard to the identification and location of enemy forces. From the point of view of Allied morale it was a wonderful thing to have inflicted a serious defeat on the Japanese aggressors only six months after Pearl Harbor, and only two days after the fall of Corregidor. The Coral Sea is of particular interest to the military historian as an illustration of the way in which relatively minor events, such as the report of an inexperienced pilot failing to detail enemy ships correctly, or the presence of a rain squall which hid one of the Japanese carriers at a crucial moment, can influence the fate of a whole force.

The Americans were not slow to learn from their mistakes, and in the next big battle, Midway, they fought with great skill.

Nimitz with seventy-six ships had to face 162 warships and auxiliaries. Nagumo had four fleet carriers and three light carriers, whilst the Americans only had three. It is a remarkable tribute to American efficiency that one of these was *Yorktown*. Repairs which in peacetime could have taken ninety days had been effected at Pearl Harbor in *two* days! In contrast, neither *Shokaku* or *Zuikaku* which had also been damaged in the Coral Sea action were ready on the Japanese side.

In addition to his fleet Nimitz had an 'unsinkable aircraft carrier' in Midway Island itself, where there were 115 planes.

The Japanese were still not aware that the Americans had broken their naval cipher: knowing when and where they meant to attack Nimitz had a tactical advantage which few commanders have enjoyed in modern warfare.

Nagumo enjoyed no such advantage, and indeed the disaster that overtook him may be attributed to the fact that he did not expect to encounter American carriers and in consequence sent out too few reconnaissance flights. Had he

appreciated that there were enemy carriers within striking distance he ought probably to have sought them out *before* attacking Midway. When before sunrise on the 4 June he sent 108 aircraft to attack the island he kept a reserve of ninety-three aircraft, armed with bombs and torpedoes. His fatal and, as it proved, mistaken decision was made about 0700 hours when he heard from the commander of his striking force that Midway required further attention, and from his reconnaissance flights that they had seen nothing. The consequence was that he was caught with the decks of his carriers crowded with aircraft unable to take off.

Midway was not only one of the decisive battles of the Second World War but of modern history. The destruction of all Nagumo's carriers gave the United States the initiative in the Pacific War, and was a terrible blow to the Japanese navy. From now on the Japanese were on the defensive, and deprived of the means of supporting the outposts of the empire they had so swiftly seized. An unusual feature of the battle was that both Nagumo and Fletcher were compelled to change their flagships, the former from *Akagi* to *Nagara*, the latter from *Yorktown* to the cruiser *Astoria*.

Both Spruance and Fletcher deserve high praise for their performance in this battle, which does not alter the fact that, like Waterloo, it was 'a damned near run thing'. As Professor Morison puts it 'for about one hundred seconds the Japanese were certain they had won the Battle of Midway, and the war.' That moment came at about 1024 hours on 4 June when the third attack of the US torpedo-bombers ended without a single hit scored and most of the aircraft destroyed. From this time onwards the Japanese navy could scarcely face the

Above left: The hulk of a Japanese cruiser after a US air attack

Above right: US Marines on Eniwetok Atoll in the Marshall Islands

Americans by day, unless they were within range of the support of land-based aircraft.

The Coral Sea and Midway showed that the day of the battleship was done. Since the Japanese could not hope to keep up with the Americans in the construction of new carriers the balance of power had now swung decisively in favour of the latter.

Whilst the Allies, in general, were agreed that the first aim of Allied strategy must be the defeat of Germany, Admiral Ernest J. King, in particular, determined to prevent the Japanese consolidating their gains, had decided to wage a 'defensive-offensive' war in the Pacific. Aware that the Japanese were planning a second attempt on Port Moresby he determined to seize Tulagi and Guadalcanal in the Solomon Islands, using the 1 US Marine Division based on New Zealand. Thus began the determined fight for ... 'an island that neither side really wanted, but which neither could afford to abandon to the enemy' (Morison).

The six months battle proved to the US Marines that they were superior to the Japanese in jungle warfare. Admiral Tanaka, a most capable and determined commander, attributed the defeat of his side to the lack of an overall plan of operations, to inferiority in the air, to forces being committed piecemeal, to bad communications, bad inter-service relations, and a tendency to underrate the enemy. 'We stumbled along from one error to another, while the enemy grew wise.' In fact the Japanese had fought bravely and though their losses on land exceeded those of the Americans, at sea things were pretty even since, oddly enough, each side lost twenty-four warships. The truth is that American superiority in numbers and equipment was beginning to tell.

From here on the Allied strategy was to work to within range of Japan, leapfrogging across the Pacific by means of a series of amphibious operations, by-passing countless Japanese island strongholds, whose garrisons soon became as useless as if they had been in prisoner of war camps. 'This', wrote General Matsuichi Ino, 'was the type of strategy we hated most. The Americans attacked and seized, with minimum losses, a relatively weak area, constructed airfields, and then proceeded to cut the supply lines ... Our strongpoints were gradually starved out. The Japanese army preferred direct assault after the German fashion, but the Americans flowed into our weaker points and submerged us, just as water seeks the weakest entry to sink a ship.' It was an amphibious application of the strategy of the indirect approach of which the late Captain Sir Basil Liddell-Hart was the exponent.

The Americans did not always get ashore scot free. At Tarawa for example they fought one of the costliest battles in their history (19/23 November 1943), in ratio to the number of troops engaged. The US Marines lost 3,000 casualties, and of 4,000 Japanese defenders only seventeen were taken. The Americans made an intensive study of the operation and learned by their mistakes, reaping the benefit during the rest of the war.

At the tactical level both sides fought with the most creditable determination. The Japanese with their spirit of 'no surrender' were always dangerous. The Americans were well-led at platoon and squad level, and accepted the fact that they were up against an enemy who had to be winkled out bunker by bunker, and cave by cave, with grenade and flame-thrower. Massive fire support, though available, was not in itself enough. The Japanese modified their tactics as time went by. At Peleliu, for example, they sited their main position well in rear of the beach, and kept a strong reserve for counterattack.

If the Americans were flexible tacticians, their strategy was to some extent bedevilled by the personal prejudices of their chiefs. King and Nimitz wished to take Formosa and assault Japan from bases on the China coast. MacArthur, yearning to liberate the Filipinos, wanted to make Luzon the jumping off place. He may have been right for much of the China coast was in Japanese hands and Formosa was very strongly held.

To the end the Japanese resisted with fanaticism. Okinawa cost the Americans 12,513 killed and 36,600 wounded in the army and navy alone. But its capture besides giving an air base for the final assault on Japan, practically cut the sea communications of all Japanese positions to the southward. As Nimitz put it: 'It has made the Japanese situation in China, Burma, and the Dutch East Indies untenable and has forced withdrawals which are now being exploited by our forces in China.'

Effectively, the Japanese were now beaten. But the problem was to make them realize it. Plans went ahead for an invasion of the Japanese home islands, but the dropping of two atomic bombs made this unnecessary.

Above left: A US Marine on Okinawa

Above right: Landing craft massed on the beaches of Okinawa

THE BATTLE OF THE CORAL SEA

By April/May, 1942, the Japanese had enjoyed a run of unbroken victories, at less cost than even they had anticipated. For the loss of only twenty-three warships (none larger than a destroyer) and sixty-seven other vessels, they had overrun the Philippines, Malaya, Burma, the Dutch East Indies, and a number of the British Pacific Islands. These successes encouraged the Japanese planners to extend the defence perimeter of Greater East Asia, and they were strengthened in this resolve by the Doolittle Raid on Tokyo on 18 April. This carrier-borne raid, designed to raise American and Chinese morale, while it caused little damage, made the Japanese take the threat of the bombing of their homeland seriously. In extending the perimeter of their conquests two choices were open to them: to strike eastwards in the central Pacific to capture Midway, gain a base within striking distance of Hawaii, and eliminate the bombing threat; or to strike south and east from Rabaul, capture Port Moresby, extend their hold on the Solomon Islands, and isolate Australia from the United States. In the event they chose to do both.

The capture of Port Moresby, the primary strategic aim of the Coral Sea operations, was entrusted to Admiral Shigeyoshi Inouye, commanding at Rabaul. The forces available to him, designated Task Force MO, were divided into five groups (**see map**):

The Port Moresby Invasion Group, eleven transports screened by destroyers, was to make straight for Port Moresby round the tip of New Guinea through the Jomard Passage.

A smaller Tulagi Invasion Group was to make for the Southern Solomons, capture the island of Tulagi, and set up a seaplane base.

A small support group was to establish a base in the Louisiade Archipelago, close to the Jomard Passage.

A Covering Group, under Rear-Admiral Goto, comprising the aircraft carrier *Shoho*, four heavy cruisers and one destroyer was to cover the Tulagi landing and then turn north-west to protect the

Port Moresby Invasion Group.

The Carrier Striking Force, under Vice-Admiral Takagi, containing the carriers *Shokaku* and *Zuikaku*, was to move south from the Central Pacific, enter the Coral Sea from the east, and cover the whole operation from United States' surface interference.

The complexity of this plan suggests that Inouye did not expect serious Allied opposition, and indeed he calculated that only one United States' carrier could be in the area at the time. However, Admiral Nimitz, C-in-C, US Pacific Fleet, knew of the Japanese plans and prepared a Task Force to meet the emergency. Task Force 17, under Admiral Fletcher, including the carrier *Yorktown*, was to be joined by Task Force 11 (Rear-Admiral Fitch), with the carrier *Lexington*. The final component of the Allies force was Task Force 44, a mixed group of Australian and US cruisers and destroyers under Rear-Admiral Crace, RN. These groups were due to rendezvous in the Coral Sea on 4 May.

But on 3 May the Japanese attack began. The island of Tulagi was occupied without opposition, and Goto, with the *Shoho* turned north-west. At 1900 hours Fletcher received news of this, and moved north. At 0630 hours on 4 May, aircraft from the *Yorktown* bombed the landings on Tulagi, registering hits on minor vessels. Shrewdly, Fletcher, resisting the temptation to follow up this success, moved south again to meet the two other Task Forces. Throughout 5 and 6 May the Japanese and US fleets searched for each other in vain. On the 5th, Takagi had entered the Coral Sea, but in perfect weather had missed the opportunity of locating Fletcher's force refuelling. Fletcher then detached the destroyer *Sims* and the tanker *Neosho* to sail south to his next fuelling rendezvous.

On 7 May at 0630 hours Fletcher detached Crace and Task Force 44 to attack the Japanese Port Moresby Invasion Group. Crace was spotted by Japanese aircraft at 0810, and Japanese land-based aircraft continued to attack

him throughout the day, under the impression that he was the main Allied force. Miraculously he survived these attacks, at some cost to the attackers. At 0600 hours, Takagi had launched reconnaissance aircraft which had located the *Sims* and *Neosho*. These, as well, were attacked in mistake for the main Allied force, the *Sims* being sunk and the *Neosho* damaged.

These Japanese errors allowed Fletcher to operate undisturbed, and aircraft from the *Yorktown* and *Lexington* located Goto's Covering Group shortly after 1100 hours. Smothered by a three-wave attack, the *Shoho* sank at 1135 hours.

Early in the day, the Japanese had realized the threat to the invasion transports, and had ordered them to turn back, but by the end of the 7th, Fletcher's position was known and Takagi's force was still fresh. Despite the loss of the *Shoho* the Japanese chances still looked favourable. Takagi determined to launch a strike during the night of the 7/8th. This proved entirely abortive, and of the twenty-seven aircraft launched, only six survived.

At 0815 hours on the 8th, Takagi and Fletcher's reconnaissance aircraft located their opposite fleets more or less simultaneously, and by 0925 both sides had launched strikes. At 1057 hours the *Shokaku* was attacked and disabled, and at 1118 hours the *Yorktown* and *Lexington* came under attack. The *Lexington*, hit several times, was eventually abandoned, scuttled and sunk.

Tactically the Battle of the Coral Sea was a draw – the Japanese lost more aircraft, the US more ships. It was the first true carrier battle – no surface ship was ever in sight of an opposing one. Strategically it was a major US victory, halting the invasion of Port Moresby, and throwing the Japanese on the defensive.

Below: USS *Lexington* on fire after being hit in a Japanese attack

Opposite: A destroyer comes alongside the *Lexington* as her crew slide down ropes into the water

Port Moresby Invasion Group

New Ireland

RABAUL
4 May

New Britain

Japanese Carrier Striking Force (Takagi)
Carriers Zuikaku and Shokaku

from Truk

NEW GUINEA

LAE

SOLOMON SEA

Bougainville

PAPUA

BUNA

Invasion Group retires

Covering Group (Goto)
Carrier Shoho and cruisers

2400, 5 May

Choiseul

SOLOMON

Santa Isabel

Support Force (Marushige)

WOODLARK

1030, 6 May
Australia–based
B-17's bomb Shoho

New Georgia

ISLANDS

0010, 5 May

PORT MORESBY

Japanese landings at Port Moresby planned for 10 May

Milne Bay 1050, 7 May

DEBOYNE IS.

MISIMA

1135, 7 May
Shoho bombed and sunk

0200, 9 May

TULAGI

FLORIDA IS

Guadalcanal

0930, 6 May

Malaita

3 May
Japanese land, establish sea-plane base

0815, 4 May
First US air strike on Tulagi

Jomard Passage

TAGULA

ROSSEL

0710, 8 May

2400, 7 May

0630, 4 May

RENNELL

San Cristobal

1400, 7 May

2400, 6 May

0010, 5 May

0945 7 May

CORAL

0630, 7 May
Crace detaches to attack Invasion Group

2400, 6 May

1755, 6 May

1930, 6 May

SEA

TF 44

0900, 8 May
Air attack launched, (Shokaku damaged)

Neosho

0930, 6 May

0700, 3 May

1118, 8 May
Yorktown damaged, Lexington hit and sinks at 1956 hrs

Task Force 17 (Fletcher)

JAPANESE OCCUPIED, 3 MAY 1942

TF 17 : Carrier Yorktown
3 cruisers, 6 destroyers

TF 11 : Carrier Lexington,
2 cruisers, 5 destroyers

TF 44 : 3 cruisers, 1 destroyer

0   NAUTICAL MILES   200

AUSTRALIA

TF's 11 and 17

Noon, 7 May
Sims and Neosho bombed.
Sims sunk; Neosho damaged, scuttled 11 May

Task Forces 11 (Fitch) and 44 (Crace) join TF 17

THE BATTLE OF MIDWAY

JAPANESE FORCES SAIL BETWEEN 25-28 MAY (DATES ARE THOSE AT MIDWAY)

The clash at Midway, the most important naval battle of the war (and one of the decisive battles of history), was the result of Japan's determination to extend the perimeter of her conquests in the Central Pacific. Both strategically and tactically its outcome was the result of several disastrous misappreciations by the Japanese commanders.

After the Battle of the Coral Sea, Yamamoto, C-in-C of the Combined Japanese Fleet, erroneously believed both the carriers *Yorktown* and the *Lexington* to have been destroyed. In fact the *Yorktown* was still very much alive and, after a miraculously swift refitting at Pearl Harbor during the last week in May, she was ready again for service. This miscalculation was understandable, but Yamamoto further deduced that the two other US carriers, *Hornet* and *Enterprise*, which had raced to take part in the Coral Sea action, were still in the South Pacific. A strike against Midway during the first week in June, he concluded, could not be opposed by a US carrier force. Accordingly he laid his plans for the Midway operation. They were characteristically complex (**Map 1**), involving nearly the whole of Japan's surface fleet. A Northern Force under Vice-Admiral Hosogaya (two light carriers, seven cruisers, and twelve destroyers) was to launch diversionary attacks on the Aleutian Islands just before the main strike at Midway. The remainder of the fleet destined for Midway was organized in three separate forces: the First Carrier Strike Force, under Vice-Admiral Nagumo (carriers *Kaga*, *Akagi*, *Soryu*, and *Hiryu*); the Midway Occupation Force, comprising the Second Fleet (Vice-Admiral Kondo), the occupation and support forces, and a minesweeping group (in all one light carrier, two battleships, two seaplane carriers, seven cruisers, twenty-five destroyers, and twelve transports carrying 51,000 men); and Yamamoto's Main Force (one light carrier, seven battleships, four cruisers, and twelve destroyers). Lastly, a screen of eighteen submarines was to operate between

Pearl Harbor and Midway. These groups were independently organized and disposed in such a way that mutual co-operation in action could not be immediate. For the purposes of the opposing US admirals, therefore, there was, in this huge armada, one overridingly important target – Nagumo's First Carrier Strike Force.

Nimitz (US C-in-C Pacific Fleet) knew of these plans and had accurate intelligence of sailing dates and timings. At his disposal were three fleet carriers carrying 250 aircraft (about the same number as on Nagumo's four carriers). In addition the fortress of Midway itself could provide a further 109 aircraft.

No time was wasted. By the end of May (before the Japanese submarine screen was in position) Nimitz' forces were at sea. They comprised Task Force 17, with the carrier *Yorktown*, under Rear-Admiral Fletcher; and Task Force 16, with the carriers *Enterprise* and *Hornet*, under Rear-Admiral Spruance. Fletcher had overall command.

Between 3 and 7 June the Japanese Northern Force carried out successful attacks on the Aleutians and, had Nimitz not known these to be diversions, might have provoked the response intended. But on 4 June, at 0430 hours, Nagumo launched his first strike against Midway (**Map 2**) to soften up the defences preparatory to landing the invasion force. Only one such strike was thought to be needed. The second wave of aircraft on Nagumo's carriers was armed to meet naval contingencies; armed, that is, with torpedoes or armour-piercing bombs.

At the same time US land-based aircraft rose from Midway to attack the approaching bombers and the Japanese fleet itself. The US aircraft were hopelessly outclassed, and the majority were destroyed, but their courage and tenacity had one important result. The commander of the Japanese airstrike signalled to Nagumo that a further strike would be necessary to subdue the island. Nagumo received this message at 0700 hours and proceeded to rearm his waiting aircraft, stripping them of their naval armament, and replacing it with high explosive and fragmentation bombs. This was a lengthy task, an hour's work at least. It was half completed at 0728 hours when Nagumo was handed a message from a spotter plane reporting the presence of ten US ships 200 miles to the north-east. If this force contained no carriers it presented no immediate threat, and the message gave no indication of its composition. Not until 0758 hours did Nagumo receive a further message from the spotter plane stating that the ten ships were five cruisers and five

destroyers. He received this message with relief, for at the same moment his force came under attack from Midway-based US bombers. As it happened, this attack did no damage, but every available Zero fighter was sent up to repel it. Then, at 0820 hours, Nagumo received another message: 'Enemy force accompanied by what appears to be a carrier.'

Nagumo's dilemma was insoluble. A strike against the approaching US carrier force would require fighter cover, but now all his Zeros required refuelling and rearming, and the rearming of his strike aircraft was not complete. Also, at 0830, the Midway strike aircraft would be returning, almost out of fuel and demanding urgent recovery. Against advice, he decided to postpone the preparation of a strike until after the Midway force had been recovered, but, as a precautionary measure, altered course 90 degrees north-east to meet the new threat at 0918 hours.

At dawn the US carriers had launched search patrols and, at 0752, the first strike was launched against Nagumo from the *Enterprise* and *Hornet*. The *Yorktown*, over an hour to the north east, did not launch a strike until 0900 hours. Both these strikes comprised Dauntless dive bombers, Devastator torpedo bombers, and Wildcat fighters.

At 0930 hours the torpedo bombers located Nagumo's force. Lacking fighter cover the low-level Devastators were massacred by the Japanese Zeros and the anti-aircraft fire of the cordon of cruisers and destroyers. Nagumo, seeing this, assumed the attacking force to have been destroyed and feverishly continued the arming of his strike. At 1025 this was complete, and on all four Japanese carriers the flight decks were crowded with waiting aircraft. But the dive bombers of all three US carriers had located the Japanese force and, at this moment, they struck. Within five minutes the *Kaga*, *Akagi*, and *Soryu* had been sunk. Only the *Hiryu*, cruising separately, was undamaged, and she was able to launch counter-strikes against the US force. Between 1200 hours and 1430 hours these strikes located and hit the *Yorktown*, rendering her uncontrollable. Abandoned at 1500 hours she was subsequently sunk by a submarine while under tow.

But this was the *Hiryu*'s last action. Aircraft from the *Enterprise* continued to attack her during the afternoon, and by 1700 hours she was damaged beyond repair. Next day she was scuttled.

Without carriers the remainder of the Japanese force was powerless. Within one day, effectively within five minutes, Japanese mastery of the sea had been destroyed. During the remainder of 4 and 5 June Yamamoto made abortive attempts to bring the US force to action with his still vastly superior surface fleet, but these were correctly and wisely avoided. From this point on in the Pacific, both on the sea and in the air, the initiative belonged to the United States.

Left: The Japanese aircraft carrier *Hiryu* on fire after a US air attack

GUADALCANAL

**7 August 1942
US 1 Marine Div**
(Vandegrift)

0740/1200,
2 Marine Regt plus 1 Para Bn
Strong resistance overcome

1/7 Feb 1943,
Japanese forces
withdraw

October,
Japanese reserves
land

17 Jan 1943,
Jap Seventeenth Army
begins withdrawal from
the Matanikau

23/26 Oct,
Maruyama's attacks
repulsed

0909,
5 Marine Regt lands
unopposed
1 Marine Regt follows

PM, 8 Aug
Henderson Field
taken

Night 7/8 Sept
Marine raiders
attack Jap base

Night 20/21 Aug,
Ichiki's detachment
destroyed

12/14 Sept,
Kawaguchi suffers
heavy losses at
'Bloody Ridge'

AMERICAN ATTACKS
JAPANESE COUNTERATTACKS
AND WITHDRAWALS
US DEFENCE PERIMETER 9 AUGUST
US POSITIONS 23 OCTOBER

EARLY DECEMBER, 1 MARINE DIV RELIEVED BY 25 INF, 2 MARINE AND AMERICAL DIVS (XIV CORPS [PATCH])

The US victory at Midway made it imperative for the Japanese to build airfields to provide the air cover that their fleet could no longer supply. In July 1942 news of the construction of an airfield by the Japanese on the Solomon Island of Guadalcanal hastened the American plans to move into the southern Solomons, and an amphibious task force under Rear-Admiral Turner was prepared. Turner's force carried the 19,000 men of Major-General Vandegrift's 1 Marine Division, and it was supported by Fletcher's three-carrier naval task force. As at Midway, Fletcher had overall command of the expedition.

In spite of the hasty composition of this force, and its inexperience of combined operations, it achieved tactical surprise. On 7 August, elements of 1 Marine Division landed unopposed on Guadalcanal. Two smaller detachments landed on the islands of Tulagi and Gavutu, valuable for their harbours and potential airfields, and encountered determined opposition. By the end of 8 August all landings had been successfully completed, and the Marines had reached Henderson Field, the site of the Japanese airstrip, to find that the Japanese had fled.

During the night of 8/9 August a naval action was fought around Savo Island at the mouth of Ironbottom Sound (see following pages), and the threat of Japanese warships forced the transports to retire, taking with them much of the landing forces' equipment. The Marines were now left to themselves, short of equipment and surrounded by waters dominated by the Japanese navy.

Between 9 and 18 August the Marines on Guadalcanal were busy strengthening the perimeter around Henderson Field, and preparing the airfield itself. They were under constant attack by Japanese ships and aircraft, and on 18 August the first Japanese troop reinforcements landed

on Guadalcanal at Taivu, 20 miles to the east of Henderson Field – one regiment under Colonel Ichiki. Ichiki's regiment moved west and, on the 21st, launched an attack against Vandegrift's position at Henderson Field. By this time the Marines had received their first aircraft, on the 20th, and were no longer as powerless in the air as before. Throughout the 21st and 22nd, Ichiki continued to launch attacks against the Marines across the Tenaru river. They were all repulsed, and eventually, after the Marine reserve regiment had worked its way behind the Japanese position, Ichiki's force was driven into the sea and destroyed. Ichiki himself committed suicide.

During 23 and 24 August the Battle of the Eastern Solomons (following pages) was fought. The Japanese were forced to retire with the loss of one carrier. This, and the presence of aircraft at Henderson Field, reduced the Japanese daytime mastery of the sea, but, with their superiority in cruisers and destroyers, they still dominated the sea at night. However, this did not prevent a party of Marine Raiders from attacking the Japanese base at Taivu on the night of 7/8 September. As well as destroying a large number of stores, the Raiders captured the details of further attacks to be

launched on Henderson Field.

On 12 September these attacks materialized. The Japanese 35 Brigade under General Kawaguchi, a far more formidable array than Ichiki's single regiment, attacked the Marine position from the east. Wave after wave was thrown in, and at one point the Japanese were within 1,000 yards of the airstrip. But they suffered appalling losses, and on the 14th Kawaguchi withdrew, leaving behind 1,200 dead and wounded.

Both sides now received reinforcements. Rushed down by sea under the cover of darkness the Japanese forces were landed night after night by the 'Tokyo Night Express' at Tenaro, to the west of Henderson Field. They comprised the headquarters of Seventeenth Army and 2 Division, about 20,000 men. Vandegrift's Marines were joined by US 7 Marines and 164 Infantry Regiment, bringing his force to 23,000.

On the night of 11/12 October another cruiser action took place off Cape Esperance (following pages), in which the US ships drove off the Japanese force, sinking a cruiser and destroyer. This upset Japanese reinforcement plants, and delayed the attack planned by the Japanese commander, General Maruyama.

By 23 October, however, Maruyama was ready. For two days he attacked Henderson Field from the south, but his forces were operating separately and lacked adequate communications. The Marines defeated each attack in detail, and by nightfall on the 26th, Maruyama broke off the engagement leaving 3,500 casualties.

It was time for the US forces to take the offensive, but the Marines on Guadalcanal were in no condition for this. Throughout November the exhausted Marines and Japanese watched each other, and not until December did the XIV Army Corps replace the Marines. The Japanese, at the same time, appalled by their losses, both at sea and on the land, decided to withdraw. Pursued by the fresh US forces, Maruyama's Seventeenth Army made its painful way west, and by 9 February the remaining 11,000 of the original 20,000 force had been evacuated from Guadalcanal.

For the Allies, the heroic Marine defence and seizure of Guadalcanal brought immense advantages. Australia and New Zealand were safe, and the Allies now stood on the flank of the outer cordon of Japan's conquests. The psychological effect of this repulse of the invincible Japanese army was incalculable.

Above right: Japanese sailors manning a machine gun on Guadalcanal

Right: US troops with tank support following the retreating Japanese

THE SOLOMON ISLANDS NAVAL BATTLES

The Marine landings on Guadalcanal brought the naval forces of each side into play. These naval clashes were related to the Guadalcanal fighting, but also had an importance of their own.

Map 1: Savo Island

A Japanese cruiser force under Vice-Admiral Mikawa was despatched on 8 August 1942, to attack the transports of the Guadalcanal landings. On the night of 8/9 August it encountered an Allied cruiser force under Rear-Admiral Crutchley. The Japanese were expertly trained and equipped for night fighting. The Allied force, being a composite one, was hampered by having no common doctrine or weapons system. Between 0100 hours and 0230 on the 9th, Mikawa's force treated the Allies, split into Northern and Southern Groups, to a dazzling display of night fighting. Avoiding the Allied destroyers *Blue* and *Ralph Talbot*, Mikawa pounced on the cruisers *Chicago* and *Canberra*, damaging both, the *Canberra* beyond repair. Turning north-east at 0138 he encountered the cruisers *Vincennes*, *Quincy*, and *Astoria*. These, too, were disabled beyond hope. The Japanese force then retired leaving four cruisers sinking. But in spite of the skill shown in this action Mikawa had failed to achieve his objective – the destruction of the invasion transports.

Map 2: The Battle of the Eastern Solomons

On 23 August 1942, an attempt to run supplies to the Japanese forces on Guadalcanal was intercepted by Task Force 61 (carriers *Saratoga*, *Enterprise*, and *Wasp*) under Vice-Admiral Fletcher. The Japanese transports were supported by a diversionary group (carrier *Ryujo*) under Hara, and a Striking Force (carriers *Zuikaku* and *Shokaku*) under Nagumo.

A strike by Fletcher on the 23rd was avoided by reversing course, but on the 24th the *Ryujo* was sighted by US search planes. A strike was launched against her, but at that moment other spotter planes sighted the *Zuikaku* and *Shokaku*. Fletcher tried to divert the strike, but communication difficulties prevented this. Only a few aircraft from the *Enterprise* located and attacked the *Shokaku*, and the main strike hit the *Ryujo*, sinking her by 1550 hours. But by 1630 hours a strike from Nagumo's carriers had found the *Enterprise*, and by 1641 had hit her. Though disabled she could still recover her aircraft. At the end of the 24th both carrier forces retired, but the Japanese Transport Group continued to head for its destination. On the 25th, Marine dive-bombers from Henderson Field discovered them, and hit the *Kinryu Maru* and the *Jintsu*. Later Flying Fortress bombers sunk the destroyer *Mutsuki*.

The Battle of the Eastern Solomons showed the Japanese the impossibility of daytime runs to reinforce Guadalcanal. The 'Tokyo Night Express' was resumed from Bougainville.

Map 3: The Battle of Cape Esperance

Another cruiser night action was fought on the night of 11/12 October 1942. An American force, under Rear-Admiral Scott, had orders to cover and escort a supply convoy to Guadalcanal, and also to ambush any Japanese naval forces approaching down the 'slot' (the narrow channel between the Eastern and Western Solomons). On the 11th Scott received news of a Japanese supply convoy moving down the slot, covered by Rear-Admiral Goto's cruiser squadron. He moved to intercept them and, at 2325 hours, the cruiser *Helena* made radar contact with the Japanese force at a range of about 14 miles. She failed to report this to Scott, who, assuming he had missed the enemy, decided to reverse course at 2332 hours. This manoeuvre dislocated his force, and at the same moment he learnt of Goto's approach. During the turn, the destroyer *Duncan* had made radar contact with the enemy and had attacked on her own initiative. At 2346 the *Helena* opened fire on the Japanese cruisers, quickly followed by the other US cruisers. Because the turn had placed destroyers between the cruisers' guns and the enemy, Scott ordered a ceasefire, but this order was ignored for long enough for the cruisers *Furutaka* and *Aoba* to be seriously hit, and for the destroyer *Fubuki* to be sunk. The Japanese cruiser *Kinugasa*, however, with her attendant destroyer *Hatsuyuki*, had turned to port on contact with the US squadron, avoiding the US cruisers' broadside. They encountered the lone *Duncan* and left her a burning hulk.

The Japanese force was now retreating, and Scott pursued them for another half hour. During the pursuit the US cruiser *Boise* was damaged by gunfire from the *Aoba*, and Scott broke off the pursuit at 0028 hours.

Cape Esperance left the Americans under the misapprehension that they had mastered the Japanese at night fighting. Goto's force had been unalert, and had failed to use their most potent weapon – the torpedo. The American tactical dispositions had been poor, but the most important aspect of Cape Esperance had been the surprise achieved by the US force – surprise made possible by the use of radar.

Map 4: The Battle of Santa Cruz

In October 1942 the Japanese launched an offensive under General Maruyama against the US Marines on Guadalcanal (see previous pages). To synchronize with this the Japanese combined fleet was to move to the north of Guadalcanal to fly aircraft to Henderson Field as soon as it was recaptured. The US Task Forces 16 and 17 (carriers *Hornet* and *Enterprise*) were ordered to sweep the area around the Santa Cruz islands, and to intercept any Japanese forces making for Guadalcanal.

At 1200 hours on 25 October an American flying-boat spotted two Japanese aircraft carriers, but a strike launched from the US carriers failed to find its target. On the 26th, however, both sides were alert. Nagumo, in command of the Japanese carrier group (the lessons of Midway still in his mind) launched his first strike at 0659 hours and immediately struck down the lifts to prepare the next strike. At this moment one of his carriers, the *Zuiho*, was attacked and put out of action by two of the *Enterprise* dive bombers. These had located the Japanese carriers at 0640 hours, and at 0730 a full strike was launched from both the *Hornet* and the *Enterprise*. Both US and Japanese strikes were in the air simultaneously, and, indeed, encountered each other on their way. At 0915 the first Japanese strike attacked the *Hornet*, hitting her with two torpedoes and six bombs. Meanwhile, at 0930 hours, the *Shokaku* was seriously hit, by US dive bombers. A second Japanese strike hit the *Enterprise*, damaging her flight deck and lift, but leaving her speed unimpaired.

With both his carriers hit, the US Admiral, Kinkaid, ordered a withdrawal, the *Hornet* abandoned and burning.

Undoubtedly a Japanese success, Santa Cruz was a Pyrrhic victory. The cost in irreplaceable air crews had been too high. Although unhit, the *Zuikaku* was virtually out of action through air crew losses. Over 100 experienced pilots had been lost.

③ **Goto's cruiser force**

Kinugasa
Furutaka
Aoba
Hatsuyuki
Fubuki

0 NAUTICAL MILES 5

2330
0028
0040 Furutaka
Kinugasa
Duncan
0012, Boise hit
Aoba hit
Furutaka hit
2346
Three van destroyers
2332
Fubuki
2346, opens fire
2325 Helena makes radar contact
Boise
2355
Farenholt
Duncan } destroyers
Laffey
San Francisco
Boise
Salt Lake City } cruisers
Helena
Buchanan } destroyers
McCalla
Farenholt
Scott's force
2303

Cape Esperance, 1 mile

④

Damaged Zuiho and Shokaku

◄······· MAIN US AND JAPANESE
·······► AIR STRIKES

Zuikaku

0 NAUTICAL MILES 150

1230
1500
1000
0930 Shokaku hit
Zuikaku Junyo
0105, 27 Oct, destroyer hit
0740 Zuiho hit
0700
carrier Junyo, 2 destroyers (Kakuta)
2 battleships, 5 cruisers, 12 destroyers
2000
0400
Advance Force (Kondo)
0920 Chikuma hit
Carrier Group* (Nagumo)
STEWART IS
0400
Striking Force
0800
0915, Hornet hit, sinks later
1015, Enterprise hit
0730
0400
Vanguard Group† (Abe)
1830
Overall commander of Japanese fleet –Adm Konda
0400
2300
carriers Enterprise and Hornet
1400

SANTA CRUZ IS

Task Forces 16 and 17 (Kinkaid)
2 carriers, 1 battleship, 6 cruisers, 14 destroyers
(1012, destroyer Porter torpedoed)

*3 carriers, 1 cruiser, 8 destroyers
†2 battleships, 4 cruisers, 7 destroyers

THE NAVAL ACTIONS OFF GUADALCANAL

In November 1942, when both sides were reinforcing their ground troops on Guadalcanal, the covering naval forces again clashed. On 12 November, eleven destroyers under Admiral Tanaka accompanied eleven transports containing 13,000 men to Guadalcanal. To cover this operation a strong group under Vice-Admiral Abe (two battleships, two cruisers, and fourteen destroyers) was sent to shell Henderson Field. Meanwhile the main Japanese carrier force moved to the north of the Solomons to provide air cover. At the same time US reinforcements arrived at Guadalcanal escorted by five cruisers and eight destroyers under Rear-Admiral Callaghan.

Learning of the approach of Abe's group, Callaghan moved to intercept relying on surprise to offset his marked inferiority. The US carrier force (under Kinkaid) was too far to the south to support. Callaghan possessed radar, and should have achieved surprise with ease. However, this priceless asset was misused, and both forces blundered into each other in the darkness at 0141 hours. A confused and violent action followed (**Map 1**). After 36 minutes both sides broke off the engagement leaving the Japanese battleship *Hiei* helpless, two of their cruisers sunk (*Akatsuki* and *Yudachi*), and all the remaining Japanese vessels damaged. The Americans had lost two cruisers sunk (*Juneau* and *Atlanta*), four destroyers (*Cushing, Barton, Aaron Ward,* and *Laffey*), and all remaining ships save one were damaged. Callaghan was killed.

This costly action prevented the Japanese reinforcements from landing, and averted the bombardment of Henderson Field. The *Hiei* was sunk on the following morning by torpedo bombers from Kinkaid's carrier *Enterprise*.

On 13 November, air activity by both sides was intense. Tanaka again started south with his transports, and during the morning of the 14th seven of these were sunk by US aircraft, along with two accompanying cruisers under Admiral Mikawa. Tanaka persevered, however, and to cover him Admiral Kondo, with the battleship *Kirishima*, four cruisers, and nine destroyers, raced southwards.

To intercept Kondo the US Task Force 64 (two battleships and four destroyers under Admiral Lee) moved up to the sound between Savo Island and Guadalcanal (**Map 2**).

At 2210 hours on the 14th a Japanese scouting group under Hashimoto, sighted Task Force 64, and the cruiser *Sendai* shadowed it. At 2300 the radar of the US ships located the *Sendai*, and at 2316 the two US battleships, *Washington* and *South Dakota*, opened fire. In the ensuing exchange the US destroyers *Preston* and *Walke* were quickly sunk, and the remaining two damaged. Shortly afterwards the *South Dakota* was hit, causing a power failure, and successfully putting her out of action. It became a battle between the *Washington* and fourteen Japanese ships. Concentrating her radar controlled guns on the *Kirishima* the *Washington* quickly sank the Japanese ship along with her attendant destroyer. The *Washington* pursued the now retreating Japanese until 0035 hours, but inflicted no further damage.

Although with almost incredible persistence Tanaka had succeeded in putting ashore some reinforcements on Guadalcanal, this was the last serious Japanese attempt to reinforce the garrison. Control of the seas around Guadalcanal passed to the Americans. While the Japanese may have given up hope of reinforcing the Guadalcanal garrison, they had no intention of abandoning it. On 30 November Tanaka and the 'Tokyo Night Express' again made a supply run to Guadalcanal. The Japanese 2nd Destroyer Flotilla, eight destroyers under Tanaka, was encountered at the entrance of Ironbottom Sound by Rear-Admiral Wright with five cruisers and seven destroyers (**Map 3**). At 2306 hours on the 30th, Wright's force made radar contact with the Japanese. But Wright instead of allowing his leading destroyers to engage the unsuspecting Japanese with torpedoes, hesitated and allowed the opportunity to pass. Then he ordered his cruisers to engage the Japanese with gunfire. The flashes alerted the Japanese, and their expert crews made ready their battle stations while the whole force was turning to engage the Americans. During this turn the outlying destroyer *Takanami* was sunk by American gunfire. The turn complete the Japanese destroyers launched torpedoes against the American ships. One cruiser was sunk and three more seriously damaged, with the loss of 400 killed.

Tassafaronga was a resounding tribute to the Japanese superiority at night fighting, and illustrated that the Americans still had to master the tool that was eventually to give them complete tactical superiority – radar.

Below left: A US naval task force in the Solomons

145

NEW GUINEA

The collapse of the Japanese attempt to capture Port Moresby from the sea (see Battle of the Coral Sea) forced them to attempt its capture overland. On the night of 21/22 July 1942, Japanese troops of the Eighteenth Army under Major-General Horii landed on the northern coast of Papua at Buna. Immediately they struck west over the Owen Stanley range by the Kokoda trail (**Map 1**). Fighting tenaciously, the Australian/US opposition, under Major-General Hering, was pushed back until, by 12 August, Horii had captured the main pass over the Owen Stanleys. Australian resistance increased, and by 26 September, although Horii was within 30 miles of Port Moresby, the efforts of Hering's men, and local Allied air superiority, brought the Japanese to a halt.

Partly under Allied pressure, and partly in response to orders from above, Horii began the long retreat over the Owen Stanleys, followed by an Australian division and a US division. By November Horii had fallen back on strong defensive positions in the Buna-Gona area, where he had landed. The Allied forces were racked by disease, exhausted, and, although learning fast, were untrained in jungle warfare. At first the Buna defences were too much for them, but on 9 December Gona was stormed by the Australians, and in January 1943, after an appalling fight, Buna too was captured.

The Allied success along the Kokoda trail left their forces in the New Guinea area in a position to form the left wing of a two-pronged encircling movement to isolate the Japanese at Rabaul. But first New Guinea itself had to be cleared. From January to December 1943, a series of small scale but brilliantly contrived combined operations were mounted against the Japanese in New Guinea (**Map 2**).

In January, 1943, a brigade of General Hering's New Guinea Force was airlifted to Wau, 30 miles west of Salamaua, and established a forward base to threaten the Japanese base there. Meanwhile General MacArthur, Allied C-in-C South West Pacific, built up his forces for an offensive.

By June the Allied forces were ready. An American amphibious landing on the 29/30th threatened Salamaua, which was simultaneously threatened from Wau by 17 Australian Brigade. These forces maintained their threatening posture in front of Salamaua until September when, on the 4th, 9 Australian Division landed to the east of Lae. At the same time US paratroops were dropped at Nadzab, and 7 Australian Division was airlifted to support them. All these forces made a converging attack on Lae, while the Allied troops investing Salamaua also took the offensive. Salamaua was taken on the 12th and Lae on the 16th.

During the rest of September and October, the new Allied commander of the New Guinea force, the Australian General Sir Thomas Blamey, thrust west and east to encircle the Huon Peninsula. With additional landings by US forces on the north coast of the peninsula, this encirclement was complete by April 1944.

The way was now clear to isolate, defeat, and most important to destroy the airfields of the remaining Japanese forces in New Guinea. From April to July 1944, the Hollandia operation was carried out, and it was among the most brilliant operations of the war. One after another the Japanese bases were isolated and destroyed. The fighting was never on a large scale, but co-operation between land, sea, and air on the Allied side was superb. By July 1944 an entire Japanese army in New Guinea had been isolated and neutralized.

Opposite: Australian troops advance against a Japanese position

Right: US paratroops landing on Numfoor island

RUSSIA

Kamchatka

ULAN BATOR ■

MONGOLIA

MANCHURIA
HARBIN
(MANCHUKUO)
MUKDEN ■

Sakhalin

Kurile Is

ATTU
KIS
15 A
194

VLADIVOSTOK

Hokkaido

SEA OF
JAPAN

18 April 1942
Doolittle's air raid on Tokyo
from carrier task force

C H I N A

PEKING ■

KOREA

SEOUL

Honshu

TOKYO
JAPAN

Amur

Hwang Ho

US strategic
direction

CHUNGKING ■
yangtse-kiang

NANKING
HANKOW

CHANGSHA

Burma Road

KUNMING

SHANGHAI

NAGASAKI
Kyushu

Shikoku

Ryukyu Is

OKINAWA
1 Apr 1945

BONIN IS

P   A   C

DELHI ■

NEPAL

KARACHI

Ganges

IMPHAL

CALCUTTA ●

LASHIO

MANDALAY ▲

CANTON

HONG KONG

Formosa
(Taiwan)

IWO JIMA
19 Feb 1945

WAKE

O   C

E

I N D I A

BOMBAY ■

BURMA

RANGOON ■

HANOI

HAINAN

Luzon 9 Jan 1945

Marianas
Islands

SAIPAN 15 July 1944

GUAM 21 July 1944

1 Feb 1944

ENIWETOK
17 Feb 1944

KWAJALEIN

Marsh
Island

BAY OF
BENGAL

THAI-
LAND

BANGKOK ■

FRENCH
INDO-CHINA

SAIGON

MANILA ●

PHILIPPINE
ISLANDS

LEYTE 20 Oct 1944

YAP

TRUK

MADRAS ●

ANDAMAN
IS

TRINCOMALEE

SOUTH CHINA
SEA

Mindanao

DAVAO

PALAU IS 15 Sept 1944

MAJURO

Caroline   Islands

MAKI

COLOMBO ■

Ceylon

NICOBAR
IS

KHOTA BHARU

N BORNEO

SARAWAK

TARAWA
20 Nov 1943

Gil
Is

Maldive
Is

MALAYA

Equator

SINGAPORE ■

Sumatra

Borneo

D U T C H   E A S T   I N D I E S

Celebes

HALMAHERA

New Guinea

ADMIRALTY
IS

29 Feb 1944

NEW
IRELAND

NAURU

OCEAN I

South-East Asia
Command
(Mountbatten)

BATAVIA ■

Java

FLORES

TIMOR

PAPUA

NEW
BRITAIN RABAUL

BOUGAINVILLE

NEW
GEORGIA

Solomon Is

NANUMEA

Ellice
Is

I N D I A N

ARAFURA SEA

TIMOR SEA

PORT
MORESBY

GUADALCANAL 7 Aug 1942

SANTA CRUZ IS

ESPIRITU-SANT

F
S

O C E A N

DARWIN

CORAL   SEA

CAIRNS

New
Hebrides

EFATE

New
Caledonia

NOUMEA

South-West
Pacific Area
(MacArthur)

A U S T R A L I A

ROCKHAMPTON

BRISBANE

NORFOLK

PERTH ●

ADELAIDE ●

SYDNEY
CANBERRA ■

TASMAN
SEA

AUCKLAND

MELBOURNE ●

WELLINGTON

NEW ZEALAND

CHRISTCHURCH ●

JAPANESE EMPIRE, 1933
LIMIT OF JAPANESE ADVANCE, July 1942
AMERICAN SUPPLY ROUTE TO AUSTRALIA
ALLIED COMMAND AREAS
SUBDIVISIONS OF PACIFIC OCEAN AREAS
BOUNDARY BETWEEN SOUTH PACIFIC AND
SOUTH-WEST PACIFIC AREAS, 2 JULY 1942
PLAN FOR AMERICAN COUNTER-OFFENSIVE
PLAN FOR ATTACK ON JAPANESE HOMELAND

7 Aug 1942   DATES OF AMERICAN LANDINGS

MERCATOR'S PROJECTION

148

tian Islands

th Pacific Area

Pacific Ocean Areas
(Nimitz)

OWAY

I   C

Hawaiian Is
OAHU
PEARL HARBOR
△ HAWAII

tral Pacific Area

N

·PALMYRA

·CHRISTMAS

JARVIS
·MALDEN

Phoenix Is

·VICTORIA

Tokelau Is
·CAROLINE

Samoa Is
·SUVOROV

·TAHITI

Cook Is   **Society Is**

Tonga Is
RAROTONGA
·TUBUAI

th Pacific Area
rmley, Halsey later)

MADEC IS

International date line (Monday)
(Sunday)

PLANNING THE US COUNTER OFFENSIVE

After the Allies had isolated Rabaul and cleared the south-west Pacific, a spirited argument developed as to where best to attack the Japanese next. At the back of the planners' minds was always the dread that, sooner or later, they would have to contemplate the invasion of the Japanese homelands themselves.

Two schools of thought arose. The first, supported by Admirals Nimitz and King, advocated a thrust straight at the weakest point of the Japanese conquests, the islands that linked Japan proper with South-East Asia – Formosa and the Ryukyus. Possession of these would place the Allies athwart the Japanese Empire, cutting it in half, and, most important of all, cutting off Japan proper from all its sources of raw materials, food, and fuel.

The second school of thought, led by General MacArthur, advocated a move up from the south-west, liberating the occupied territories as a major objective in themselves.

The dispute between these two views was not simply a straightforward service wrangle. If anything it was the outcome of intense personal rivalry between MacArthur and King. Strategically, the Formosa plan was unquestionably superior, and it speaks volumes for MacArthur's personality and tenacity that the compromise eventually arranged by President Roosevelt heavily favoured the MacArthur Philippine plan.

Whichever course was adopted, the price was going to be high. Japan's delusive hope was that the Allies, and particularly America, would expend their strength at great cost against the jungle-clad island fortresses on the perimeter of their empire, and, becoming discouraged, sue for a negotiated peace. No such considerations occurred to the Allies, however. Operations in the Far East and Pacific, while still to some extent held back by the 'Germany First' policy, were aimed at the defeat and unconditional surrender of Japan.

Right: Japanese troops patrolling on Guam before the US counterattack began

THE BATTLE FOR THE SOLOMONS

The drive through the Solomons was a preview of how the whole of the Pacific island war was to be waged (**Map 1**); a series of outflanking operations to secure the key airbases, followed by two or three month build-up for the next 'hop'. The inset map shows the Elkton Plan to surround and neutralize the Japanese forces in the Solomons and New Guinea. The advance up the Solomons was to form the right hand of its two pincers.

The two key islands to the Solomons campaign were New Georgia (**Map 2**) and Bougainville (**Map 3**). Successful landings on these would isolate the Japanese on the more northerly islands, and put commanding air bases into Allied hands.

Between February and June 1943, preparations were in hand for an attack on New Georgia. In February the Russell Islands were seized, and in June Rendova Island, within artillery range of New Georgia, was captured.

On 2 July, US 43 Division and part of 37, supported by a naval task force, landed at Munda on the western end of New Georgia. Other small units had already established footholds in the east. Under the command of Major-General Hester the US troops attacked the Japanese base at Munda, encountering savage opposition. On 25 July, US 25 Division was thrown into the fight, and the Allied force, now commanded by Major-General Griswold captured the airfield on 5 August. By the 25th all resistance in New Georgia was at an end.

Also during August a US combat team landed on Vella Lavella, north-west of New Georgia (**Map 1**), to establish a base there, outflanking the Japanese on Kolombangara. In mid-September New Zealand troops cleared the remainder of Vella Lavella and the Japanese were compelled to withdraw from Kolombangara.

By October the next stage of the Allied thrust was ready. On 27 October, a feint assault on the island of

Map 3

LEGEND:
- US BEACH-HEAD NIGHT, 1 NOVEMBER
- FRONT LINES AT DATES SHOWN
- AIRFIELDS UNDER CONSTRUCTION

③

MILES 0 — 4
KILOMETRES 0 — 6

Laruma

Numa Numa Trail

26 Nov

Koromokina

Piva

Piva

Trails defended by parts Jap 23 Inf Regt

'Hellzapoppin' Ridge

East-West Trail

37 Div

Piva Fields

7 Nov

3 Marine Div
5 Nov
Part Jap 23 Inf Regt

1 Nov

15 Dec

Torokina

0400/0600, 7 Nov Part Jap 17 Div from Rabaul. Eliminated 8 Nov

PURUATA I

Opened 9 Dec

Cape Torokina

3 Raider Bn

0722, 1 November 1943 'CHERRYBLOSSOM' 3 Marine Div (Turnage)

Empress Augusta Bay

Map 4

④

AIRFIELDS

MILES 0 — 5
KM 0 — 8

12 March
Part 7 Cav Div

PITYILU 30 Mar

HAUWEI

NDRILO 1 Apr

15 March
Part 7 and 8
Cav Divs

Seeadler Harbour

11 Mar

Part 7 and 12
Cav Divs

Los Negros

Lugos Mission

BUTJO LUO

LORENGAU

Number One Road

OLD ROSSUN

ROSSUM

Manus Island

29 February 1944 Part 7 Cav Div

Hyane Harbour

MOMOTE

25 March
End of Japanese
resistance

27 February
Alamo Scouts
reconnoitre

Operation 'CARTWHEEL' map

KAVIENG

RABAUL

Operation 'CARTWHEEL'

NEW GUINEA

PAPUA

LAE

Jap Eighteenth Army (Adachi)

SOLOMON ISLANDS
Jap Seventeenth Army (Hyakutake)

Command boundary

GUADALCANAL

PORT MORESBY

Milne Bay

South-west Pacific Area (MacArthur)

South Pacific Area (Halsey)

AUSTRALIA

Final 'Elkton Plan' (26 April 1943)

Solomon Islands map

15 February
3 NZ Div

BUKA

nis

Tenekau

Bougainville

Kieta

PACIFIC OCEAN

SOLOMON ISLANDS

'BLISSFUL' (diversion for 'Cherryblossom')
28 October
2 Mar Para Bn
(withdraws 3 Nov)

ress Augusta Bay

Kara

Kahili

BIUN

VOZA

Choiseul

SHORTLAND IS

FAURO

SAGIGAI

The Slot

TREASURY IS

RYBLOSSOM'
mber
ne Div

VELLA LAVELLA

KOLOMBANGARA

4 July

(New Georgia Sound)

Santa Isabel

'GOODTIME'
27 October
8 NZ Bde Group

15 Aug

MUNDA

13 Aug

New Georgia

RENDOVA

VANGUNI

'TOENAILS'
30 June
US 43 Inf Div

RUSSELL IS
BANIKA

FLORIDA IS

Malaita

'CLEANSLATE'
21 February 1943
US assault bns

PAVUVU

Henderson Field

Guadalcanal
7 Aug 1942/7 Feb 1943

San Cristobal

nd 1942

Choiseul (Operation Blissful), obscured the real objective, Bougainville. On 27 October New Zealand troops had captured Treasury Island (**Map 1**).

On 1 November, US 3 Marine Division went ashore at Empress Augusta Bay (**Map 3**). By the end of the year, in spite of Japanese counterattacks, the Americans held a defensive perimeter ten miles wide and five miles deep, and had made Augusta Bay into a naval base with three operating airstrips. The eastern arm of the Elkton Plan was complete.

The western arm depended on the clearing of New Guinea and Papua (see New Guinea), and the occupation of the Admiralty and St Matthias groups. The New Guinea campaign in 1943 had captured and cleared the small islands of Trobriand and Woodlark in the Solomon Sea, and landings had been effected on the western tip of New Britain.

On 29 February 1944, a reconnaissance in force by US 1 Cavalry Division swiftly became an invasion of Los Negros in the Admiralty group (**Map 4**). Two more US divisions were landed during the first two weeks of March, and by 25 March all Japanese resistance was at an end. At the same time US 1 Marine Division had landed on the northern coast of New Britain, and units of Fortieth Army and 1 Marine Division moved along the coast to join up with them (**Map 1**).

Thus by the end of March 1944 the pincers of the Elkton Plan were complete. The Japanese bases on New Britain and New Ireland remained isolated till the end of the war.

CLEARING THE MARSHALLS

While MacArthur's forces in the South-West Pacific were completing the encirclement of Rabaul (previous pages), the drive against the Japanese in the West Central Pacific was proceeding under Admiral Nimitz.

Between January and October 1943, men, ships, and aircraft in enormous numbers began to assemble in Hawaii, the Fijis, and the New Hebrides. By October Nimitz could deploy the Fifth Fleet (Vice-Admiral Spruance) comprising seven battleships, seven heavy and three light cruisers, eight carriers, and thirty-four destroyers; the Fifth Amphibious Force (Turner) carrying more than 100,000 troops; and the V Amphibious Corps (Major-General 'Howling Mad' Smith). In addition to naval air cover, Nimitz could call on the Seventh Army Air Force (Major-General Hale) operating from the Ellice Islands. Also, after the completion of the Solomons operation, he had the naval and marine elements that had previously comprised Halsey's Third Fleet.

Nimitz's first target was the Gilbert Islands, to provide bases for the next step, the capture of the Marshall Islands (**Map 1**). Possession of these two atoll groups would put him in a position to threaten the Japanese naval base at Truk. In the Gilberts, the Japanese defences were based on the two largest atolls, Makin and Tarawa.

From 13–20 November Makin and Tarawa were thoroughly strafed by Army Air Force bombers, and then subjected to heavy naval gunfire. Between 20 and 23 November the atoll of Makin was cleared and occupied with little difficulty. The main US losses were, in fact, incurred at sea where the carrier *Liscombe Bay* was sunk by a Japanese submarine.

Tarawa, however, was another matter. The atoll was a roughly triangular string of small islands and coral reefs (**Map 2**). The main Japanese stronghold was Betio (**Map 3**), a flat, sandy 300-acre

③

2 Marine Div
(C. Smith)

21 Nov
1 bn, 8 Regt

20 Nov
2 Regt

20 Nov
2 bns, 8 Regt

Long Pier

Red 1   Red 2   Red 3

Landing beaches ▶

Green beach
21/22 Nov
2 bns,
6 Regt

● JAPANESE STRONGPOINTS
US POSITIONS AT
━━━ 1800, 20 NOVEMBER 1943
•••••••• " 21
━ ━ ━ " 22
🌴🌴 WOODED AREAS (PALMS)
0   YARDS   1000

N

Betio

Airstrip

1305, 23 Nov
Last Japanese
pocket eliminated

Night, 22/23 Nov
Japanese counterattacks

1310, 23 Nov

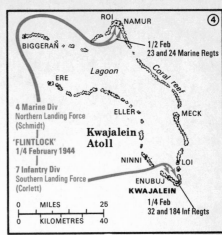

④

ROI NAMUR

BIGGERAŇ

1/2 Feb
23 and 24 Marine Regts

ERE

Lagoon

ELLER   MECK

Coral reef

4 Marine Div
Northern Landing Force
(Schmidt)
'FLINTLOCK'
1/4 February 1944

7 Infantry Div
Southern Landing Force
(Corlett)

**Kwajalein
Atoll**

NINNI   LOI

ENUBUJ
KWAJALEIN

1/4 Feb
32 and 184 Inf Regts

0   MILES   25
0   KILOMETRES   40

⑤

0   MILES   20
0   KILOMETRES   30

ENGEBI

ROJOA

17/19 Feb
Two bns, 22 Marine Regt

**Eniwetok
Atoll**

RIGILI

Invasion
fleet

22/23 Feb Three bns,
22 Marine Regt

PARRY

ENIWETOK

19/21 Feb
Two bns, 106 Regt;
one bn, 22 Marine Regt

'CATCHPOLE'
17/23 February, 1944
Landing Forces
(Watson)

island, honeycombed with underground shelters, pillboxes, and strong points. Insufficient US reconnaissance had failed to reveal that the inner coral reef of Betio itself was too shallow to allow landing craft to approach.

Despite the heavy preliminary bombardment, when the assault waves of 2 Marine Division went in on 20 November, they encountered intense resistance from the Japanese garrison under Rear-Admiral Shibasaki. Most of the landing craft grounded on the inner reef and the Marines were compelled to wade several hundred yards under intense criss-cross fire. By nightfall on the 20th, 1,500 of the 5,000 Marines put ashore were casualties. During the night, tanks, guns, and ammunition were landed, and, during the 21st and 22nd, inch-by-inch frontal assaults drove the Japanese back. Most of the defenders were killed in a suicidal counterattack on the night of the 22nd, and on the 23rd the last pocket of Japanese resistance on Betio was eliminated. Of the 4,700 Japanese on the island only 100 were taken prisoner (of these only 17 were combat troops). The rest were dead. The Marines lost nearly 1,000 dead and over 2,000 wounded.

Safely installed in the Gilberts, the US forces were, by February 1944, ready to tackle their next target, the Marshalls. Here the centre of the Japanese defences was Kwajalein Atoll (**Map 4**), a large, spread-out lagoon with small islands at its northern and southern ends. Operation Flintlock was carried out by 4 Marine Division under Schmidt, and 7 Infantry Division under Corlett. They were carried by Turner's Fifth Amphibious Force, and Admiral Mitscher's East Carrier Task Force swept ahead of them to neutralize Japanese air power in the Marshalls. On 1 and 2 February, 23 and 24 Marine Regiments landed on Roi and Namur at the north end of the lagoon. At the same time 32 and 184 Infantry

Regiments tackled Kwajalein itself. The Japanese garrisons fought to the death in both places, but, learning from the lessons of Tarawa, the US forces were able to overrun them with relatively few losses (372 dead out of 41,000 landed). Of 8,000 Japanese troops 7,870 were killed.

The final step in the Marshalls campaign was the capture of Eniwetok Atoll, to the north-west of Kwajalein. Turner's Amphibious Force again put the Marines ashore. On 17 February, two battalions of the 22 Marine Regiment landed on Engebi (**Map 5**), encountering little opposition. But on 19 and 22 February, further battalions of 22 Regiment, and two battalions of 106 Infantry Regiment were landed on Eniwetok and Parry islands. The Japanese garrisons fought desperately and to the death. All 2,000 defenders were killed.

Left: US Marines in action in the jungle

153

CLEARING THE MARIANAS

Some 1,000 miles to the north-west of the Marshalls lay the next objective of Nimitz's trans-Pacific drive – the Mariana Islands. The main Japanese defences here rested on three large islands, Saipan and Tinian (**Map 1**), and Guam (**Map 2**). Again Turner's Fifth Amphibious Force, 530 warships and auxiliaries carrying over 127,000 troops of 'Howling Mad' Smith's V Amphibious Corps, rendezvoused off Eniwetok Atoll. Ahead of it, Mitscher's Task Force 58 had softened up the island defences of Saipan destroying 200 Japanese aircraft and twelve or more cargo ships.

On 15 June Turner's force arrived off Saipan. They faced the Japanese Thirty-first Army, under the overall command of Admiral Nagumo. Landings by 2 and 4 Marine Divisions on eight beaches were hotly contested, but by nightfall a beachhead had been established. Heavy resistance, however, compelled Smith to commit the 27 Infantry Division on the 17th, and the departure of his naval support on the 19th to take part in the Battle of the Philippine Sea hampered his operations still further. Not until 9 July did Japanese resistance end, after a Japanese counterattack on 7 July had been wiped out by 4 Marine Division.

Casualties on Saipan were high. 3,126 US dead, and 27,000 Japanese dead – virtually the whole garrison.

From 9 July to 24, 2 and 4 Marine Divisions reorganized themselves for the assault on Tinian. Again the Japanese fought furiously, expending enormous numbers on suicidal counter-attacks. By 31 July the island had been cleared from north to south.

On 21 July, 3 Marine and 77 Army Divisions landed on Guam, supplemented by 1 Marine Brigade. Two landings were made, north and south of the Orote Peninsula. After a struggle, costing 1,400 US killed and 10,000 Japanese killed, the island fell.

Opposite: Japanese dead and a wrecked tank on Saipan

Below: US Marines landing on the beach of Guam

① 'FORAGER'
15 June /1 August 1944
Northern Troops and
Landing Force
(H. Smith, Schmidt later)

9 July
End of effective Japanese resistance

7 July
Final Japanese counterattack

Marpi Pt

Coral Reefs

Mt Marpi
MAKUNSHA

Saipan

15 June
Feint attack
by reserve regts

Tanapag
Harbour

4 Marine
Div
4 July
30 June

Mutcho Pt
GARAPAN

Mt Tipo Pale

Mt Tapotchau   ▲ Purple Heart Ridge

17 June
27 Inf Div (reserve)
(R. Smith, Griner later)

15 June
2 Marine Div
(Watson)

Kagman
Peninsula

Afetna Pt

15 June
CHARAN KANOA
4 Marine Div
(Schmidt)

ASLITO

Magicienne
Bay

24 July
4 Marine Div
(Cates)

Ushi Pt

Saipan Channel

28 June

Nafutan Pt

25 July
2 Marine Div

Mt Maga ▲

Night 24/25 July
Japanese counterattack fails

Mt Lasso ▲

Asiga Bay
28 July

P A C I F I C

4 Marine
Div

2 Marine
Div

Tinian

30 July

O C E A N

TINIAN
(Sunharon
Harbour)

31 July
Attacks begin on last
Japanese defences

24 July
2 Marine Div (reserve)
launches feint attack

Lalo Pt

1 August
End of effective Japanese resistance
after final counterattack fails

---- US POSITIONS AT DATES SHOWN
✈ AIRFIELDS

0   MILES   8
0   KILOMETRES   12

✈ To Guam

154

② 'FORAGER'
21 July/10 August 1944
Southern Troops and
Landing Force
(Geiger)

10 August
End of effective
Japanese resistance

ACIFIC OCEAN

0829, 21 July
3 Marine Div
(Turnage)

Mt Machanao

1 Marine Bde
FINAGUAYAC

Pati Pt

UPI

TAGUAC

LULOG

3 Marine
Div

6 Aug

Mt Santa Rosa

Tumon
Bay

DEDEDO

77 Inf Div

Asan Pt   Adelup Pt

Mt Barrigada

CABRAS I   ASAN   AGANA   1 Aug

Orote   Piti Navy Yard
Peninsula
29 July

Mt Chachao
Mt Alutom
Mt Tenjo

Guam

0830, 21 July
1 Prov Marine
Bde (Shepherd)
Followed later by
77 Inf Div (reserve)
(Bruce)

AGAT
Apra
Harbour

Bangi Pt

Mt Alifan

Coral Reef

MATA

Mt Lamlan

INARAJAN

UMATAC

JAPANESE COUNTERATTACKS
ON NIGHT OF 25/26 JULY
AIRFIELD

0   MILES   10
0   KILOMETRES   15

Ajayan
Pt

Last Japanese soldier surrendered in 1972

THE BATTLE OF THE PHILIPPINE SEA

After the capture of the Marshalls, the next US objective was of such strategic importance that the Japanese could not let it go unchallenged. Possession of the Marianas would put the US in a position to cut the homeland of Japan off from the Philippines and her other South-East Asian possessions. When the US assault fell upon the Marianas (previous pages), the Japanese First Mobile Fleet under Ozawa, and a Southern Force under Ugaki, were sent to give battle. US submarines reported the rendezvous of these groups on 16 June, and the US Task Force 58, under Mitscher, was prepared to meet Ozawa (**Map 1**). The US force totalled seven heavy and eight light carriers, seven battleships, eight heavy and thirteen light cruisers, and sixty-nine destroyers. To oppose this the Japanese had only five heavy and four light carriers, five battleships, eleven heavy and two light cruisers, and twenty-eight destroyers.

Early on June 19, Ozawa's scouting planes spotted Mitscher's force and immediately, at 0830 hours, strike aircraft were launched (**Map 2**). Further strikes were launched at 0900 hours. However, the US radar gave warning of the approach of these aircraft, and fighters were sent up to intercept them fully 50 miles before they reached the US fleet. More than 200 aircraft were shot down, eliminating Ozawa's first strike. Meanwhile US submarines had located Ozawa's force and had attacked. At 0905 hours the carrier *Taiho* was torpedoed and sunk, and at 1220 hours the *Shokaku* was also hit,

sinking finally at 1624 hours. A second strike by Ozawa at 1400 hours was misdirected, and was intercepted by US fighters on its way to Guam. By nightfall the battle was over. So heavy had the Japanese air losses been that the US crewmen dubbed the battle 'The Great Marianas Turkey Shoot'. Two carriers and over 300 aircraft had been lost, against some thirty US aircraft and slight damage to a battleship.

On the 20th (**Map 3**) Mitscher pursued Ozawa's force, but did not make contact until the afternoon. At 1624 hours he launched a strike which, at 1844 hours, sunk the carrier *Hiyo* and two oilers. Twenty US aircraft were lost, and Ozawa lost a further sixty-five. Realizing the magnitude of his defeat, he retired hastily towards Okinawa.

The Battle of the Philippine Sea dealt irreparable damage to Japanese sea power. Not only the loss of carriers and aircraft, but the loss of over 460 irreplaceable trained aircrews, was crippling.

Opposite: A near miss on a US carrier during the Battle of the Philippine Sea

Below: US sailors watch a Japanese aircraft crash into the sea

② **Van Force** (Kurita)
carriers: Chitose,
Chiyoda, Zuiho

Task Force 58
15 carriers plus supporting units

Japanese fleet

0830, 19 June
First strike launched

1000, 19 June
US planes return from
raid on Guam. Japanese
strike planes sighted

1200, 18 June

2000

1628,
Taiho sinks

1400
Second strike launched from forces
'A' and 'B', 49 planes misdirected

1600

Guam

Forces 'A' (Ozawa)
and 'B' (Joshima)
carriers: Taiho, Zuikaku,
Shokaku, Junyo, Hiyo,
Ryuho

0900/0930
First strikes launched
by forces 'A' and 'B'
0905
Taiho torpedoed by
submarine Albacore

1220
Shokaku torpedoed
by submarine Cavalla

1624, Shokaku sinks

US fighters intercept
Japanese aircraft

SITUATION 19 JUNE 1944

③

0   NAUTICAL MILES   200

**Japanese fleet
withdraws**

2045
80 returning US aircraft crash,
attempting night landing on carriers

1844
US air attacks sink
Hiyo and 2 oil tankers,
Zuikaku and Chiyoda
damaged

1600, 19 June

1624, 20 June
US strike planes launched

Japanese fleet
sails NW to attempt
refuelling

1200

Task Force 58

Guam

SITUATION 20 JUNE 1944

157

THE BATTLE OF LEYTE GULF 1

The capture of the Marianas and the completion of the Solomons/New Guinea operations prepared the way for the next move of the war. Nimitz favoured a drive against Formosa or China, but General MacArthur insisted on a move to free the Philippines, (not only for military and political reasons, but because he himself had vowed to return there). President Roosevelt favoured the MacArthur plan, and arrangements were made for a move by both MacArthur's and Nimitz's forces against the southern Philippine island of Leyte.

The force given this task was General Krueger's US Sixth Army. Following intensive bombardment by Admiral Olendorf's gun-fire-support group, Sibert's X Corps and Hodge's XXIV Corps landed, on 20 October, on the Eastern shore of Leyte (**Map 1**). By nightfall a beachhead was established, and 132,400 men had moved ashore. 200,000 tons of supplies had been landed.

These landings were lightly opposed by the Japanese 16 Division, while General Yamashita, Japanese C-in-C in the Philippines, reinforced Leyte from Luzon and the Visayas, building up the Japanese Thirty-fifth Army. However, by mid-December US aircraft had brought to a standstill all Japanese shipping in the Leyte waters. Throughout October and November the Sixth Army made slow progress. The X Corps, using overland and amphibious movements, thrust north of the beachhead to try to outflank Suzuki's Thirty-fifth Army from the north. XXIV Corps, having made a hook to the south, attacked Ormoc, the key to the Japanese defences. Then, in December the northern and southern 'hooks' converged, and, using amphibious landings for further outflanking movements, cut Suzuki off from his last remaining naval base. All organized resistance ended by Christmas day. Japanese casualties had been 70,000; American 15,584. In the meantime Sibert's X Corps had also secured a foothold on Samar. The Japanese, rightly appreciating that a successful US landing in the Philippines would cut their empire in two, severing the homeland from the Southern Resources Area with its supplies of food and fuel, decided to destroy the landings on the eastern coast of Leyte and their attendant naval escorts. The plan to achieve this, optimistically called the 'Sho' (victory) Plan, was put into operation in late October 1944 shortly after the US forces had begun landing on Leyte.

The whole of the Japanese Combined Fleet moved from widely scattered bases (**Map 2**). Ozawa's Northern Force, or Carrier 'Decoy' Force (the four remaining carriers, two battleships, four cruisers, and eight destroyers), steamed south from Japan to lure the US Third Fleet (eight heavy and eight light carriers, six battleships, three heavy and nine light cruisers, fifty-eight destroyers, and more than 1,000 planes), under Halsey away from the landings. Kurita's Force 'A' (two superbattleships, three other battleships, twelve cruisers, and fifteen destroyers), sailed east from Borneo to traverse the San Bernardino Strait and attack the landings from the north. A second force from Borneo, Force 'C' under Vice-Admiral Nishimura (two battleships, one heavy cruiser, and four destroyers), backed up by the Second Striking Force under Vice-Admiral Shima (two heavy and one light cruisers and four destroyers), was to pass through the Surigao Strait to attack the landings from the south (**Map 2**).

On 23 October the US submarines *Darter* and *Dace* spotted Kurita's First Striking Force. Not only did they send word to Halsey, but they sank two heavy cruisers *Atago* and *Maya*. Kurita, continuing into the Sibuyan Sea, was attacked by aircraft from Mitscher's Task Force 38 (the carrier element of Halsey's Third Fleet). After nearly two days of incessant bombardment the super-battleship *Musashi* was sunk at 1000 hours on the 24th. Late on the 24th Kurita turned and headed west again, and Halsey assumed that he was retreating. Meanwhile Japanese aircraft from Clark Field on Luzon attacked part of Task Force 38 and succeeded in sinking the light carrier *Princeton*. Unknown to Halsey, after dark, Kurita changed course again and headed for San Bernardino Strait.

Opposite: The crew of an escort carrier take cover from a Japanese dive bomber

Right: The US fleet under Japanese air attack during the invasion of Leyte

POSITIONS OF US CARRIER TASK GROUPS, 0600, 24 OCTOBER
TIMES ARE THOSE FOR 24 OCTOBER UNLESS OTHERWISE INDICATED

0   NAUTICAL MILES   300

Carrier 'Decoy' Force (Ozawa)   0100

0000, 25th

1140

0600, 25th

Group 'A' (Matsuda)   0822, 25th

2000

2241

Task Force 38 (Halsey's Third Fleet) steams north to engage Ozawa's force

2345

2000

C. Engaño

Luzon

TG 38.3 (Sherman)

Clark Field

Princeton

Second Striking Force (Shima)

0935 Carrier Princeton hit, sinks at 1630

PHILIPPINE ISLANDS

MANILA

TG 38.2 (Bogan)

1200, 23 Oct

Mindoro

1026/1530 US air strikes. Battleship Musashi sinks at 1935, cruiser Myoko retires damaged

Sibuyan Sea

1000

Masbate

San Bernardino Str

0600, 25th

TG 38.4 (Davison)

CALAMIAN GROUP

1200, 23 Oct

Panay

Samar

Force 'A' (Kurita)

0632, 23 Oct US Submarines sink cruisers Atago and Maya, Takao retires damaged

Leyte

0400, 25th

US Seventh Fleet (Kinkaid)

Negros

Cebu

Surigao Str

Bohol

1000

Palawan

2000

2330

TG 38.1 (McCain) to Ulithi

0918

1000

Force 'C' (Nishimura)

Mindanao

1200, 23 Oct

Sulu Sea

First Striking Force (Kurita)

BRITISH NORTH BORNEO

Sails 22 Oct

BRUNEI

②

THE BATTLE OF LEYTE GULF 2

Warned of the approach of Nishimura and Shima from the south, Kinkaid, in command of the US Seventh Fleet at the landings, ordered Olendorf's gun-fire support group (Task Group 77) to intercept them. On the night of the 24th Olendorf drew up his battleships he deployed his approach of Nishimura's force. In front of his battleships he deployed his cruisers, and in front of them his destroyers (**Map 1**). Between 0300 hours and 0340 on the 25th destroyer attacks on Nishimura's flanks torpedoed the battleship *Fuso* and four destroyers. The remainder of Nishimura's force, in line ahead, ran into Olendorf's cruisers and battleships. Olendorf was in the classic naval position of having crossed his opponents' 'T'. In the ensuing forty minutes the whole of Nishimura's force, save one destroyer, had been wiped out. Nishimura went down with his flagship, *Yamashiro*.

Shima's force, bringing up the rear, had already suffered the loss of a cruiser, torpedoed by a PT boat. Attempting to retire, Shima's own flagship, the *Nachi*, collided with a crippled ship of Nishimura's force. One more cruiser was lost next day as Shima withdrew. Olendorf turned back after a short pursuit, knowing that he might well have to fight again to protect the landings.

Halsey, meanwhile, convinced that Kurita was permanently out of the fight, steamed north after Ozawa's Decoy Force, failing to inform Kinkaid of this. Early on 25 October, Kurita surprised Rear-Admiral Sprague commanding Taffy 3, an escort carrier group of Kinkaid's Seventh Fleet. With only six escort carriers, three destroyers, and four destroyer escorts, he found himself giving battle to four battleships, six heavy cruisers, and ten destroyers. His aircraft were armed for land operations, and were almost helpless against the Japanese ships. In an amazing two-hour running fight Sprague staved off disaster, using his destroyers skilfully to keep the Japanese

160

at their distance (**Map 2**). He was assisted by aircraft from other escort carrier groups, but nonetheless one carrier, *Gambier Bay*, and three destroyers were lost. Persistent and superb destroyer action by the US force succeeded in sinking three Japanese cruisers.

At 0923 hours, when Sprague's force could hardly have held out any longer, Kurita decided to withdraw. The aircraft from other escort carriers had misled him into supposing that he had engaged Task Force 38 which was in reality many miles away to the north. His decision was strengthened by reports that Nishimura's force had been destroyed. Within a few hours of success Kurita turned to make off homewards via the San Bernardino Strait.

Sprague's ordeal was not quite over, however. Returning southward he was attacked by Japanese land-based aircraft, including the first Kamikaze missions, and the carrier *St Lo* was sunk.

Halsey's headlong rush northwards to catch Ozawa paid off in the small hours of the morning of the 25th (**Map 3**). At 0220 hours Mitscher's search aircraft located Ozawa, and by 0845 hours the first of four strikes was on the way. Ozawa, most of whose few remaining aircraft had been put ashore to operate as land-based forces, had nothing to oppose these strikes. Throughout the day the strikes continued as Ozawa fled north. By nightfall all four Japanese carriers had been sunk, and five other ships. Only two battleships, two cruisers, and six destroyers escaped.

The four-phased Battle of Leyte Gulf shattered Japan's seapower for ever. Four carriers, three battleships, six heavy and four light cruisers, eleven destroyers and a submarine were sunk. Almost every other Japanese ship was in some way damaged. 500 aircraft and a total of 10,000 men were lost. These were casualties that could never be made good.

Right: The battleships of Task Group 77 in line ahead off Leyte

0 NAUTICAL MILES 60

③

2041
Ozawa turns to
assist Hatsusuki

2330

2059
Destroyer Hatsusuki sunk
by Cruiser Group
1800
2050

4
2000

1526
Zuiho sunk by
third air strike
3

1414
Zuikaku sunk by
third air strike
1830

0000

1200

1, 2

0235

0700
Matsuda's group
rejoins Ozawa
1800

1900

1630

1415

1219

Task Groups 38.3, 38.4

0400

Group 'A'
(Matsuda)
2 battleships
1 cruiser
4 destroyers

1115
Task Group 38.2 turns
to intercept Kurita's force*

1115
TF 34 turns to
intercept Kurita's force*

0822

Carrier 'Decoy' Force
(Ozawa)

carriers:
Zuikaku, Zuiho, Chitose,
Chiyoda
battleships:
Isu† Hyuga†
cruisers:
Isuzu, Oyoda, Tama†
plus 9 destroyers

†to Group 'A' later

Cruiser Group
(DuBose) 4 cruisers, 10 destroyers

1655
Chiyoda sunk by Cruiser Group
(damaged by first air strike

0937
Chitose sunk by
first air strike

Destroyer Akitsuki sunk
by first air strike

Task Force 38 (Mitscher)
10 carriers, 22 destroyers
plus ships in Cruiser Group

Task Force 34 (Lee)
formed, 0240, 25 Oct
from part of TF 38

6 battleships, 4 cruisers
8 destroyers

*retiring towards San Bernardino Strait
after "The Battle off Samar"

Mitscher's air strikes
1   0845–0930
2   1000–1010
3   1300–1500
4   1710–1740

CLEARING THE PHILIPPINES

After the capture of Leyte in December 1944 the way was open for a US attack on the main Philippine Island, Luzon.

Between 2 and 8 January, the Sixth Army (General Krueger), moved from Leyte to Lingayen Gulf on Luzon, carried by the Seventh Fleet. The Japanese air bases on Formosa, that might have harassed the landings, were neutralized by aircraft from Halsey's carriers and by aircraft operating from China. Although US aircraft from Leyte and Mindoro tried to neutralize the aircraft on Luzon itself, Olendorf's gun-fire-support group lost heavily to Kamikaze pilots – both on the way

up, and during the preliminary bombardment. One carrier was sunk, and another damaged. The battleship *New Mexico*, one heavy, and four light cruisers, and several other ships were damaged. On 9 January the Sixth Army went ashore in Lingayen Gulf. The Japanese commander, General Yamashita, commanding the Japanese Fourteenth Army, decided not to contest the landing. The US forces landed on a two corps front, four divisions abreast. On the left, I Corps (General Swift); on the right XIV Corps (General Griswold). Griswold's corps pushed aside Japanese delaying

①

0930 hrs, 9 January 1945
US Sixth Army (Krueger)

I Corps (Swift)
6 Div and 43 Div

XIV Corps (Griswold)
37 Div and 40 Div

Jap Fourteenth Area Army (Yamashita)

17 Jan

29 Jan
XI Corps (Hall)

15 Feb
Regt of XI Corps

21 Feb
Bataan cleared

31 Jan
Majority 11 Abn Div

3 Feb
Remainder drop by parachute. Light opposition

Command boundary
US Sixth Army
US Eighth Army, 1 Jan 1945

15 December 1944
Western Visayan Task Force
(Dunckel) lands. Light opposition.
Other landings between 21 December and 22 January

CAMIGUIN

23 June
Part 511 Para Inf Regt
APARRI

LAOAG
GONZAGA

26 June
Contact

VIGAN
19 Apr

TUGUEGARAO
25 June

Cordillera Central
Sierra Madre
Cagayan

BONTOC

ILAGAN
19 June

L u z o n

26 Mar
SAN FERNANDO
BAUANG
BAGUIO BAYOMBONG
AGOO
DAMORTIS ROSARIO BAMBANG
LINGAYEN TAYUG
CARMEN
SAN JOSE 13 Feb
Zambales Mts
TARLAC **CABANATUAN** 24 Jan
21 Jan GAPAN
IBA **BAMBAN**
Clark Field
PORAC
Del Carmen Field **SAN FERNANDO**
SAN ANTONIO DANILUPIHAN CALUMPIT
OLONGAPO 5 Feb
Bataan **MANILA**
Peninsula Manila Nielson & Nichols Fields
Bay
CAVITE
CORREGIDOR
28 Feb *Laguna de Bay*
NASUGBU MAUBAN 10 Apr
Tagaytay Ridge ATIMONAN
TIAONG LUCENA SIAIN
BATANGAS CALAUAG 14 Apr
LUBANG IS *Balayan Bay*
XXXX
CALAPAN BOAC
24 Jan
XXXX

M i n d o r o

4 Feb/3 March
Battle for Manila

Lamon Bay

DAET

Bicol Peninsula
NAGA

2 May
Contact

CATANDUANES

LEGASPI 1 April
158 Regt CT

BURIAS
IROSIN
San Bernardino Str

S i b u y a n
S e a

SAN JOSE

Jap defence sectors

Shobo Group
(Yamashita)
152,000 men

Kembu Group
(Tsukada)
30,000 men

Shimbu Group
(Yokoyama)
80,000 men

Luzon
6 Jan

MANILA

Samar

2 Jan
Leyte

US Seventh Fleet
(Oldendorf)
carrying US Sixth Army
200,000 men

Mindanao

OCCUPIED BY US FORCES, 1 Jan 1945

YAMASHITA'S HEADQUARTERS

HELD BY JAPANESE REMNANTS UP TO END OF WAR

0   MILES   100
0   KILOMETRES   150

forces and pressed on to Clark Field, which he reached by 23 January.

On the left of the beachhead, however, Swift's I Corps had heavier going against the bulk of Yamashita's Shobo Group.

Between 29 January and 4 February, task forces from General Eichelberger's Eighth Army made landings on the north and south of Manila Bay. On the north XI Corps under General Hall landed at San Antonio and drove straight across the top of the Bataan Peninsula. To the south 11 Airborne Division landed at Nasugbu, to make straight for Manila itself. For a whole month, 3 February to 4 March, the Americans fought their way into Manila. Elements of Griswold's corps, approaching from the north, split. Part continued to attack Manila from the north, and part executed a flanking movement to link up with 11 Airborne Division in the south. By 22 February the Japanese had been driven back into the old walled city where, ignoring Yamashita's orders, they conducted a street by street defence. When the last resistance ended the city was rubble and 16,000 Japanese lay dead.

In the same month, Corregidor was captured. On 16 February paratroopers of 11 Airborne Division dropped on its tiny golf course, supported by an amphibious landing from Bataan. By the 27th the fortress was clear. US ships began to move into Manila bay, and on 13 April the bay's last fortification, Fort Drum, the 'Concrete Battleship', was overcome by pouring petrol down the ventilators and lighting it, cooking the garrison inside.

Between April and August the weight of Sixth Army turned east, north, and south in a series of assaults against Yamashita's mountain strongholds. When Yamashita surrendered at the end of the war, he still had organized forces of about 50,000 men.

Luzon was the largest single campaign undertaken by the Americans in the Pacific. Their losses were 7,933 killed and 32,732 wounded. The Japanese lost 192,000 killed.

At the same time as the Luzon campaign, Eichelberger's Eighth Army was tackling the remaining Philippine Islands garrisoned by elements of the Japanese Thirty-fifth Army, in all some 102,000 men, mainly concentrated on Mindanao. Between February and July, 1945, Eighth Army task forces conducted more than fifty amphibious operations. The pattern rarely varied. The landing would be followed by a Japanese withdrawal into the interior, US forces would secure the island, and mopping-up would be left to the active Filippino guerrilla units.

On Mindanao itself, however, Suzuki, having escaped from Leyte, put up a sterner resistance. Concentric landings from north, east, and south finally isolated his forces into two groups, in which they remained until the end of the war.

Left: US troops climbing into their landing craft before the landings in Lingayen Gulf

IWO JIMA

The seizure of Iwo Jima, so costly that it was to eclipse even Tarawa in US Marine Corps legend, was dictated by several considerations. First, although distant from Japan, it was a part of the Japanese homeland, and its capture would be a deep psychological shock to the Japanese, military and civilian alike. Second, it was within fighter range of Tokyo, and US bomber losses demanded that their raids enjoy fighter protection. Third, crippled or fuelless bombers would be able to make a landfall there.

Nobody pretended however, that Iwo Jima could be taken easily. A mere eight square miles, wholly devoid of cover, and dominated at one end by the sugar-loaf massif of Mount Suribachi, it was garrisoned by 22,000 Japanese army and navy troops under Major-General Kuribayashi. 'Honeycombed' is a cliché, but no other word can describe the complex of tunnels, gun emplacements, pillboxes, and caves that the Japanese had created on Iwo Jima.

On 19 February 1945, after the most prolonged and intense bombardment in the Pacific war (a 72-day softening up by B–24 and B–25 bombers, followed by a pre-assault barrage fired by the US navy for three days), 4 and 5 Marine Divisions, with the 3rd in reserve, were put ashore by Schmidt's V Amphibious Corps. For the first few minutes they encountered only sporadic resistance. Either the garrison had been overestimated, or the barrage had done its job more than well. After twenty minutes, however, the fire of all the defenders' weapons, artillery, mortars, and small arms, opened up on the exposed Marine positions. Brilliant though the co-ordination of this fireplan was, the Japanese had left it just too late. They had allowed the Marines to land with all the equipment they needed, and to establish a large enough beachhead to land more. By the end of the day 30,000 Marines had been landed, and had swarmed right across the neck of the island. With them had come tanks, bulldozers, and artillery.

For the following three days the Marines fought for the control of Suribachi, and by the 23rd had achieved this with the historic raising of the Stars and Stripes on its summit. But the fall of Suribachi did not mean the fall of Iwo Jima. The north-east of the island remained to be conquered, and this was to take until 26 March. The maze of underground defences and the closeness of the opposing forces made the fighting of this phase more like the First World War than the Second. There was little room to manoeuvre round the defenders' flanks: every assault was a frontal attack, using the tactics of fire and movement to shoot the men forward. It was extremely costly.

Some 6,821 US Marines and sailors lost their lives on Iwo Jima, and almost all of the 22,000-man Japanese garrison was killed.

Below: Landing craft approaching Iwo Jima

Opposite above: Supplies being unloaded on the beachhead at Iwo Jima

Oppposite below: A rocket barrage on Japanese positions during the final stages of the advance

OKINAWA

The final preliminary to an invasion of Japan itself was the capture of Okinawa, the main island of the Ryukyu group, the southernmost islands of Japan. It was held by the 130,000 men of the Japanese Thirty-second Army, under Lieutenant-General Ushijima. Unlike the other Pacific islands (with the exception of some parts of the Philippines) Okinawa was quite densely populated, having a civilian population of about 450,000.

From 14 to 31 March preliminary air operations were undertaken to isolate and soften-up the target. Japanese air bases on Formosa and the islands surrounding Okinawa were attacked by US and British carrier forces, both of which paid a toll to

Kamikaze pilots. But of the 196 Kamikaze attacks launched, 169 were destroyed before reaching their targets.

From 23 March onwards, Okinawa itself was subjected to a continuous air and artillery strafing. Neighbouring small islands were captured to provide fleet anchorages and bases. On 1 April, Operation Iceberg began. General Buckner's Tenth Army, one Army corps and one Marine corps, landed at the southern end of Okinawa. On the left, the Marine III Amphibious Corps was to push north and secure the whole northern end of the island in just over a fortnight. On the right, however, Hodge's XXIV Corps ran against formidable Japanese defences – the Shuri Line. Buckner was faced with a difficult decision. Should he attack the Shuri defences frontally, or outflank them with another amphibious landing in their rear? The frontal assault would be costly, but the amphibious operation might split his force in the presence of a formidable enemy. In the event he did both, but in the meantime, on 3/4 May, the Japanese had obliged him with one of their now inevitable suicidal counterattacks. It was repulsed with the loss of 5,000 Japanese, and the hitherto concealed Japanese positions on the Shuri Line were given

away. From 11 to 21 May Buckner's forces tore at the Japanese defences in appalling weather conditions. They broke through, and Ushijima, disengaging, retreated to the hill masses of the southern tip of the island. A massive two-pronged attack overwhelmed the final resistance by 21 June.

Japanese losses on Okinawa were staggering. The known dead totalled 107,500 and probably a further 20,000 died sealed in their cave hideouts. About 4,000 Japanese aircraft were lost in combat, and an equal number from other causes. But for the first time Japanese soldiers had surrendered in appreciable numbers – 7,400 prisoners were taken.

The US Tenth Army lost 7,613 killed, including Lieutenant-General Buckner, and 31,800 wounded. The US Navy's casualties were 4,900 killed and 4,800 wounded. In addition, thirty-four ships and aircraft were sunk and 368 damaged.

Below: Marines assault a Japanese strongpoint

Opposite above: Part of the preliminary bombardment before the landings on Okinawa

Opposite below: Men of 6 Marine Division advancing into Naha, the capital of Okinawa

THE END IN THE PACIFIC

With the invasion of Okinawa, the American forces were now faced with their last and greatest challenge – the invasion of the home islands of Japan (opposite). The fanatical resistance which had been encountered at every stage of the Pacific War gave the American planners no reason to hope or expect that a surrender would be forthcoming, and the combined staffs of General MacArthur and Admiral Nimitz began to prepare for an eventual invasion. Landings on southern Kyushu were to be made on 1 November 1945 in Operation Olympic and on Honshu on 1 March 1946 in Operation Coronet. The operations were then to be extended and pushed ahead until all Japanese resistance had been overcome.

The forces to be assembled for these two operations would have been the largest amphibious assault force ever raised. While the earlier landings would use forces already in the Pacific, the second landings would utilize men and equipment redeployed from Europe. It was assumed that the landings would be resolutely opposed by the still-powerful forces remaining on the Japanese islands, and the planners were pessimistic about the likely casualty rate which the operation would entail.

It was against this background that President Truman was presented with the decision as to whether to use the atomic bomb to force the Japanese surrender. He decided that the immediate advantage in saving lives outweighed the disadvantages of unleashing a new and unthinkably powerful form of warfare on the world, and on 6 August 1945 the Superfortress 'Enola Gay' dropped the first atomic bomb on Hiroshima. In one minute more than 78,500 people died and many more were to be struck down in the weeks which followed, but a surrender ultimatum to Japan was ignored. On 9 August a second bomb was dropped at Nagasaki, and Japan surrendered. The war in the Pacific was over.

The Russian attack on Manchuria was a nine-day wonder of logistics, staff work, and planning. This was almost the only occasion in the war when the Japanese did not put up a stiff resistance. The campaign was the result of Russia's need to get her foot into the Far Eastern door before peace shut it. It had been long planned, and long delayed, but the atomic bombing of Hiroshima and Nagasaki prompted Russia to speed into action.

Manchuria was garrisoned by nearly one million Japanese troops of the Kwantung Army under General Yamada. On 8 August Russia declared war on Japan, and on 9 August Marshal Malinovsky's Trans-Baikal Front moved into Manchuria from the north, west, and east. The Kwantung Army was no match for the armoured and motorized units under Malinovsky's command. By 18 August the whole of Manchuria had been overrun.

Right: Smoke billowing 20,000 feet over Nagasaki after the second atomic raid

Jap Sixteenth Area Army
Kyushu
TSUNO
FUKUSHIMA
KOBAYASHI
MIYAZAKI
SENDAI
KUSHIKINO
KAGOSHIMA
MIYAKONOJO
SHUBISHI
KANOYA
Satsuma Pen
Araake Bay
KOSHIKI RETTO
28 Oct
UJI GUNTO
Kagoshima Bay
Sata Misaki
KISAKAKI SHIMA
KURO SHIMA
KUCHINOERABU SHIMA
TANEGA SHIMA
YAKU SHIMA
27 Oct
40 Inf Div
US V Amphib Corps
27 Oct
158 Regtl Cbt Team

US IX Corps (reserve)
US I Corps
US XI Corps

OPERATION 'OLYMPIC'
PLANNED LANDINGS
POSSIBLE LANDINGS
LANDINGS

0 — 60 MILES
0 — 80 KILOMETRES

Sakhalin

RUSSIA

Jap Fifth Area Army
5 infantry divs

Hokkaido

OTARU
SAPPORO
HAKODATE

S E A   O F
J A P A N

HACHINOHE

AKITA

P A C I F I C
O C E A N

① **Jap First General Army HQ** (Sugiyama) Eleventh, Twelfth & Thirteenth Area Armies

② **Jap Second General Army HQ** (Hata) Fifth, Fifteenth & Sixteenth Area Armies

Jap Eleventh Area Army
6 infantry divs

Jap Twelfth Area Army
18 infantry divs
2 armoured divs

SADO
NIIGATA
SENDAI

Honshu

KANAZAWA

Kanto Plain
TOKYO

Jap Thirty-sixth Army (reserve) and Air General Army

KOREA
SEOUL

Jap Seventeenth Area Army

Jap Fifteenth Area Army
8 infantry divs

Jap Thirteenth Area Army
6 infantry divs

KYOTO
HIROSHIMA
KOBE OSAKA
NAGOYA

Shimonoseki Str

Jap Sixteenth Area Army
14 infantry divs
2 armoured bdes

FUKUOKA
Kyushu
SENDAI
MIYAZAKI
Shikoku

TANEGA SHIMA

Feint
30 Oct/1 Nov

US Eighth Army
(Eichelberger)
X Corps (Sibert)
3 infantry divs
XIV Corps (Griswold)
3 infantry divs
XIII Corps (Gillem)
2 armoured divs

US First Army
(C. H. Hodges)
III Amphibious Corps
(Geiger) 3 marine divs
XXIV Corps
(J. R. Hodges) 3 infantry divs

OPERATION 'CORONET'
tentatively scheduled for 1 March 1946 (Y-Day)

US V Amphib Corps (Schmidt)
2 Marine, 3 Marine and 5 Marine Divs

40 Inf Div
27/28 Oct

US XI Corps (Hall)
1 Cav (Armd) Div
43 Inf and American Divs

US I Corps (Swift)
25 Inf, 33 Inf and 41 Inf Divs

US IX Corps (Rider)
77 Inf, 83 Inf and 98 Inf Divs (reserve corps)

OPERATION 'OLYMPIC' scheduled 1 November 1945 (X-Day)
US Sixth Army (Krueger)

⊙ JAPANESE AREA ARMY HEADQUARTERS
—·—·— JAPANESE AREA ARMY BOUNDARY

0 — MILES — 300
0 — KILOMETRES — 500

OPERATION 'CORONET'
0 — MILES — 40
0 — KM — 60

KUMAGAYA
KOGA
Kanto Plain
Armour to isolate Tokyo
TOKYO
YOKOHAMA
Tokyo Bay
Kujikurihama Beach
Sagami Bay
Boso Pen

Honshu
SHIZUOKO
O'SHIMA
Pre Y-day landings

US First Army
US Eighth Army

THE BURMA CAMPAIGN

'If the armies and government of
Generalissimo Chiang Kai-shek had
been finally defeated, Japan would
have been left free to exploit the
tremendous resources of China
without harassment. It might have
made it possible when the United
States and Britain had finished
the job in Europe, and assaulted the
Japanese home islands, for the
government to flee to China, and
continue the war on a great and
rich land mass.'
General George C. Marshall

Opposite: Japanese officers laying down
their swords in surrender

One does not lightly differ from the strategic opinions of so distinguished a soldier as General Marshall, and it may, therefore be some consolation to the veterans of the Fourteenth Army that without their efforts China could not have been kept in the fight. Even after the Burma Road was cut at Lashio on 29 April 1942 the Allies had continued to fly supplies to the Chinese over 'the Hump', a flight which meant clearing the Himalayas at an altitude of 23,000 feet. At first these supplies amounted to about 10,000 tons a month.

The Allies, in the words of Lieutenant-General Joseph W. Stilwell – *alias* 'Vinegar Joe' – had taken 'a hell of a beating' in the first Burma campaign. Even so by the end of 1942 the British had begun to think of going over to the offensive. Early in 1943 they made a thrust down the Arakan coast with the object of recapturing Akyab and its airfield, but this proved a costly failure. The truth is that morale was low at this time. The Japanese soldier had come to be regarded as a kind of Superman. A high sick rate is usually an indication of low morale. In 1942 for every man wounded 120 were being sent back sick. At the end of the year one division, 17,000 strong, had 5,000 sick. Malaria, dysentery, mite typhus, and skin diseases all took their toll.

It was at this time that Brigadier Orde Wingate appeared on the scene. Experience of guerilla warfare in Palestine and Abyssinia had led him to conceive the idea of long-range penetration, and this he had contrived to 'sell' to Winston Churchill, who was often receptive to unorthodox ideas and willing to encourage a commander who wanted to fight. Wingate was allowed to raise a 'private army', the Chindits, and with this force he waged war beyond the Chindwin from February to May 1943. His men cut the Mandalay–Myitkyina railway in seventy-five places – exploits which generally speaking left the Japanese unimpressed, for, unlike the Germans, they were not particularly sensitive about being raided. But, thanks

to the Press, the morale effect on the Allies was quite different. Although the Chindits had endured terrible hardships and had been compelled to abandon many of their sick and wounded, they had shown that they could take on the Japanese in the jungle. The myth of the Japanese Superman began to dissolve. Wingate had moreover demonstrated the value of air supply. He himself enjoyed in the eyes of the British public a reputation akin to that of T. E. Lawrence in the First World War, and, despite his eccentricities, he was clearly a very talented soldier. At the same time he was unscrupulous about getting his own way, and having direct access to the Prime Minister, an unwarrantable by-passing of the normal military channels – was now able, at the expense of Fourteenth Army, to build his brigade into a division.

In August 1943 another young and brilliant commander came on the scene. This was Lord Louis Mountbatten, a member of the British Royal Family. At the beginning of the war he had been a dashing destroyer captain. Later he had scored notable successes as Chief of Combined Operations. Now at the early age of forty-three he was made Supreme Commander of the newly created South-East-Asia Command (SEAC). It would be wrong to underrate Mountbatten as a strategist, but his great asset was that he had an inspiring personality. His brand of leadership appealed to the men of his command, and his tireless visits to every kind of unit were a very real factor in raising morale. In this sphere he was as effective as Montgomery himself. But morale is not only a question of enthusiasm, but of discipline. The improvement in Fourteenth Army was partly a question of improving its health, and to some extent this was simply a matter of discipline. The strictest health precautions were needed, for example in seeing that every man took his daily mepacrine tablet to prevent malaria.

Mountbatten's immediate object was to reopen land communications

with China. To this end American engineers, with coolie labour, had been building the Ledo road, begun in December 1942 and eventually completed in January 1945. This was to be extended so as to join the old Burma Road at Mongyu near Lashio. Fuel pipelines were to be built from Calcutta to Assam, and parallel to the Ledo road. Supplies over the Hump were to be increased to 20,000 tons a month.

The key to the reconquest of Burma was air supply. As Admiral Mountbatten himself pointed out:

'It was not just a question of auxiliary air supply, because 96 per cent of our supplies to the Fourteenth Army went by air. In the course of this campaign we lifted 615,000 tons of supplies to the armies, three quarters of it by the US Air Force and one quarter by the Royal Air Force; 315,000 reinforcements were flown in, . . . 110,000 casualties were flown out, . . . in our best month – March 1945 – we actually lifted 94,300 tons. During that time the American Air Transport Command were building up their 'Hump' traffic, so that by July they had reached their peak of 77,500 tons per month.'

Despite this administrative effort and backing the motto of the Fourteenth Army was 'God helps those who help themselves'. The feat of improvisation which brought into being the flotilla that made possible the Irrawaddy crossing is a classic example.

No amount of administrative skill will win wars without soldiers prepared to fight with the skill and determination of the men who defended Imphal and Kohima. But stout-hearted soldiers will still be defeated if they are not well commanded. In Sir William Slim the Fourteenth Army had a general of the highest calibre.

4 ·········
Areas covered by
maps –

6 ·········
5 ·········
9 ·········
7 ·········
8 ·········
3 ·········

INDIA

KOHIMA •

IMPHAL •

LEDO •

FORT HERTZ

MYITKYINA •

INDAW •
BHAMO •

CHINA

Irrawaddy

Chindwin

10 ·········

11 ·········
1 ·········

12 ·········

2 ·········

AKYAB •

B U R M A

LASHIO

MANDALAY •

Irrawaddy

Sittang

Salween

THAILAND

RANGOON ■

0   MILES   200
0   KILOMETRES   300

Opposite left: Japanese representatives being
marched to sign surrender terms in Hong Kong

Opposite right: Troops boarding landing craft
for the seaborne attack on Ramree Island

Right: A British officer searches a Japanese
after the surrender

Above right: A Bren-gun carrier during the
advance to Mandalay

173

THE ARAKAN BATTLES

Chittagong 60 miles
21 Sept 1942
14 Ind Div (Lloyd)
begin first counterattack
from Chittagong

14 IND DIV'S POSITIONS
- ·—·—· 31 DECEMBER 1942
- — — — 31 JAN/END FEB 1943
- ———— 25 MAY
- ◄—— ATTACKS BY JAP 55 DIV AND 213 REGT 4 MAR / 14 MAY 1943

COX'S BAZAR

INDIA   BURMA

TUMBRU

BAWLI BAZAR   GOPPE BAZAR

NHILI

TEKNAF   Tunnels   BUTHIDAUNG 7 May

MAUNGDAW   'Soutcol' (flank guard)
14 May   A r a k a n

ZEDIDAUNG

123 Ind Inf Bde   Miyawaki Column

HTIZWE 18 Mar   Tanahashi Column

RATHEDAUNG

INDIN 6 Apr
47 and 55 Ind Inf Bdes

B a y   o f   B e n g a l   **Jap 213 Regt**

DONBAIK
Foul Point

AKYAB   AKYAB

End Feb 1943
Jap 55 Div (Koga)
from Prome area

MILES 0 — 30
KILOMETRES 0 — 40

After the series of reverses during 1942 that drove the British first into surrender at Singapore and then headlong defeat in Burma, General Wavell, commanding the Allied forces in India, realized that a counter-invasion of Burma was out of the question until late 1943 at the very earliest, but wished to raise the morale of his men by success in small scale, carefully planned operations. These were to have the additional benefit of providing up to date experience on combat with the Japanese. For the first of these small offensives, Wavell chose the Arakan, operations being directed against the island post of Akyab, from which the Japanese could bomb Chittagong and Calcutta.

The 14 Indian Division advanced carefully from its base at Chittagong to the forward base at Cox's Bazar by sea and overland along a very poor road (**Map 1**). From Cox's Bazar onwards, the only means of advance was fair weather tracks. The British advance continued cautiously against skilful Japanese delaying tactics, but gave the Japanese commander in Burma, General Iida, time to move up his 55 Division in time to halt 14 Indian Division in front of Donbaik and Rathedaung.

After a stalemate lasting from January to March 1943 the Japanese counterattacked, both frontally and over the mountains to the east that the British had considered more or less impassable. The 14 Indian Division retreated in some disorder, leaving the Japanese still holding the Arakan, and the British troops further impressed by Japanese fighting abilities.

In December 1943 the British, in the form of Christison's XV Corps, once again tried to advance on Akyab (**Map 2**). The Japanese, who were starting to plan an invasion of eastern India by Mutaguchi's Fifteenth Army, soon halted the British along the line Maungdaw–Buthidaung and prepared a counterstroke. While the Doi Column pinned down the 5 and

7 Indian Divisions, the Sakurai Column moved through the 'impassable' eastern flank jungle and mountains and cut off the two Indian divisions. General Slim, commanding Allied forces operating against Burma from India, refused to contemplate a withdrawal and decided to supply the encircled divisions by air. After bitter fighting, the two surrounded divisions made contact with each other on 24 February and in turn cut off part of the Japanese 55 Division. Between March and April XV Corps finally broke through the Japanese defence and began the advance on Akyab again, only to be halted by the need to send reinforcements to Imphal.

Above: Gurkha troops at a camp on the Arakan

Opposite: Indian gunners in action during the offensive in the Arakan

81 West Afr Div
(Woolner)
in reserve

BAWLI BAZAR

Groppe Pass

GOPPE BAZAR

XV CORPS FORWARD POSITIONS, DEC 1943
XV CORPS ATTACKS END DEC 1943/FEB 1944
JAPANESE FRONT, 3 FEBRUARY
DISPOSITION OF XV CORPS UNITS, 3 FEBRUARY
JAPANESE COUNTERATTACK 3/24 FEBRUARY

MILES 0 — 6
KILOMETRES 0 — 10

XV Corps
(Christison)

MYAUKE

81 West Afr Div
(Woolner)

5 Ind Div
(Briggs)

Mayu Range

Kubo Force

TAUNG BAZAR

4 Feb

0 MLS 10

BAWLI BAZAR

NHILA

BURMA

Teknaf Pen

Naf R

BUTHIDAUNG

TEKNAF

MAUNGDAW

Bay of Bengal

Kalapanzin

INGYAUNG

Tanahashi Force

7 Ind Div HQ

Laung C.

7 Ind Div
(Messervy)

KWAZON

5/6 Feb

CHOTA MAUNGHNAMA

6 Feb

Ngakyedauk C.

AWLANBYIN

Tanahashi and Kubo Forces

5 Ind Div HQ

WABYIN

Ngakyedauk Pass

SINZWEYA

6/24 Feb Admin box besieged

6/7 Feb

KYAUKYIT

Doi Column

LETWEDET

Tunnels Road (All weather)

BUTHIDAUNG

DABRUGYAUNG

3 Feb, assembly area

Jap 55 Div (Hanaya)

OPERATION "HA-GO"
3/24 February 1944
Sakurai Column

MAUNGDAW 9 Jan

RAZABIL

Kalapanzin

THE CHINDIT OPERATIONS

At the same time as he initiated the first venture into the Arakan, Wavell also gave permission for a second operation that might bolster Allied morale – Wingate's first 'Chindit' operation by 77 Indian Brigade. The aim of the brigade was to operate for lengthy periods behind the Japanese lines, cutting communications, gathering Intelligence, and causing confusion, relying on air supply for essentials before finally pulling back through the Japanese lines. Above all the idea was to demonstrate that British, Indian, and Ghurka troops could take on and beat the Japanese.

The brigade was split into two groups, the Southern one crossing the Chindwin first as a diversion for the larger Northern Group (**Map 1**). Both then advanced in a easterly direction, causing as much damage as they could to Japanese communications. Supply caused difficulty at first as it was not realized that drops could be made in jungle, and much time was wasted in finding open dropping zones. Little damage was caused as the groups advanced to the Irrawaddy, but the Japanese were massing forces against the Chindits, and the advance became very difficult after the Irrawaddy had been crossed. The remains of the two Groups joined up on 24 March, the day Wingate was ordered to return to India. Wingate's last plan to cut the Mandalay–Lashio railway had to be abandoned. The various columns made their way back during late March and April.

Losses were over 33 per cent, too high to justify the small amount of damage inflicted, but the operation was a definite propaganda and morale success, and many valuable lessons were learnt.

Meanwhile General Joseph Stilwell, commanding in the American and Chinese forces in southern China, disappointed by the fact that there was to be no major Allied offensive in Burma in 1943, and fearing a Japanese thrust into north-eastern India, where the vital supply road from Ledo to China was being built, decided to advance on Myitkyina (**Map 2**). Japanese resistance was tough in the Hukawng Valley, but Stilwell was able to resume his advance after a

month's delay on 24 December 1943.
But in January 1944 the Japanese
18 Division again halted the Chinese
advance until late February, when the
US 5307 Provisional Regiment under
Brigadier-General F. Merrill arrived.
This allowed the development of the
tactics that led to renewed advances:
Chinese pinning attacks combined
with American flanking movements.

To complement Stilwell's advance,
a second Chindit operation was
mounted. The main force was flown
in by glider and later by transport
aircraft to the area indicated, while
another brigade marched from Ledo.
The Chindits were to harass Japanese
communications by establishing
'blocking points' such as 'White City'
and preventing supplies being moved
up against Stilwell. Wingate was killed
in an air crash on 25 March and was
succeeded by Major-General
W. Lentaigne. Finally exhausted, most
of the Chindits were flown out from
Lake Indawgyi in June and July,
leaving 77 Brigade to take Mogaung
and 16 Brigade to co-operate as best it
could with the prickly Stilwell.

In May the exhausted and disease-
ridden Marauders, now commanded
by Colonel C. N. Hunter, failed to take
Myitkyina, but after the fall of
Mogaung, a combined Allied force
finally took the town on 3/4 August as
the Japanese evacuated it.

Opposite: Chindits prepare to blow up
a bridge

Above: A Chindit mortar crew in action
Below: A supply drop being made near
'White City'

THE JAPANESE ADVANCE TO KOHIMA AND IMPHAL

In Burma, the Japanese Burma Area Army (Lieutenant-General Shozo Kawabe) had ordered the Fifteenth Army (Lieutenant-General Renya Mutaguchi) to start the movement of the three of its four divisions that were to take part in the invasion of India (Operation 'U-GO') on 7/8 March 1944. This invasion, which had been long in the planning, was not a strategic offensive but rather a strategic defensive move, designed to safeguard the Japanese position in Burma by spoiling the Allied offensive that was clearly being prepared. Mutaguchi's offensive had two main objectives: the occupation of the plain on which lie Imphal and Kohima, in Manipur, which was the only practical jumping off point for an Allied invasion of central Burma from India, and the cutting of the single railway to Assam in north-east India, over which most of the supplies for China and Stilwell's forces operating against Burma were carried.

In line with the forces facing them, Scoones' XV Corps, the Japanese sent one division against Kohima, and two against the larger centre of Imphal. The British were expecting the offensive, but even so were taken by surprise by the sheer speed of the Japanese advance. Nevertheless, the British withdrew in good order, those units which were cut off mostly being able to fight their way back to their parent formations.

Kohima was cut off by the Japanese 31 Division on 4 April, and Imphal by the Japanese 15 and 33 Divisions a day later. Slim, though surprised, had his plans ready: the two garrisons were to hold out, being supplied by air, while XXXIII Corps, which was to relieve them, finished assembling at Dimapur.

Above right: A British soldier keeps watch on a Japanese supply track

Right: Searching for snipers in the Kohima area

Legend

← JAPANESE ADVANCE 7 MARCH /11 APRIL 1944
AREAS EVACUATED BY IV CORPS DURING JAPANESE ADVANCE
AREAS HELD BY IV CORPS
① SEQUENCE OF MOVEMENTS OF 23 IND DIV
ALL-WEATHER ROADS
FAIR-WEATHER ROADS
TRACKS
INDIA-BURMA BOUNDARY

MILES 0 — 30
KILOMETRES 0 — 40

Main map labels

To Dimapur
ZUBZA
KOHIMA
JOTSOMA
PHAKEKEDZUMI
JESSAMI 1 Apr
Assam Regt
KHARASOM
Mol-he ▲
LAYSHI
138 Regt
MAO SONGSANG
SOMRA
TAMANTHI
MARAM
Part 58 Regt (31 Div) followed later by 124 Regt
Part 58 Regt
FORT KEARY
KANGPOKPI
HOMALIN
Uya
To Indaw

15/21 March 50 Para Bde from Kohima
UKHRUL 21 Mar
49 Bde (23 Ind Div) ①

Night, 15/16 March
Jap 31 Div (Sato)

15 Div
KANGLATONGBI 29 Mar
Nungshigum ▲ 6 Apr
LITAN
SANGSHAK
MOLLEN
51, parts 60 and 67 Regts
Chindwin

IV CORPS (Scoones)
IMPHAL
17 Ind Light Div 50 Para Bde
19/29 March 5 Ind Div arrives from Arakan
23 Ind Div ① ④ (In reserve) (Roberts) 254 Tank Bde
HUMINE
'V' Force
1 Indian National Army Div attached to Jap 15 & 31 Divs

To Silchar
BISHENPUR
WANGJING
THANAN

Night, 15/16 March
Jap 15 Div (Yamauchi)

23 Ind Div ③
TORBUNG
PALEL
20 IND DIV
Part 60 Regt
Shenam Saddle
Nippon Hill ▲
THAUNGDUT

7/8 March 1944
OPERATION 'U-GO'
Jap Fifteenth Army (Mutaguchi)

CHURACHANDPUR
SHUGANU
MOREH
TAMU
20 IND DIV (Gracey)
SITTAUNG

B U R M A

MOMBI
WITOK 11 Mar
MAW
I N D I A

HENGTAM
YUWA

37 and 49 Bde (23 Ind Div) ②
MILESTONE 100
109
214 Regt
Yamamoto's Columns (Part 33 Div)

215 Regt
TONGZANG
MAWLAIK

MUALNUAM 12 Mar
YAZAGYO
17 IND DIV (Cowan)
TIDDIM

Night, 7/8 March
Jap 33 Div (Yanagida)

FORT WHITE
KALEWA
MUALBEM 9 Mar
213 Regt
KALEMYO

Inset map (bottom right)

OVER 1500 FT
APPROXIMATE FRONT LINE, 7 MARCH 1944
MILES 0 — 300

Himalaya Mts
BHUTAN
LEDO
Brahmaputra
GAUHATI
DIMAPUR
KOHIMA
A s s a m
SILCHAR
IMPHAL
Manipur
Chindwin
I N D I A
AREA COVERED BY MAIN MAP
Ganges
CALCUTTA
CHITTAGONG
MANDALAY
Irrawaddy
Bay of Bengal
AKYAB
B U R M A

THE BATTLE AT KOHIMA AND IMPHAL

The investment of Kohima by the Japanese was completed on 7 April 1944 (**Map 1**), and there then followed twelve days of desperate struggle by the small garrison to hold off the constant Japanese attacks until help could arrive. The relief operation was entrusted to Stopford's XXXIII Corps, which pushed on its British 2 Division as soon as possible. On 14 April its leading brigade overwhelmed the Japanese road-block at Zubza and pushed on to relieve 161 Indian Brigade trapped in Jotsoma. The 2 Division's 5 Brigade then pushed on to relieve Kohima itself on 18 April.

After reinforcing the garrison, 5 Brigade pulled back to take part in a sweeping pincer movement intended to trap the Japanese, with 5 Brigade cutting down from the north and 4 Brigade up from the south. The counterattack was only partially successful, however, 5 Brigade linking up with the garrison on Firs Hill on the 27th, but 4 Brigade being held on Mount Pulebadze and not managing to take GPT Ridge until 4 May.

On 4 May an attack by 6 and 33 Brigades to take the Japanese line between the District Commissioner's Bungalow and Jail Hill failed in the face of stubborn Japanese resistance, and the attack was called off on the 7th. It was renewed on 11 May and the hills were retaken on the 13th.

An attack on Hunters Hill and Gun Spur by 33 Brigade was repulsed between 15 and 31 May, as was an attack to clear Aradura Spur in the south between 25 and 28 May but a final attack by 7 Indian Division broke through the Japanese positions around the Naga Village on 1 June and allowed 5 Brigade to outflank the Aradura Spur on 3 June, this last making the final Japanese positions at Kohima untenable. The battle had been won. The 2 Division advanced south.

Meanwhile, to the south IV Corps

had been involved in a desperate
struggle around Imphal (**Map 2**). The
original defence perimeter had proved
too large, and even the inner one was
penetrated by the Japanese in attacks
towards Ningthoukhong, Palel,
Nungshigum, and Sengmai, attacks
that were only held after some of the
most vicious fighting seen in the
theatre. Supply dropping and landing
proved more difficult than had been
imagined, and both sides found
themselves quickly on the edge of
starvation. Additional forces were
flown in by Slim throughout the siege
to replace these losses, until the British
strength in Imphal was about 100,000
men.

Despite this, the Japanese continued
to fight superlatively in the face of
overwhelming odds to prevent the
relief of Imphal by British 2 Division
advancing from Kohima, and it was
not until 22 June that IV and
XXXIII Corps met at Milestone 107
on the road between the sites of the
two sieges, the longer of which, that of
Imphal, had lasted 88 days.

The remnants of the Japanese
Fifteenth Army started to pull back to
the River Chindwin, with British air
and land forces hard on their heels.
They did not entirely disintegrate in
the face of this massive British
counteroffensive, but nevertheless the
campaign had cost them some 65,000
dead.

Above right: Mortars firing on Japanese
positions near Imphal

THE ADVANCE TO MANDALAY AND MEIKTILA

After their defeats at Kohima and Imphal, the Japanese were pressed back steadily across the Kabaw Valley and to the Chindwin by the British Fourteenth Army (Lieutenant-General W. Slim), which now prepared to cross this major barrier at a number of points.

The disaster that had befallen the Japanese Fifteenth Army brought disgrace to Kawabe, who was replaced as commander of the Burma Area Army by General Hoyotaro Kimura, and to Mutaguchi, who was replaced as commander of the Fifteenth Army by Lieutenant-General Shihachi Katamura. Kimura spent the summer

months rebuilding his shattered forces, and planned to allow the Allies to push on into central Burma, where their overextended lines of communications, combined with the shortened Japanese lines, would allow his ten divisions to inflict a crushing reverse on Lieutenant-General O. Leese's Allied Land Forces South-East Asia, made up of Stilwell's Northern Combat Area Command, the British Fourteenth Army, and the XV Corps in the Arakan.

Operation Extended Capital, the crossing of the Chindwin and advance on Mandalay, started on 19 November with IV Corps at Sittaung and XXXIII Corps at Mawlaik and Kalewa (**Map 1**). The three bridge-heads were secure by 4 December. The British pushed on and met up with advance elements of Stilwell's command on 15 December at Banmauk, and by the end of the year the Allied forces were closing on the Irrawaddy line from Katha to Seikpyu.

Of all the Allied leaders in Burma, Slim was the only one to appreciate what Kimura was attempting to do, as well as his intention of destroying the Fourteenth Army as it crossed the Irrawaddy north of Mandalay. So leaving 19 Division to act as a decoy for IV Corps in this area, he had

secretly switched the corps to the south of XXXIII Corps, to cross the river at Pakokku and cut off the Fifteenth and Thirty-third Armies.

Slim was proved right when 19 Division was heavily counterattacked when it crossed the Irrawaddy at Thabeikkyin on 11 January. Further south, and closer to Mandalay, XXXIII Corps had also advertised its intentions so as to draw Japanese forces away from the area in which IV Corps was to make the major crossings – at Pakokku still further to the south. On 12 February, XXXIII Corps started its operations to cross the Irrawaddy at Ngazun, and immediately ran into heavy opposition, just as 19 Division had at Thabeikkyin in January. But when IV Corps started its crossing at Nyaungu just south of Pakokku on 13 February, only light opposition was encountered. Slim's analysis of the Japanese intentions, and his deception to exploit them, had proved accurate.

As planned, the main effort was now to be made by IV Corps, to cut the Japanese lines of communication from the south by a swift eastward advance. Thus the corps' 17 Indian Division rushed forward from the bridgehead to Meiktila (**Map 2**), which it took from astounded Japanese rear area troops on 3 March. Meanwhile, the defence of IV Corps' bridgehead was entrusted to 4 Indian Division.

Meiktila, and the nerve centre of rail communications in the area, was clearly the key to the situation, to the almost complete exclusion of the larger city of Mandalay, and both sides acted promptly. The 17 Division dug itself in and Kimura virtually denuded the defences of Mandalay to provide a force sufficiently powerful to retake Meiktila. Confused fighting continued up to 15 March before the Japanese were able to invest 17 Division in Meiktila with parts of three divisions. Bitter fighting raged up to 29 March, when Kimura realized that his position was no longer tenable: with most of his troops involved around Meiktila and its vital communications to Rangoon, the British were advancing steadily on Mandalay against the weakened Japanese defence. So Kimura decided to pull back, which he did with considerable skill through the smaller rail junction at Thazi, to the east of Meiktila.

To the north, XXXIII Corps had kept the defence of Mandalay pinned down while 19 Division finally took the city in heavy house to house fighting on 20 March. Freed of the need to keep Mandalay's defence pinned, XXXIII Corps was then able to advance south to relieve the hard-pressed 17 Division in Meiktila.

Opposite left: Gurkha troops approach Mandalay

Below: Supplies being brought down the Chindwin

THE CAPTURE OF RANGOON

The monsoon season was now nearly upon Burma, and Slim ordered his forces into a rapid drive on Rangoon, so that he could make full use of his armour before the rains rendered it useless. The Japanese, almost completely exhausted, still offered some resistance, but their lines of communications were harassed by the Burma National Army under General Aung San, which had been ordered north to help Kimura's forces but had revolted.

The British, driving on from Meiktila, advanced along the lines of the Irrawaddy in the west and the Sittang in the east, with the eastern drive soon pulling ahead (**Map 1 opposite**). The monsoon broke on 1 May, and the next day 17 Indian Division entered Pegu. On the other side of the Pegu Yoma, 20 Indian Division took Prome on 3 May.

Both these drives were beaten to the capture of Rangoon by XV Corps from Akyab. Operation Dracula brought 26 Indian Division round from Arakan by sea and landed it south of Rangoon on 2 May. The Japanese realized that their position was untenable and evacuated the city, which was occupied by 26 Division on the 3rd. The 17 and 26 Indian Divisions met at Hlegu on 6 May. XV Corps seaborne operation which resulted in the capture of Rangoon was made possible by the third and last Arakan campaign, Operation Talon (**Map 2**). Kimura, who wished to fight the decisive battle for Burma around Mandalay and Meiktila, had stripped the defences of Arakan to the minimum, and there was little to hold XV Corps when it advanced on Akyab from 12 December 1944. Akyab itself was taken on 4 January 1945 and the whole coast secured in a series of amphibious landings at Myebon, Kangow, and Ramree island.

The war in southern Burma ended without further major battles, just a series of skirmishes between the Allied forces consolidating their positions in the main areas and the Japanese holding out between the west coast and the Irrawaddy, the Irrawaddy and Sittang, and between the Sittang and Thailand, all areas rendered virtually impenetrable by the monsoon.

Above right: Indian troops assault a village after the Rangoon landings

Below right: A 25-pounder being brought ashore during the landings

Opposite right: Indian troops advance under cover of smoke

Map

OPERATION 'TALON' : XV Corps (Christison) ②

82 W Afr Div
81 W Afr Div
MAUNGDAW
HTIZWE
74 Bde (25 Ind Div)
DONBAIK
23 Dec
Foul Point
MYOHAUNG
SEIKPYU
Irrawaddy

Jap Twenty-eighth Army (Sakurai)

AKYAB 4 Jan
MYEBON
NGAPE
AN
0942, 21 Jan 1945
71 Bde (26 Ind Div)
Jap 54 Div
KYAUKPYU
LETPAN
Ramree
MAYIN
RAMREE 9 Feb
TAUNGUP

Bay of Bengal

CHEDUBA

0 MILES 60
0 KILOMETRES 80

Op 'Dracula' 26 Ind Div for Rangoon landing on 2 May

Br XXXIII Corps (Stopford)

Br IV Corps (Messervy)

MANDALAY

KYAUKSE

7 Ind Div

PAKOKKU

MYINGYAN
Br 2 Div

19 Ind Div

Jap Thirty-third Army (Honda)

NYAUNGU

Mt Pope
19 Apr

MEIKTILA

THAZI

TAUNG-GYI

SEIKPYU

CHAUK

KYAUKPADANG
12 Apr

YINDAW

17 Ind Div

KALAW

SALIN
25 Apr

YENANGYAUNG
21 Apr

5 Ind Div

PYAWBWE

Jap Twenty-eighth Army (Sakurai)

Jap Fifteenth Army (Katamura)

YAMETHIN

Southern Shan Hills

MINBU

20 Ind Div

TATKON

MAGWE

TAUNGDWINGYI
15 Apr

Karen levies blow roads

MYINGYUN

PYINMANA
19 Apr

LOIKAW

LEWE

THAWATTI

Burma Area Army (Kimura)

YEDASHE
21 Apr

BAWLAKE

ALLANMYO

THAYETMYO
5 May

KAMA

TOUNGOO
22 Apr

PROME
3 May

SHWEDAUNG

5 Ind Div

PYU

PAUNGDE

MYANAUNG

PENWEGON
25 Apr

17 Ind Div

NYAUNGLEBIN

SHWEGYIN

LETPADAN

THARRAWAW

HENZADA

PAYAGYI
30 Apr

WAW

BILIN

3 May 1945
Rangoon occupied unopposed

PEGU
2 May

HLEGU

BASSEIN

MINGALADON

6 May Contact

RANGOON

SYIRAM

KYAUKTAN

Gulf of Martaban

FRONT LINE, 9 APRIL 1945

DRIVE BY BR FOURTEENTH ARMY (SLIM)

OVER 1500 FT

Op 'Dracula'
2 May
26 Ind Div

1 May
2/3 Gurkha Para Bn

0   MILES   80

0   KILOMETRES   120

THE WAR IN NORTHERN BURMA

Stilwell's last advance in northern Burma started on 15 October 1944, and was a large scale pincer movement intended to trap Lieutenant-General Masaki Honda's Thirty-third Army between his own Northern Combat Area Command and the Chinese Y Force (General Wei Li-huang). Progress was slow but sure.

In China, however, matters were desperate, and when Stilwell recommended measures that Chiang Kai-shek ought to take, the latter demanded that Stilwell be replaced. Major-General A. Wedemeyer took over from him as chief-of-staff to Chiang and Lieutenant-General D. Sultan as head of the Northern Combat Area Command.

The British, American, and Chinese forces continued south, the Chinese 22 Division crossing the Irrawaddy at Shwegu on 7 November as the first part of the closing pincer movement. The movement was held up for a month, however, by the Japanese defence of Bhamo, which ended only on 15 December, when survivors of the garrison fought their way out to rejoin 56 Division south-east of Bhamo. At this point Chiang Kai-shek removed two divisions for service elsewhere in China, and Sultan had to alter Stilwell's plan from an envelopment to just opening the road from Bhamo via Namkham to the Burma Road.

The advance continued into the new year, and the two arms met at Mongyu on 27 January. The Japanese 56 Division managed to slip away, but the Burma Road had been reopened. The campaign in northern Burma ended after the Japanese had resisted the advancing Allies all the way to Lashio and Kyaukme. The British 36 Division reached Mandalay and returned to Fourteenth Army control on 21 March.

Right: General Stilwell watching his troops cross a river

THE WAR IN CHINA

Japan's war against China had started in 1937, and initial successes had come thick and fast against a weak and poor China, already divided by the conflict between the Nationalists under Generalissimo Chiang Kai-shek and the Communists under Mao Tse-tung. Although a truce between the two Chinese parties was established, their rivalry was to dog the Chinese war effort throughout the Second World War. By 1939 Japan held most of China as far west as a line from French Indo-China in the south to the south-eastern border of Outer Mongolia in the north, and as these comprised the richest areas of China, Japan was content to hold here. America in particular was sympathetic to the Chinese cause, and enormous quantities of material were shipped to China, during the war via the Burma Road or 'Over the Hump' by aircraft. Perhaps as important, General Joseph Stilwell was loaned to Chiang as his chief-of-staff and military adviser in retraining the Chinese army.

1942 saw little action as the Japanese were too tied up with the opening and initial consolidation phases of their war against the Western Allies and the Chinese were too weak.

1943 was used by the Japanese for 'rice offensives', designed to give new formations battle experience against weak opposition and to seize the rice crop from previously unoccupied areas. The Chinese were at their lowest ebb and could offer no real resistance until the end of the year, when they managed to repulse, with American air support, one rice offensive in the Battle of Changteh. A dispute between Stilwell and Brigadier-General Claire Chennault about priority of supplies for the Chinese army or the Chinese air-force had been decided in the latter's favour, and the new US 14th Air Force as it became started to inflict severe damage on the Japanese all over China and as far away as Formosa. Increased hostility towards the Communists also weakened Chiang's already overextended forces.

1944 was marked by a *de facto* truce with the Communists, which allowed greater activity against the Japanese. But the Japanese, disturbed by the success of the 14th Air Force operating from airfields at Linchow, Kwerlin, Lingling, Hengyang, and Chihkiong, launched Operation ICHI-GO in April to capture these and force China out of the war. The Chinese defence crumbled alarmingly, though there were local successes, but the offensive in northern Burma had to be called off and the loss of the 14th Air Force's airfields hindered the US advance in the Pacific. The situation was finally stabilized on 10 December.

1945 saw further Japanese offensives to consolidate their previous year's gains, but the threatening situation in Manchuria and his own overextended deployment led General Okamura, commanding the China Expeditionary Army, to shift much of his strength north, which allowed the Chinese to cut off the corridor to Indo-China. The position remained approximately thus until the end of the war, when the civil war between the Nationalists and the Communists was soon resumed.

RUSSIA
FIGHTS
BACK

Opposite: Raising the Red Flag over the
ruins of the Reichstag in Berlin

Hitler, when he launched Barbarossa, had miscalculated Russian military strength. Even so his initial onslaught had inflicted terrible casualties, and if he had not, like Napoleon before him, entered Moscow itself he had come perilously near it. When planning the campaign Hitler had, according to Colonel-General Halder, expressed the opinion that the seizure of Moscow 'was not so very important'. When late in the year the Germans did begin their onslaught against the Russian capital they did so without proper logistic preparation and were foiled not only by the weather but by the inadequacy of their own resources. Although the long Russian retreat was by no means the calculated withdrawal that Stalin would have had people believe, it did give time for the organization of new Russian armies. In December 1941 German intelligence still credited the enemy with 280 rifle or cavalry divisions and forty-four mechanized or armoured brigades. The remarkable resilience of the Russians was demonstrated by their great winter counteroffensive.

Even so they were disappointed by its results for they had hoped that this winter campaign would wipe out an exhausted enemy. But the Germans proved to have more staying power than they calculated. Stalin, it seems, held a meeting on 5 January, and without so much as asking for anyone else's opinion, announced that the time was opportune for a general counter-offensive. This led to a dissipation of effort. Nor were the various offensives, which involved six different Fronts, closely co-ordinated from the strategic point of view. Had the Russians concentrated on the destruction of Army Group Centre they might have achieved better results. It must be appreciated that the Russians, though better prepared administratively for winter warfare, also suffered from the weather. They too felt the cold; they too needed food and ammunition. The great Soviet counteroffensive eventually lost its momentum because the lines of

communication were becoming too long as it progressed westwards. Moreover their state of training was still poor. Inexperienced commanders with untrained staffs tended to use their tanks in penny packets and to hound their infantry into action without properly co-ordinated artillery support. In truth the Red Army operated in a fashion very strange to the armies of the Western Allies, where it was not the thing for the higher commanders to become involved in the details of the tactical battle. This is well-illustrated by Colonel Albert Seaton in his account of the attack on 6 Rumanian Corps on the Stalingrad Front on 20 November 1942: 'The Red Army system of command and control was very different from that in use in western armies, and instead of commanding the attack by map, radio and liaison officers, all higher commanders, even the front commander himself, would establish battle command posts on prominent ground within sight of the enemy. This meant that in the sectors selected for the main attack within one or two thousand yards of the forward defended localities, regimental, divisional, army and front commanders would be watching the progress of the battle, each commander being accompanied by his personal staff, signallers, orderlies and clerks, and his artillery commander and the commanders of his main arms. The front commander would in addition have a telephonic or short wave radio telephonic rear link to Moscow and Stalin.' The Russian dictator was just as prone to interfere in operations and personnel selection as was the German.

By this stage the tide of war was turning against an over-extended Germany. The Allied victories at El Alamein, Stalingrad, and Tunis were landmarks on the road back to the *Reich*. Hitler's strategy was over-ambitious. He thrust to the Caucasus and the Volga simultaneously when his resources were scarcely adequate for even one of these objectives. Unable, as he was to tell Goebbels (8 May 1943), to overcome the

problems of movement and supply he had left his unfortunate soldiers, as usual in Russia, to live from hand to mouth. Even had he allowed Paulus to try to break out of Stalingrad the move would probably have failed for lack of fuel. Göring's assurances that the place could be supplied by air were valueless. Nobody else on the staff of the Luftwaffe believed them.

Hitler did not have to cut the Volga at Stalingrad. By fighting the Russians in a built-up area he played into their hands, for the Soviet troops, outclassed in open warfare, were formidable in the ruins of a city. As Eremenko put it: 'the greatest error of the German High Command was to underestimate the power of the Soviet nation and its armed forces, at the same time overestimating its own ability.' When, as occasionally happened, the German generals were able to persuade Hitler to give them a free hand they were still capable of scoring a telling success. An example was von Manstein's daring counter-attack with Army Group South, which brought to an end the hitherto successful Soviet offensive in the winter 1942–3. Von Manstein and von Kluge, having prevailed upon Hitler to allow them to shorten the front and build up a reserve by withdrawing troops from the line, were able to counterattack with advantage in the Ukraine. With three experienced and fresh Panzer divisions (*Leibstandarte*, *Das Reich*, and *Totenkopf*) they were too much for tired opponents who had temporarily outrun their supports and supplies.

On 31 May 1943 there was a conference in Berlin. When it was over General Guderian seized Hitler's hand and asked to be allowed to speak to him. The Führer listened and Guderian urged him to abandon the plan for a summer offensive on the Russian Front on the grounds that 'the great commitment would certainly not bring us equivalent gains; our defensive preparations in the West were sure to suffer considerably. I ended', Guderian writes, 'with the question: "Why do you want to attack in the East at all this year?" Here Keitel joined in, with the words: "We must attack for political reasons." I replied: "How many people do you think even know where Kursk is? It's a matter of profound indifference to the world whether we hold Kursk or not. I repeat my question: Why do we want to attack in the East at all this year?" Hitler's reply was: "You're quite right. Whenever I think of this attack my stomach turns over." Well it might.'

Kursk, the greatest armoured battle of all time, was a costly failure. The German offensive lost its momentum in the first 48 hours. The Anglo-American landings in Sicily gave Hitler the opportunity to break off an unprofitable operation in which he had never really believed. He was now in the situation, dreaded by German strategists, compelled to fight on land on two European fronts. 'The time was soon to come,' as Colonel Seaton points out, 'when a number of German formations were permanently lost to the war effort as they were shunted throughout Europe in an effort to plug gaps.' Soviet historians would have us believe that the Kursk battle compelled the Germans to withdraw divisions from the Mediterranean thus permitting the Allies to land in Sicily and leading to the defeat of Italy. It is evident, however, that in the long term the Italian campaign and that in Normandy eased the pressure on the Eastern Front whilst, in the short term, the Sicily landings provided the occasions for Hitler to break off the Kursk battle. What he did not appreciate, since he still underestimated them, was that the Russians were about to launch their own summer offensive. He had irretrievably lost the initiative on the Eastern Front. Even had Hitler wished to make peace, nobody was so stupid as to trust him to keep any terms he might make. And as for the Russians, who had suffered so much, they were determined to drive their tanks through the ruins of Berlin. Hitler himself recognized that the situation had changed. In his Directive No. 51 (3 November 1943) we read: 'The danger

in the East remains, but a greater danger now appears in the West; an Anglo-Saxon landing! In the East, the vast extent of the territory makes possible for us to lose ground, even on a large scale, without a fatal blow being dealt to the nervous system of Germany.' He now began to reinforce the defences in the West, especially the areas from which the V-1 and V-2 campaign against England was to be waged. Thus the Germans some 3,000,000 strong found themselves facing some 5,700,000 Russians, who greatly outnumbered them in tanks and guns, and who, thanks largely to the Americans, were well-supplied, and to whom the White half-track had given a new mobility. Hitler spoke of losing ground, but at a time when he should have withdrawn at least to the Bug, he still hoped to retake Kiev and to make an offensive in the Crimea.

In January 1944 at long last the Russians raised the thirty month siege of Leningrad (St Petersburg), then in February the Russians reached the northern frontier of Rumania. This was the occasion for Hitler to dismiss his greatest general, von Manstein – that master of manoeuvre. He now reverted wholeheartedly to his idea of an inflexible defence – 'All that counts now is to cling stubbornly to what we hold' . . . His choice to carry out this plan was the bold, inexhaustible Field-Marshal Walther Model, a determined fighting man, who did not belong to any high-born Prussian clan. Truly Hitler's tactical ideas were those of the Somme and Verdun. He can hardly be classed as a subtle tactician, and he was not the man to learn from his mistakes – if only because, like most dictators, he was not given to the admission that he ever made any. If 1944 became for the Russians 'The Year of the Ten Victories' it was largely thanks to Hitler, who as late as 2 April could announce 'The Russians have exhausted and divided their forces', could declare that it was imperative to hold firmly to the Crimea, and to hold or win back the line of the Dniester.

Hitler's judgment, never of the best, became decidedly warped after the attempt on his life on 20 July 1944. Guderian tells us that 'the deep distrust he already felt for mankind in general, and for General Staff Corps officers and generals in particular, now became profound hatred . . . in his case what had been hardness became cruelty, while a tendency to bluff became plain dishonesty. He often lied without hesitation, and assumed that others lied to him . . . It had already been difficult enough to deal with him; it now became a torture that grew steadily worse from month to month.' But he still had courtiers like Göring and Ribbentrop to bolster his self-esteem, and he still trusted *treuer* Heinrich Himmler, who had no kind of pretension to high military command, to command the Replacement Army. And as late as 20 April 1945 Field-Marshal Schörner, who after a meteoric rise, now commanded Army Group Centre, could visit him in the famous bunker in Berlin and restore him to good spirits and optimism. But by that time the Third Reich was dissolving in a crazy dream world.

Irrespective of all his strategic and tactical errors Hitler himself brought about the ultimate defeat of his Germany when by a gross political misjudgment he condemned her to wage the two-front war which every good German strategist from Frederick the Great onwards has always dreaded.

Opposite left: Civilians of Bryansk greet the Red Army

Opposite right: A Soviet assault begins

Above left: Troops crossing the Dniepr under fire

Above right: Soviet troops advancing in the Ukraine

THE RED ARMY ATTACKS IN THE SOUTH

Hitler's changes of mind in 1941 had robbed his forces both of the prize of Moscow and of any decisive gains in the south. As 1942 opened the German forces in the east were deployed from Finland to the Crimea in a series of huge defensive camps (nicknamed 'hedgehogs'), between which the tide of Russian counteroffensives ebbed and flowed. In the south the Germans held all the territory up to a line from Kharkov to Taganrog on the Sea of Azov, including all of the Crimea save Sevastopol and the Kerch peninsula (**Map 1**). In this area the major German hedgehogs were Kharkov, Artemovsk, and Taganrog.

In spite of their staggering losses in 1941, the Russian's were able to maintain a constant pressure on the Germans throughout the winter of 1941/42. Part of the reason for this was that the Russians, with the whole of their eastern empire at their back, were able almost immediately to make up their manpower losses, particularly in the infantry, with first rate, hardy troops. The importance of their losses in armour was to some extent mitigated by the frost, which for long periods immobilized German tanks and aircraft. Therefore the Russian winter counteroffensives, hastily planned and lacking in strong logistic support though they were, enjoyed considerable success. But the bulk of the German forces, esconced in their hedgehogs, were not effected.

One such counteroffensive, planned for Kostenko's South-West Front and Malinovsky's South Front to take place in January 1942, was to be launched across the River Donets between Kharkov and Artemovsk, wheeling south to trap the German forces in Artemovsk and Taganrog and freeing ports on the north coast of the Sea of Azov. A smaller force was to wheel north to attack the hedgehog of Kharkov.

Launched on 18 January, this attack did not meet its objectives (**Map 2**). The Russian Sixth, Fifty-seventh, and Ninth Armies of the South-West Front encountered sharp opposition from the German Sixth and Seventeenth Armies. By 31 January, although they had established a substantial salient in German-occupied territory, they were still far from their objectives. Elements of Fifty-seventh Army, thrusting south in accordance with the plan, were repulsed by the German Group 'Mackensen', hastily brought into action by the commander of Army Group South, Bock, to save the lateral railway communication from Pavlograd to Taganrog.

In March the spring thaws brought activity on both sides to a halt. Apart from the difficulties of movement, both sides were at the end of extended lines of supply, and short of all vital matériel. Not until May was either side ready for further action.

On 12 May Kostenko's South-West Front took the offensive again in an attempt to make good one of the objectives of his original plan by encircling Kharkov (**Map 3**). But by this time the Germans were able to move outside their hedgehogs, and their armies had been substantially reinforced. (A total of fifty-one new divisions from the satellite countries, Italy, Rumania, Hungary, and Slovakia, and one Spanish volunteer division had been added to the German armies in the east in April 1942). Also their tanks and aircraft were superior to anything the Russians could bring against them at the time. Kostenko's attacks were halted and turned back, and the German Sixth Army and Group Kleist were able to eliminate the Russian salient and push back their line east of Kharkov. These operations, codenamed 'Fridericus I', were completed by the end of May.

Also in May Manstein's Eleventh Army cleared the Kerch Peninsula, inflicting 150,000 casualties on the Russians, and renewed attacks on Sevastopol, but it was not until 18 June that any significant progress was made (**Map 4**). In a series of concerted attacks the German LIV Corps from the north, the Rumanian Mountain Corps from the east, and the German XXX Corps from the south closed in on Sevastopol. They were helped by the largest artillery piece ever to grace a siege train. Eventually an amphibious assault by LIV Corps sealed the fate of the city and between 30 June and 2 July the remnants of the Russian garrison were evacuated by sea. They had lost a further 100,000 men.

Right: German troops surrender during the Russian spring attacks

Below right: Sailors loading a gun for shipment to besieged Sevastopol

193

THE DRIVE TO THE VOLGA

The situation that faced Hitler in the spring of 1942 was very different to that which had faced him a year before. Then his armies had been everywhere victorious. Of his enemies only Britain remained in the field, and she with scant effect. But in 1942 his magnificent armies had lost their cutting edge. Huge numbers of them were committed deep in Russia with no prospect of release. The United States had entered the war, and the prospect of a war on two fronts, Germany's recurrent nightmare, was imminent. Above all, as his economic advisers never ceased to remind him, Germany's oil situation was critical,

and Hitler made the goal of his 1942 campaign the capture of the Caucasus oilfields. His initial aim was to occupy the oilfields in the northern part of the Caucasus, and to establish a defensive line along the River Don from Voronezh to Stalingrad (**Map 1**). To this end he planned first to burst through the Russian front between Kursk and Rostov. He reorganized Bock's Army Group South into Army Group A (Field-Marshal List), and Army Group B (initially under Bock; from 13 July under General Weichs). Army Group A was to thrust south into the Caucasus, capture the oilfields, and defeat the Russian forces facing it. Army Group B was to establish the protective front along the Don, but at this stage Hitler gave it a second objective – Stalingrad itself (**Map 2**). From being a covering operation the task of Army Group B became a major offensive while Army Group A was ordered to occupy all the oilfields to a line from Batumi to Baku. Even as a protective flank the role of Army Group B was radically unsound. A glance at the map will show that a concerted Russian thrust from the Stalingrad area towards Rostov, enjoying the protection of the 'elbow' of the Don on its right flank, could easily sever Army Group A from Army

Group B. Now Hitler planned to disperse the effort of his armies still further by giving them two major objectives to be taken simultaneously.

On 28 June the German summer offensive opened with a drive by the German Second Army and the Fourth Panzer Army against Voronezh. On 30 June the German Sixth Army (General Paulus) began its drive down the Donets Corridor (**Map 3**). It was not until 9 July that Army Group A broke into the Donets Basin and headed south to cross the Don between Rostov and Tsirilyansky. With Army Group A poised to cross the Don, and Army Group B racing for the Don elbow and Stalingrad, Hitler made the second of three moves that ruined the campaign, and sowed the seeds of his defeat. The first had been his change of plan on 13 July designating Stalingrad a major objective. Now, on 17 July, fearful that Army Group A would not be powerful enough to force the Don crossings, he diverted the Fourth Panzer Army from the eastward drive against Stalingrad to the southern drive against the Caucasus. In spite of this diversion, Army Group B was able to clear the Don elbow and arrive on the Volga north of Stalingrad by 23 August. But without Fourth

194

Panzer Army its progress was slow.

In spite of their decline in men, matériel, and morale during the long winter sieges, Hitler's armies carried out his extraordinary orders with remarkable success. By 29 July, Army Group A and Fourth Panzer Army had driven a deep wedge into the Caucasus, reaching to within 70 miles of the Caspian sea. The Russian Trans-Caucasus Front was threatened with separation and complete disruption.

At this point Hitler made the third of his mistakes. Enraged by the slow progress of Sixth Army, he ordered the Fourth Panzer Army to turn round yet again and rejoin Army Group B in its attacks toward Stalingrad. List and the German Chief-of-Staff, Halder, daring to protest at these moves, were relieved of their appointments. Army Group A, under the distant and erratic personal command of the Führer, was left holding a front of 500 miles in the Caucasus and at the same time trying to maintain an offensive to gain the original objective of the Batumi–Baku line. Not surprisingly, no significant progress was made.

Hitler's total failure to grasp even the most elementary military principles was not the only difficulty his armies had to contend with in 1942. The losses of Russian manpower of 1941 had been made good from the subject peoples of the Soviet empire in Asia. These were recruited mainly into the infantry and cavalry, and though, because of their illiteracy, tactical plans had to be simple, they were possessed of matchless endurance and tenacity. From a general's point of view they were ideal troops, needing minimal logistic backing. In the field of armour, too, the Russians had the edge over their opponents by the summer of 1942. The T34 tank, just coming into service, though simple to the point of crudity, was, in the crucial ratio of gun, armour, and speed, superior to anything the Germans could show against it. By mid-August any serious attempt to secure the oilfields was as good as over, and Hitler had diverted all his energies to the attack on Stalingrad.

Left: German artillery bombards a Russian position

Above right: German infantry advancing across the steppes

195

THE ASSAULT ON STALINGRAD

In 1942 Stalingrad was a city of 500,000 inhabitants straggling for 18 miles along the western bank of the Volga. Its industrial importance was considerable. It was a large inland port, and its factories produced over a quarter of the Russians' tractors and vehicles, as well as tanks, guns, and weapons. In the immediate vicinity of Stalingrad the Volga pursued a serpentine course through a number of different channels, posing a formidable bridging problem and making it virtually impossible for the Germans to invest the city from the east. An obvious solution to this problem was to establish a bridgehead north (upstream) of the city, stop all river traffic and prevent the reinforcement of the city. In spite of fact that they reached the Volga on 23 August (**Map 1**) the Germans failed to do this. Anyway their slow advance, caused by the removal of Fourth Panzer Army, had already allowed the Russians considerably to strengthen the defences of Stalingrad.

On 17 August, Paulus' Sixth Army struck across the Don, and the now-restored Fourth Panzer Army advanced from the south (**Map 1**). The Russian Fourth Tank, First Tank, and Fifty-first Armies fell back before them, and by the end of the month the Germans had squeezed the Russian defenders into a small perimeter some 30 miles by 18 miles. At this stage various alternatives were still open to the Germans: an upstream crossing, encirclement, siege – all could have been attempted. But they elected to carry the city by direct attack. The result was one of the most terrible battles of the war. Stalin's determination not to lose the city of his name, and Hitler's equal determination to take it, blinded both sides to other tactical and strategic considerations. Stalingrad became the Verdun of the Second World War.

By 12 September the Russian perimeter had been reduced to a total of 30 miles and the battle for the city

proper began. Street by street, house by house, the Germans fought their way towards the Volga. The brunt of the fighting fell on the infantry, much of it at appallingly close quarters. By 13 October the river had been reached in the south, but in the north the factory area remained unconquered (**Map 2**). The attackers were exhausted, and Hitler ordered a change in tactics. Instead of a direct assault the city was to be reduced by artillery fire and bombardment, followed by a steady advance by the ground troops. This was next to nonsense. As the Allies were to find to their cost at Monte Cassino, heaps of rubble make better defensive positions even than standing buildings. All this order succeeded in doing was to make the task of the attacking troops still more difficult. By 18 November, although elements of Sixth Army had reached the river in the north, the Russian Sixty-second Army still held substantial areas on the west bank (**Map 2**).

By 18 November (the approximate date of the onset of the Russian winter freeze) Hitler had failed to carry either of the twin objectives of his 1942 summer campaign. He had succeeded in placing his armies in untenable positions with large gaps between them, tenuous supply lines and weakly defended, extended flanks direly vulnerable to Russian counterattack.

Above right: The first German troops arrive on the outskirts of Stalingrad

Right: A German anti-tank gun in action amid the ruins of Stalingrad

196

197

THE RUSSIAN COUNTER ATTACKS

On 19 November 1942 came the Russian counterattack that the extended German flank in south Russia had been inviting since July. Timed to coincide with the frosts and the Allied landings in North Africa, this offensive had been long in preparation. Both planning and execution were excellent, and demonstrated how far the Red Army had come in these respects since 1941.

From north of the Don the South-West Front (Vatutin) and the Don Front (Rokossovsky) were to drive south, pinching out the Don elbow, and trapping the German forces between the Don and the Volga (**Map 1**). A day later, 20 November the Stalingrad Front (Eremenko) was to attack westward to meet up with the northern attack and complete the encirclement of the Germans in Stalingrad. The two forces met on 23 November, and the German Army Group B under Weichs was only just able to reel back in time to save itself from total defeat. Sixth Army and part of Fourth Panzer Army, however, were completely trapped. On the same day (23 November) five encircled Rumanian divisions in the north surrendered.

Although the Russians had achieved encirclement, they were not yet sufficiently organized to prevent Paulus and the German Sixth Army from breaking out. This he was urged to do by Weichs, but the chain of command between Weichs and Paulus had been bypassed by Hitler, who assumed direct command of Sixth Army himself. On hearing of the Russian offensive, even Hitler was at first inclined to order Paulus to escape, but he was easily persuaded to order him to stay put when Göring undertook to supply Sixth Army by air to the tune of 500 tons of supplies per day. Like many of Göring's assurances this was wildly unrealistic, but it was enough for Hitler. Paulus was ordered to form 'Fortress Stalingrad', and plans to relieve him were put in train.

Manstein's Eleventh Army was moved from the Leningrad front, renamed Army Group Don and allotted the task of opening a corridor

198

to Sixth Army, re-establishing its
supply lines, and restoring the original
front. Manstein organized his force in
two groups, Group Hoth south of the
Don (**Map 2**) and Operational Group
Hollidt north of the river. His plan
(largely dictated by Hitler) was to
attack Yeremenko's Stalingrad Front,
roll it back, and then, in concert with
Paulus attacking from Stalingrad, fall
on Rokossovsky's Don Front.

On 12 December Manstein launched
his offensive. For two days progress
was brisk, but Russian opposition was
stiffened by reinforcements and
Manstein's pace became slower.
However by 23 December he had got
within 30 miles of Stalingrad. His
position here became so critical that
he defied Hitler and sent Paulus a
message ordering him to abandon
what he could not carry and break
out of Stalingrad to join forces with
Group Hoth on the Myshkova. Paulus
again refused to act on his own
initiative, and declined to leave
Stalingrad without direct authority
from Hitler. This was the nearest that
the attempt to relieve Paulus came to
success.

Above left: A Stuka over Stalingrad

Left: German troops in a snow storm during
the attempt to relieve Stalingrad

THE END AT STALINGRAD

Manstein's order to Paulus to break out and join him was prompted by the increasing insecurity of his own position. Operation Group Hollidt (see **Map 2** on previous page) found its front on the Chir threatened by Vatutin's South-West Front, and on 24 December, a day after Manstein's message to Paulus, the Russian South-West and Stalingrad Fronts erupted onto Manstein's tired forces (**Map 1**) leaving Rokossovsky's Don Front to invest Stalingrad. On Christmas Day Manstein was in full retreat, and by the end of the month had been driven back beyond all hope of relieving Stalingrad. It was all he could do, indeed, to try to keep open a narrow corridor east of Rostov to permit the withdrawal of Kleists' Army Group A, threatened with complete isolation in the Caucasus.

In Stalingrad itself Paulus' position was desperate. His force was dwindling rapidly through disease, battle casualties, but most of all through frostbite. His first estimated requirement of 700 tons of supplies per day was based on his then existing reserves. These reserves exhausted, his needs were at least double that. In spite of valiant efforts, the Luftwaffe was unable to make good Göring's vain-glorious boast. Between 23 November 1942, and the Russian capture of the airfields in early 1943, airlifted supplies into Stalingrad never averaged more than 70–80 tons per day.

At the moment of encirclement the German force in Stalingrad numbered some 200,000. The Russians were slow to realize the extent of their success – at first they thought they had trapped a pocket of a few divisions. On 8 January Rokossovsky called on Paulus to capitulate. This being refused, he launched an offensive against the German perimeter on 10 January (**Map 2**). Surrounded by seven Russian armies, Sixth Army's fate was a foregone conclusion, but Hitler would countenance no surrender. By 13 January the Russians had pinched out the western end of the German position, and by the 14th had captured the most important airfield, Pitomnik. By the 25th the remaining airfield had been lost, and Paulus' last contact with the outside world was gone. By 31 January there was nothing left for Paulus to defend. Continued fighting would merely involve the slaughter of his troops. The whole of Sixth Army except XI Corps laid down their arms, and XI Corps followed suit on 2 February.

It has been estimated that the matériel lost at Stalingrad represented six months of German production. Of the original 200,000 beleaguered Germans 100,000 had been killed and 34,000 evacuated by air. The remainder surrendered. In addition the Luftwaffe lost nearly 500 transport planes. Far more serious than these losses was the psychological effect of Stalingrad. The invincible Wehrmacht had suffered a resounding, shattering defeat. Coupled with the Allied successes in Africa this disaster preshadowed for both the Allies and the Axis the probable outcome of the war. The German generals, too, who had seen their armies and campaign wrecked by interference, suffered a sharp decline in confidence at a moment when their Russian counterparts were gaining both confidence and competence with every week that went by.

Opposite: A mortar crew supports advancing Russian infantry

Below left: Russian troops in the ruins of Stalingrad

Opposite below: Field Marshal von Paulus after the surrender at Stalingrad

GERMAN PERIMETER ON NIGHT OF 8/9 JAN 1943

FRONT LINE ON NIGHT OF 13 JAN

" " " " " 17 JAN

GERMAN POCKETS, 25 JAN/2 FEB

201

THE ADVANCE TO KHARKOV

The battles to encircle Stalingrad placed the Russian Stalingrad Front in a position to strike straight at Rostov and sever Kleists' Army Group A from the German forces to the north. Such an event would be catastrophic for Kleist, and a simultaneous offensive by the Russian Trans-Caucasus Front would seal his fate. Already, by the end of December 1942, the Stalingrad Front was within 70 miles of Rostov, and when the Northern Group of the Trans-Caucasus Front attacked from the River Terek (**Map 1**) on 1 January 1943, Kleist's position was so perilous that

he had no alternative but to fall back as fast as possible. Manstein, in charge of Army Group Don (later Army Group South), fought desperately to keep open the Rostov corridor for Kleist's escape. Only the First Panzer Army escaped through this corridor. By 14 February Rostov had fallen to the Russians, and the remainder of Kleist's Army Group A had been compelled to take refuge in the Taman peninsula. Here simultaneous attacks by the Black Sea Group and Northern Group of the Trans-Caucasus Front drove Kleist back into a still smaller bridgehead around Novorossiysk.

Here for the time being, in strong positions, he was able to hold out.

North of the Don the last and greatest act of the 1942/43 winter campaign was enacted. On 12 January, on a front stretching from Orel to Rostov (**Map 2**) four Russian Fronts, the Bryansk Front, Voronezh Front, South-West Front, and South Front (a regrouping of Stalingrad Front), broke out and fell upon Army Group Don in the south and Army Group B under Weichs. Their objective was Kharkov. On the right flank of the Russian offensive their armour literally flooded westward, surrounding elements of the German Second Army, and forcing the rest of it to fall back well beyond Kursk. In the centre Kharkov fell early in February to troops of the Russian Fortieth Army and Third Tank Army. In the south, the Russian left, the Germans fared somewhat better. By brilliant handling of his reserves Manstein was able to halt the Russian offensives and, then, in the face of numerical odds of seven to one, to counterattack the vulnerable Russian salients, recapture Kharkov, and establish a slightly more favourable line along the Donets before the spring thaw brought movement to an end at the end of March. Near miraculous though Manstein's achievement was, the Russian winter offensive had struck a decisive blow at German power. Their losses had been crippling. Accurate figures do not exist but estimates put the German dead during the winter battles of 1942/43 at over 1,000,000. The Russians claimed the destruction or capture of 5,000 aircraft, 9,000 tanks, 20,000 guns, and thousands of trucks and other vehicles. Russian losses, even more difficult to establish, were probably just as great, but they at least had the satisfaction of having recaptured all the territory lost in 1942, and of the knowledge that their strength was now many times greater than the Germans, and growing.

Opposite above: Soviet troops storm a water obstacle

Above right: A Soviet anti-tank gun supports advancing infantry

THE BATTLE OF KURSK

The success of the Russian offensive in the first months of 1943, and the German counterattacks in the south left a huge salient around Kursk, a bulge that the Germans were determined to pinch out (**Map 1**). The period March to June 1943 was one of relative inactivity on the Eastern Front. Both sides had lost heavily during the winter, and both needed a long period of recuperation. Yet, to the Germans, such a period was not without peril. With American and British aid now flowing freely, Russian recuperative power was greater than German, and any prolonged pause favoured their chances.

Operation Citadel, the plan to eliminate the Kursk salient, was scheduled for the beginning of July. Two German armies, Ninth and Fourth Panzer, enormously strong in armour were to attack north and south of the salient respectively. The Russian's were well aware of the weakness of the salient, and had been at pains to strengthen it. Two Fronts, Central and Voronezh, occupied the salient, and eight concentric lines of defence had been built. They constituted the most formidable defences the Germans had ever prepared to assault. The result, now called the Battle of Kursk, was the biggest tank battle ever fought, involving over two million men, 6,000 tanks, and 4,000 aircraft. Although best known as a tank battle, Kursk was also an important air battle, and the Luftwaffe's loss of supremacy in the air is as important and interesting as the Wehrmacht's loss of supremacy in armour.

From the start Operation Citadel was doomed. Not only were the Germans attacking forces numerically inferior to their own, but the Russians were well aware of their intentions, both in broad outline and in detail – the reward of good Intelligence and of the work of the 'Lucy' spy ring operating from Switzerland.

On 5 July the German offensive opened, slightly behind schedule as a result of a preventive Russian bombardment that had hit the German forward areas as they were forming up. In the north Ninth Army

gained a mere six miles at the cost of
25,000 killed, and 200 tanks and
200 aircraft lost (**Map 3**). By the 10th
the whole of the German strike force
in the north had been committed with
no further gains.

In the south Manstein's forces
enjoyed greater success. A wedge
25 miles deep was driven into the
Russian defences, but again at
high cost – 10,000 men and 350 tanks
lost (**Map 2**). Reinforcements from
the Russian Steppe Front, stationed in
reserve, halted Manstein's attacks.

Between 12 and 15 July the Russian
forces took to the offensive (**Map 3**),
and by the 20th all Russian formations
were advancing and the Germans were
in full retreat. By the 23rd the
Germans were back beyond their start
lines, and Citadel had been destroyed
without coming even distantly within
sight of success. But the Russians were
not going to stop there. In the north,
Army Group Centre was compelled
to abandon Orel, and was forced back
to the Hagen Line. In the south the
Voronezh and Steppe Fronts
converged on Kharkov and, by
22 August, the Germans began to
withdraw from the town, finally
abandoning it to the Russians on
23 August. Manstein, keeping his
forces intact as skillfully as ever,
defied Hitler's order to stand fast,
and fell back towards the Dniepr.

Opposite: A Soviet anti-tank gun is moved
into position

Below: Russian tanks during the
Kursk counterattacks

205

THE DNIEPR AND SMOLENSK BATTLES

Kursk marked the end of German mass efforts in the east. Hitler, alarmed by the Allied landings in Sicily, had transferred many of his best divisions to the west. His generals in the east, now hopelessly outnumbered by the great masses of Russian armour, hung on grimly and with great skill, keeping their forces intact, and giving ground grudgingly and always at a cost.

From July to December 1943, the Russians launched a series of blows along the whole length of the Eastern Front from Smolensk to Rostov. By 23 August their line lay from the Donets in the south, through Kharkov,

to the Dvina north of Smolensk
(see map). Three German Army
Groups were faced by eight Russian
Fronts. By September 16 the Russians
were threatening Smolensk in the
north and Kiev in the centre. In the
south the Donets was crossed and the
Dniepr bend was being approached.
By the end of September the Russians
were on the Dniepr along most of its
length, and Smolensk had fallen. Also
during September the German Army
Group A was rescued in the nick of
time from its Caucasus bridgehead to
operate on the right of Manstein's
Army Group South. By the end of the
year the Russians had crossed the
Dniepr in great force around Kiev
(which fell on 6 November) and in
Manstein's sector in the south.
Manstein's insistence that the German
Seventeenth Army be evacuated
from the Crimea was overruled by
Hitler in another of his 'No Retreat'
orders. By the end of the year it was
cut off in the Crimean peninsula.

The Russian forces had pressed
these offensives against very skilled
and determined opposition, and in
spite of their enormous territorial
gains they had lost heavily in
men and matériel.

Left: Russian infantry in action on the banks
of the Dniepr

Below left: The first Russian troops crossing
the Dniepr on a makeshift bridge

THE RELIEF OF LENINGRAD

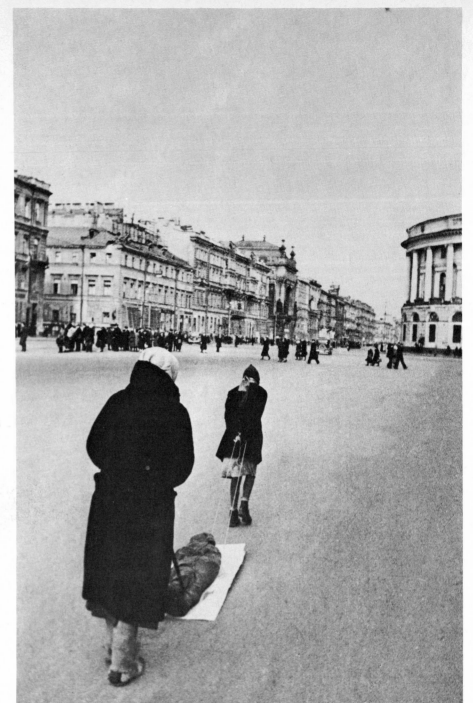

In 1941 the advancing German forces bypassed Leningrad and advanced on the left bank of the Neva to Lake Ladoga. This manoeuvre trapped the Russian forces in Leningrad (and other Russian forces around Oranienbaum cutting them off from the rest of Russia (see The Attack on Leningrad). For 900 days Leningrad remained isolated, without supplies of food, fuel or arms. By the end of the siege its citizens were dying of hunger, cold, and disease at the rate of 20,000 a day. In addition to their other sufferings, the inhabitants had to endure constant German bombardment. But a combination of patriotism, fear of German occupation, and severe Soviet discipline kept the Leningraders active throughout the siege. Production never entirely ceased in the factories; vigilante organizations were always at hand, however hungry and enfeebled, to put out fires, clear up rubble, construct defences.

There is some evidence that Stalin allowed the siege to go on longer than he needed for political reasons connected with his dislike of the Leningraders independent spirit, and a feud between him and the Leningrad party leader, Zhdanov. Nonetheless some relief operations were attempted. In August 1942 the Leningrad Front and the Volkhov Front (**Map 1**) planned to raise the siege by severing

208

the German-held corridor between
Tosno and Lake Ladoga, and with
a thrust north of Pushkin to link up
with the Oranienbaum forces. The
attempt lasted from 19 August to the
end of September, but was checked at
all points by the German Eighteenth
Army.

It was not until January 1943 that
the Leningraders received their first
gleam of hope. On 11 January another
concerted effort by the Leningrad
Front and Volkhov Front succeeded in
securing a narrow corridor south of
Lake Ladoga. Through this a thin
trickle of supplies was able to reach
Leningrad (**Map 2**), and with this
Leningrad had to be content for the
remainder of 1943.

Real release for the Leningraders
did not come until January 1944.
Between 14 January and 19 January
three Russian Fronts, Leningrad
Front, Volkhov Front, and 2 Baltic
Front launched attacks against the
German Army Group North. By
27 January the Moscow–Leningrad
railway was cleared (**Map 3**).
Novgorod fell to the Russian
Fifty-ninth Army on 19 January, and
the threat of encirclement compelled
the withdrawal of the whole of Army
Group North out of the area east of
Lake Chudskoye. By 1 March the
Russians had reached the River
Narva in the north, Pskov in the
centre, and Pustoshka in the south.

Opposite above: Nevsky Prospekt during the
siege of Leningrad

Above: A Russian patrol sets out during
fighting south of Lake Ilmen

THE BATTLES IN THE UKRAINE

While Leningrad was being relieved in the north, the German forces in south Russia were given no rest. On 24 December 1943, and 5 January 1944, the 1 and 2 Ukrainian Fronts erupted from their bridgeheads over the Dniepr, falling upon Manstein and Kleist's Army Groups and trapping the German First Panzer Army. Instant counterattacks by Manstein bogged down in blizzards and appalling weather. The Russian advance continued towards the Rivers Bug and Dniestr in spite of desperate counterattacks by Manstein (see map).

Meanwhile the trapped First Panzer Army conducted a brilliant behind-lines rearguard action. An improvised airlift kept the army supplied, and eventually it fought its way out almost completely intact south of Tarnopol. To the south Army Group A had also taken a considerable beating. Attacked by 2 and 4 Ukrainian Fronts, Kleist fell back to Odessa, leaving behind surrounded elements of Sixth and Eighth Armies. On 10 April he was compelled to abandon Odessa, and by mid-April the Russian front had been extended from Odessa in the south nearly to Brest Litovsk in the north.

With the Russians poised on the borders of Poland and in the foothills of the Carpathians the German situation in the east was desperate. The abandoned Seventeenth Army was cleared out of the Crimea by troops of the 4 Ukrainian Front during April (see inset) and Sevastopol finally fell on 12 May.

Hitler, infuriated by these losses, relieved Manstein and Kleist of their commands. Model replaced Manstein in command of Army Group North Ukraine, and Schörner replaced Kleist in charge of Army Group South Ukraine.

In summary it must be stressed that the tenacity of the German generals in south Russia in the face of the Russian onslaught was nothing short of miraculous. Manstein, in particular, since being called in to relieve Stalingrad, had fought continuously, untiringly, and at great cost to the Russians.

Below: German sentries on the alert as a flare goes up

Opposite below: During the spring offensive, Russian infantry attack with tank support

THE THRUST INTO POLAND

Following the appalling reverses of the winter of 1943/44 the only course open to the Germans in the east was to fall back to a shorter front and reorganize on strong defensive positions sited in depth. If the pause during the spring thaws of 1944 had been occupied in doing this, there might have been some hope of blunting the Russian offensives of the summer of 1944. But Hitler's obsession with holding territory at all costs left his forces dangerously overextended, holding a vast 1,400-mile front with scant reserves.

The Russian blow fell at the end of June. On the 23rd three Russian Fronts, 1, 2, and 3 Belorussian, under the overall command of Marshal Zhukov (now deputy supreme commander) struck at General Busch's Army Group Centre. A simultaneous outburst of partisan activity in Busch's rear came close to destroying his communications, and when Zhukov's forces (supported by a density of almost 400 guns *per mile* of front) assaulted on a 350-mile front (see map) he was unable to co-ordinate the movements of his formations. Russian air superiority was complete, many Luftwaffe units having already been taken west. Busch's army group was torn apart. By 4 July Minsk had fallen, and to the north 1 Baltic Front was driving for Riga. By the end of July, Vilnyus and Brest Litovsk were in Russian hands. Twenty-five out of Busch's thirty-three divisions had been trapped, and the Russians claimed 158,000 captured, almost 400,000 dead, 2,000 tanks, 10,000 guns, and 57,000 motor vehicles captured or destroyed. Hitler instantly replaced Busch with Model. By the end of August Zhukov's offensive had reached the gates of Warsaw in the south, and Riga in the north. The Russians stood on the frontiers of East Prussia. The German Army Group North was threatened with being trapped with its back to the Baltic, and Model, now

commanding what was left of Army Group Centre, only just succeeded in stopping the Russians in front of Warsaw. (In this he was assisted by the Russians themselves who paused before Warsaw to resupply and to allow the German SS to crush the non-communist Warsaw insurrection.)

To the south of Warsaw the Russian 1 and 4 Ukrainian Fronts had surged through Lvov, isolating elements of the Army Group North Ukraine, and by the end of August had reached and crossed the Vistula.

In two months the Russian armies had advanced 450 miles, and had outstripped their own supply capabilities. Operations on this front came, temporarily, to a halt.

Opposite above: Soviet infantry disembark from tanks in preparation for an attack

Opposite below: Members of the Polish Home Army whose rising in Warsaw was crushed

OCCUPPIED BY RUSSIAN FORCES,

JAN/APR 1944

JUNE/AUG 1944

0 MILES 200

0 KILOMETRES 300

FINLAND

L. Onega

L. Ladoga

HELSINKI

LENINGRAD

TALLINN

BALTIC SEA

Estonia

PSKOV

Volga

Latvia

RIGA

MOSCOW

Lithuania

Dvina

KAUNAS

SMOLENSK

TULA

E PRUSSIA

Minsk

OREL

Vistula

BIALYSTOK

Bug

RUSSIA

WARSAW

LUBLIN

KURSK

POLAND

KIEV

LVOV

ZHITOMIR

KHARKOV

Dnieper

HUNGARY

VINNITSA

Dniester

KRIVOY ROG

Prut

ODESSA 15 Apr

RUMANIA

SEVASTOPOL

BUCHAREST

BLACK SEA

213

CLEARING THE BALTIC STATES

The defeat of Finland was undertaken in June 1944 by the Russian Karelian Front under Meretskov. There is some irony in reflecting that the last time the Russians had conquered Finland it had been as the ally of Nazi Germany. From the south, operating on both sides of Lake Ladoga, units of the Karelian Front attacked the strong Finnish fortifications, between Lake Ladoga and the sea and on the east of the lake, between 8 June and 11 July. West of the lake (**Map 1**) they enjoyed success. The formidable Mannerheim Line was breached, and on 20 June Viipuri was captured. East of the lake, although the Russian attacks were repulsed at the Finnish U Line, the Murmansk railway had been cleared, and the Finns had been pushed back from their positions between Lake Ladoga and Lake Onega.

Below right: Civilians take cover during fighting in Karelia

In the north, the Russian Fourteenth Army pushed the German Twentieth Mountain Army off its positions on the Litsa, and by executing amphibious landings on its flanks, forced it back into Norway by the end of October (**Map 2**). In the same sector the Russian Nineteenth Army pushed units of the Twentieth Mountain Army back to Salla, clearing the last German/Finnish troops from Russian soil.

Having withdrawn from Leningrad in January 1944, the German Army Group North was, by July, situated in the Baltic states with its back to the sea. It was placed in extreme jeopardy by Zhukov's successful offensive against Army Group Centre, which threatened to destroy its corridor of escape to Germany, and bottle it up in the Baltic states. Guderian (by July 1944 Chief of the German General Staff) tried to persuade Hitler of its peril, but Hitler clung to his 'No

Retreat' principle until it was too late. At the same time that the Russian 3 Belorussian Front seized Vilnyus, the 1 Baltic Front drove for Memel and Riga, separating Army Group North from Army Group Centre, cutting off its retreat, and forcing it back until by the end of September it was locked up in the Kurland Peninsula. Here the bulk of it remained blockaded until the end of the war, although some units were taken off by the German navy. Meanwhile 2 and 3 Baltic Fronts and the Leningrad Front had overrun Estonia and Latvia, capturing Riga on 15 October (**Map 3**).

Left: German paratroops prepare for action on the borders of East Prussia

CLEARING THE BALKANS

Zhukov's June/July attacks in Belorussia pushed out a large salient that left the German Army Group South Ukraine on the southern or 'under' side of it. If driven further south this Army Group might well lose contact with the other German Eastern Front groups, and if this were done swiftly enough the pursuing Russian forces might well cut off the German armies in Greece and the Balkans from their homeland (see map).

In this, due to the speed of their own advance, and Hitler's now predictable delay in ordering a withdrawal, the Russians very nearly succeeded. On 20 August 1944, the 2 and 3 Ukrainian Fronts under Malinovsky and Tolbukhin attacked Friessner's Army Group South Ukraine, trapping the German Sixth Army and the Rumanian Third Army (see map). They drove south, reaching the Danube by 29 August. On 30 August the bulk of the Russian forces turned west and then north, overrunning Rumania by 24 September. A smaller group of 3 Ukrainian Front headed south over the Danube into Bulgaria, forcing the withdrawal of elements of Weichs' Army Group F.

By early October Rumania and
Bulgaria were in Russian hands, and
the German Army Groups E and F
were within an ace of being trapped in
southern Yugoslavia and Greece. In
the nick of time they retreated north
and west, and took up a position on
the right of Friessner's retreating Army
Group South Ukraine. During October
the two Russian Fronts, supported
by the 4 Ukrainian Front on the right,
overran the larger part of Hungary.
And during November, December,
and January the remainder of
Hungary, up to Lake Balaton and the
Czechoslovak border, fell. Budapest,
encircled on 24 December, held out
until 14 February 1945.

The Russian advance through
Rumania, Bulgaria, and Hungary
was made much easier by the activities
of Tito's Yugoslav partisans, and by
the defection of Rumania and Bulgaria
to the Allied cause.

Right: Russian troops enter Bucharest

Below: Soviet artillery in the Carpathians

217

THE DRIVE TO THE ODER

Their advances of 1944 had brought the Russians to the borders of East Prussia, and by January 1945 they were ready to invade the German Fatherland for the first time since 1914. On 12 January Rokossovsky's 2 Belorussian Front, fielding nine armies (**Map 1**), fell upon the German Second Army along the Narew north of Warsaw. The Russian Forty-seventh Army encircled Warsaw, which fell on 17 January. The remainder of Rokossovsky's forces drove north-west along the right bank of the Vistula towards Danzig, isolating Reinhardt's Army Group Centre. To the north of Rokossovsky the Russian 3 Belorussian Front and the 1 Baltic Front also closed in on Army Group Centre forcing it back until, by 8 February, the Germans occupied a few isolated pockets along the Bay of Danzig. More than 500,000 German troops were cut off, but during April and March these pockets were successfully evacuated by the German navy. On 9 May the remaining German beachheads surrendered.

The operations of the German Baltic Fleet, which had included the evacuation of part of Army Group North from the Kurland Peninsula, succeeded in rescuing an estimated million and a half fugitives, many wounded, and four army divisions. The cost, due to lack of air cover, was virtually the whole strength of the fleet. Only the cruisers *Prinz Eugen* and *Nürnberg* were still afloat at the end of April.

At the same time as Rokossovsky's attack north of the Vistula (**Map 1**), the Russian 1 Belorussian Front (Zhukov) and the 1 Ukrainian Front (Konev) launched an assault on a wide front from Warsaw to Jasto in the south. In one of the most massive, costly, and fastest advances of the war Zhukov's forces had reached the Oder by 31 January. Pockets of German resistance were bypassed and mopped up at leisure. Russian armies of over 1,500,000 men, supported by 28,000 guns, 3,300 tanks, and 10,000 aircraft, faced German forces of 596,000 men, 8,230 guns, 700 tanks, and 1,300 aircraft. Against odds like these the Germans could not contend. Army Groups Vistula and A were torn apart (**Map 2**). Torun, Poznan, and Breslau were surrounded and held out for some time, but the remainder of the German armies were swept back. By 24 February Pomerania in the north, and Silesia in the south, had fallen, so that the Russian forces presented a solid front along the Oder less than 40 miles from Berlin.

Opposite: Russian artillery bombard German positions before an assault

Right: German anti-tank guns going to the front

FRONT LINES

11 JANUARY 1945
17 JANUARY
1 FEBRUARY, 8 FEB (E PRUSSIA)
20 FEB (POMERANIA), 24 FEB (SILESIA)
31 MARCH
5 MAY
GERMAN COUNTERATTACKS
GERMAN POCKETS
PRE-WAR BOUNDARIES

MILES 0 — 100
KILOMETRES 0 — 160

*Heinrici later, then Student

THE INVASIONS OF AUSTRIA AND HUNGARY

After the fall of Budapest on 14 February 1945 the Russian 2 and 3 Ukrainian Fronts stood poised to overrun the rest of Hungary and strike at Vienna. However, on 6 March 1945, Hitler, in a desperate attempt to save the Balaton oil fields, launched a counterattack north and south of Lake Balaton. North of the Lake the Sixth SS Panzer Army was to break out and strike north and south to Budapest and Baja, establishing a line along the Danube. South of the lake, Second Panzer Army was also to strike towards the Danube – due east. In hideously muddy conditions this counterattack, codenamed *Frühlingserwachen*, was ground to a halt by weather, lack of fuel, and stiff opposition. On 16 March the Russians resumed their advance against Army Group South. By 4 April they were within five miles of Vienna, which finally fell on 14 April.

Right: German troops move forward during the abortive 'Frühlingserwachen' offensive

220

THE DRIVE INTO CZECHOSLOVAKIA

RUSSIAN AND ALLIED ATTACKS

- 12 JAN/18 FEB 1945
- 26 MARCH/30 APRIL
- 10 MARCH/5 MAY
- 6 MAY/12 MAY
- ······ LINE REACHED BY RUSSIAN AND AMERICAN FORCES, 12 MAY 1945
- ─·─·─ INTERNATIONAL BOUNDARIES 1938

After the fall of Berlin (next page) only one sizeable German force was left in Europe – Schörner's Army Group Centre now in Czechoslovakia. In spite of madcap Nazi plans to form a 'national redoubt' on the German/ Czechoslovak border based on this force, Schörner's position was without hope. On three sides, north, east, and south the Russians surrounded him. From the west Patton's US Third Army was approaching. But his armies, numbering nearly 1,000,000 men, held the Reich's last important industrial area.

The Russian 2 and 4 Ukrainian Fronts had already by 6 March overrun much of Slovakia (see map). By 6 May they were well into Moravia, having occupied more than a half of Czechoslovakia. At the same time Czech partisans in Prague and elsewhere rose against the Germans, capturing much of Prague and further disrupting the German forces, especially their communications.

On 8 May an all-enveloping Russian offensive began. From the north troops of Konev's 1 Ukrainian Front bore down on Prague, while 2, 3, and 4 Ukrainian Fronts struck from the south and east. Prague was liberated on 9 May, and contact with the US Third Army made on 12 May along a line from Karlovy Vary to Linz. On 11 May, completely surrounded, Schörner surrendered. After nearly six years, the war in Europe was over.

Above: A Russian tank knocked out during the Czech campaign

OCCUPIED BY RUSSIAN FORCES

- AUG/DEC 1944
- DEC 1944/APR 1945
- APR/MAY 1945

THE BATTLE OF BERLIN

Once safely ensconced on the Oder the Russians were able to prepare for the Red Army's greatest exploit – the capture of Berlin. Zhukov's 1 Belorussian Front, and Konev's 1 Ukrainian Front were given the task of taking Berlin and driving beyond to establish the Russian armies on the Elbe. In spite of the losses they had taken, the Germans were still able to deploy 1,000,000 men in the defence of Berlin, situated in strong defensive positions on the west bank of the Oder. Although between them Konev and Zhukov could command nearly 2,500,000 men, their task was not going to be an

easy one. Simultaneously, in the north, Rokossovsky's 2 Belorussian Front was to occupy all of northern Prussia up the Elbe.

Employing an unprecedented artillery concentration of one gun per 13 feet of front, Zhukov and Konev opened their bombardment of the German forces on 16 April. It was the prelude to one of the most ferocious slogging matches of the war, the Germans, having few illusions as to what a Russian breakthrough would mean, fighting desperately. In two days, 18 April, only small bridgeheads 3–7 miles deep had been established (see main map). But by 20 April the German resistance on the Oder had been smashed, and the Russian advance to encircle and capture Berlin could continue. By 25 April Konev and Zhukov's armies had met on the west of Berlin. On the same day Russian and US forces made contact on the Elbe at Torgau. Apart from the garrison of Berlin itself, all that remained of the Wehrmacht in Germany itself was a few isolated remnants of Army Groups Centre and Vistula, all trying desperately to surrender to the Western Allies rather than the Russians.

At the moment of encirclement Berlin contained 2,000,000 civilian

inhabitants and about 30,000 garrison troops. Since January the city had been preparing for a siege, but its defences were rudimentary – certainly no match for the enormous Russian forces encircling them. Even so the Russian attack on the city of Berlin was no walk-over. Every street – every house – was bitterly contested.

On 26 April Zhukov's armies from the north, and Konev's from the south drove in on the Berlin defences. Two days of fighting brought Zhukov's armies to the River Spree in the Moabit area (see map below). From the south Konev's forces had advanced almost to the Tiergarten. Both threatened to cut the city in half – east from west. Between them lay the Reichstag and Hitler's command bunker in the garden of the Chancellery. The distance between the two Russian forces was less than a mile, and some idea of the savagery of the Berlin fighting is given by the fact that it was not until 2 May that they met across the Charlottenberg Chaussee. In the meantime the Reichstag had fallen on 30 April, and Hitler had killed himself, naming as his successor Admiral Dönitz.

MILES 40
KILOMETRES 60

BALTIC SEA

Rügen

STRALSUND
RIBNITZ
ROSTOCK
WISMAR
British Second Army
GRIEFSWALD
DEMMIN
ANKLAM
PEENEMÜNDE
Usedom
SWINEMÜNDE
19A
Stettiner Haff
UECKERMÜNDE
FRIEDLAND
Third Pz Army
STETTIN

2 Belorussian Front (Rokossovsky)
attacks AM 20 April
2SA

STARGARD

GÜSTROW
SCHWERIN
NEUBRANDENBURG
PACEWALK
65A
70A

Army Group Vistula
(Heinrici, then Tippelskirch acting for Student)

PARCHIM
Müritz
WAREN
NEUSTRELITZ
PRENZLAU
SCHWEDT
65A
70A
49A

LUDWIGSLUST
WITTSTOCK
PRITZWALK
TEMPLIN
49A

DÖMITZ
LENZEN
WITTENBERGE
Elbe
ZEHDENICK
ANGERMÜNDE
61A

US Ninth Army
61A
NEURUPPIN
Operational Group Steiner
Oder-Havel Canal
EBERSWALDE
61A
Pol1A
2GTA

1 Belorussian Front (Zhukov)
attacks 0500 hrs, 16 April

Pol1A
Rhinkanal
18 Apr
ORANIENBURG
2GTA
BERNAU
PRÖTZEL
47A
3SA
5SA
Warta

STENDAL
RATHENOW
47A
47A
STRAUSBERG
3SA
SEELOW
8GA
KÜSTRIN

TANGERMÜNDE
KETZIN
BERLIN
5SA 1GTA
1GTA
3A

Havel
POTSDAM
8GA
FÜRSTENWALDE
69A
FRANKFURT an der Oder

GENTHIN
BRANDENBURG
3A
28A
3A
33A

BURG
Twelfth Army
BEELITZ
3GTA
ZOSSEN
BEESKOW
EISENHÜTTENSTADT
Oder

MAGDEBURG
69A
BELZIG
4GTA
LUCKENWALDE
MARKISCH BUCHHOLZ
Ninth Army & part Fourth Pz Army

33A
ZERBST
JÜTERBOG
BARUTH
GUBEN

US First Army
DESSAU
BERNBURG
Saale
WITTENBERG
13A
LUCKAU
LÜBBEN
Spree

1 Ukrainian Front (Konev)
attacks 0615 hrs, 16 April

US front 25 April
SCHLIEBEN
HERZBERG
FINSTERWALDE
COTTBUS
22 Apr
FORST
3GA

18 Apr
Mulde
TORGAU
Elbe
5GA
3GTA
TRIEBEL
13A
5GA
4GTA

HALLE
EILENBURG
25 April 1945 US and Russian forces make contact
Army Group Centre (Schörner)
Fourth Pz Army
ELSTERWALDE
SPREMBERG
Neisse
28A

LEIPZIG
RIESA
GROSSENHAIN
HOYERSWERDE
KAMENZ
Pol2A
NIESKY
52A

FRONT LINES
15 APRIL 1945
18 APRIL
25 APRIL
6 MAY
GERMAN DEFENCE LINES
GERMAN POCKETS
GERMAN COUNTERATTACKS
ANGLO-AMERICAN ATTACKS
ANGLO-AMERICAN FRONTS AT DATES SHOWN

MEISSEN
BAUTZEN
GÖRLITZ
RADEBERG
Seventeenth Army
COLDITZ
DRESDEN

223

THE WAR IN NORTH-WEST EUROPE

Opposite: US troops go ashore
on D-Day

On 6 June nine Allied divisions invaded Normandy over the open beaches between the Cherbourg Peninsula and the mouth of the River Orne at Ouistreham. Ten weeks later when the Allies broke out from Normandy they had destroyed the German Seventh Army, some 500,000 strong. Yet on the first day of the invasion the Allies landed a force which was scarcely the equivalent of ten divisions: six infantry divisions; three airborne divisions; two Commando brigades; and one Ranger battalion. In all 5,300 ships and craft were to put ashore 150,000 men and 1,500 tanks during the first forty-eight hours of the Second Front. There were 12,000 aircraft in support.

On sea and in the air the German defenders were completely outclassed, but Field-Marshal von Rundstedt, the Commander-in-Chief, West, had sixty divisions, including eleven armoured divisions, with which to defend Holland, Belgium, and France. Of these, six, including one Panzer division, were in or near the area of the beachhead. With so many troops at his disposal it was well within the bounds of possibility the Germans would either crush the invaders on the beaches, or with a swift concentration of a mass of armour break into the beachhead before the Allies could get set and consolidate. In order to prevent these unpleasant possibilities the Allies devised the most elaborate and successful deception plan which military history records.

The objects of this plan were to persuade Hitler and his entourage that the Normandy assault was just a cunning diversion, and that the main invasion must be expected elsewhere, probably in the Pas de Calais. The idea was to prevent the Germans reinforcing Seventh Army from the nineteen divisions of Fifteenth Army, which included some of their best formations. Had this happened in the early days of the invasion when bad weather delayed the build-up, smashed

one of the artificial (Mulberry) harbours and hampered air support, it is by no means certain that Montgomery could have continued to hold the original bridgehead. The British had been remarkably successful in rounding up German agents working in England. This greatly facilitated the Allied deception team's task of selling fake intelligence to the enemy. By 31 May 1944 German intelligence credited the Allies with the equivalent of eighty-seven combat divisions, including eight airborne, in Britain. In fact there were less than fifty-two, and only thirty-seven were available for operations on the continent. Some of these would not be going to France until seven months after D-Day. It is no exaggeration to say that the German Fifteenth Army was kept idle for seven crucial weeks by a Phantom Army, the US First Army Group (FUSAG), under General George S. Patton, Jr., which was waiting with its twenty-five large formations, and perhaps five airborne divisions, to embark in South-East England and pounce on the Pas de Calais. Since Hitler himself expected an attack in that area it is little wonder that the Germans bought the Allied deception plan. Another Phantom Army, the 'Fourth' under Lieutenant-General Sir A. F. A. N. Thorne (Commander-in-Chief, Northern Command) was 'assembled' in Scotland with the object of discouraging any movement of German troops from Norway to France. Hitler, convinced of the importance of Norway, was receptive to the suggestion that it was imperilled.

Montgomery's campaign in Normandy went more or less according to plan. There were times when he was criticized, quite unfairly, because it was going more slowly than some hoped. He can, of course, be criticized upon points of detail. It may be, for example, that the employment of an airborne division in Operation Goodwood (the attack on Caen) might have made all the difference at a moment when

victory was almost within his grasp, but for all his tactical soundness, Montgomery was an unimaginative general.

As the end of the battle of Normandy came in sight a serious inter-Allied controversy blew up: the Broad Front/Narrow Front question.

There was a brief moment round about 4 September when, at least in Rundstedt's view the Allies might have broken through the shattered German front. If he was correct Montgomery's idea of thrusting with a solid mass of some forty divisions towards Antwerp, Brussels, Aachen, and Cologne, may have been right. But the Americans were now the senior partners in the alliance and Bradley has told us what was in their minds: 'The first or predominantly American plan called for emphasis on a thrust to the Reich straight through the middle of France to the Saar and beyond the Saar to the Rhine in the vicinity of Frankfurt . . . Both the First and Third American Armies . . . would be required for this major effort.'

In the event the Allies approached the German frontier on a broad front, and Eisenhower ended up in a situation not unlike that of Joffre in 1914. Had his whole army been of one nation it would have been a grave error. As things were it was perhaps inevitable. The American nation would never have stood for the British and the Canadians reaping all the glory.

Montgomery was still determined – although the Russians were still the other side of the Vistula – to gain a foothold beyond the Rhine before winter. Hence his somewhat belated and ambitious Operation Market Garden (the airborne landing at Arnhem). At a time when the Allies were still being supplied over the open beaches of Normandy he would probably have done better to concentrate upon clearing the seaward approaches of the port of Antwerp.

The dramatic German offensive in the Ardennes, which took the

Americans by surprise, showed Eisenhower in a good light. He had but a small reserve but this he deployed to advantage. The Allied air forces, thinking the German army no longer capable of a counteroffensive had failed to detect its concentration. The defence of Bastogne was a splendid demonstration of what the American soldier can do when he means business. In the event the offensive only succeeded in destroying Hitler's last effective reserves. When the time came for the Allies to cross the formidable obstacle of the Lower Rhine the Germans found themselves left with too few troops to defend it. There were three more rivers to cross before Hamburg should fall, but the war was as good as won.

Touring his victorious troops soon after the surrender Montgomery told them that the Western Allies had won for four main reasons. Firstly, the Germans' mistakes; second, Allied domination of the air; third, Anglo-American co-operation; fourth, the fighting qualities of the British, Canadian, and American soldiers. As so often he had got to the heart of the matter.

For most of the German mistakes Hitler himself must bear the blame, for it was no longer the great General Staff that controlled operations but the Führer himself. The flair for military affairs which he occasionally showed in the earlier part of the war, had long since abandoned him. He had spent his last reserves in the Ardennes offensive. He had clung to the Reichswald too long. Like so many bad generals he wished to hold everything, and ended up by being weak everywhere. He believed only such Intelligence as fitted in with his own prejudices and mistrusted the majority of his best qualified commanders.

Allied air supremacy was a pearl of great price, even though the Allied air marshals may be said to have got out of political control, and might have given direct support to the other services in a more generous – not to say more

accurate – fashion. It is not easy, on moral grounds, to justify their policy of area bombing. Herman Göring, who consistently exaggerated the strength and capabilities of the Luftwaffe, must take some of the credit for the fact that the Allied airmen got the upper hand.

For Anglo-American co-operation Eisenhower must take much of the credit. His strategic errors, due in part to lack of proper political direction, are obvious enough. Nevertheless he could get on with Churchill and Alanbrooke and Montgomery and won the liking and trust of the British as well as the American soldier. His own generals, Bradley and Patton were men who needed a firm superior. Patton, despite his arrogant temper, was a thruster with real talent. Bradley, though an effective writer, was what Napoleon would have called *bon gènèral ordinaire*, or as Montgomery once rather maliciously is said to have described another – British – colleague, 'a good, plain cook'.

Most of the Allied generals have either found biographers or have given us their own recollections. An exception is one of the best of them: General Sir Miles Dempsey. As Major L. F. Ellis says: 'He was always in firm control of all that was done by Second Army. Much of his day was usually spent in visits to formations chiefly involved, to confer with commanders on their problems and progress and to give them clear and concise verbal orders. The directives he received left him little scope for any conspicuous initiative but his understanding of Montgomery's purpose, his own knowledge of the troops he commanded and his quiet and steady personality continued to give both his superior and his subordinates confidence in his judgement and in his leadership.' Given the character of Montgomery and the nature of Second Army he was the ideal man for his job.

The fighting qualities of the British, Canadian, and American soldiers is a subject of great interest, but it is a vast one for in the nature of things the various

formations varied in quality and experience. The great majority of those who went to France in 1944 had never been in action before, but they were on the whole pretty well trained. It is no exaggeration to say that early disasters at Dunkirk and elsewhere had led the Allies to overhaul their tactics, a process in which the Commandos, paratroops, and Rangers led the way, if only by arousing in the ordinary infantry divisions a spirit of emulation. One of the chief lessons of modern warfare is that however much air or gunfire support may be available, the infantryman and the tank crew must sooner or later come to close quarters with the enemy and fight it out. A very experienced soldier and historian, Major-General H. Essame, writes: 'There is some truth in the statement that he who has not fought the Germans does not know what war is.' They remained formidable to the end when 'they were outfought on the Western front by troops, . . . as well-trained, as well-led and as tough as themselves'.

PREPARATION FOR D-DAY

As agreed at the Trident Conference in Washington in 1943, the Western Allies laid plans for an invasion of Europe in 1944. Ignoring the fact that they already held a foothold in Europe, Italy, the American and British planners yielded to political pressures and selected France as the target of a cross-channel assault. The Normandy beaches between Cherbourg and Le Havre were chosen as the targets of this attack for a number of reasons. First, the area was in easy reach of the fighter bases of southern England. Secondly, the beaches and the countryside inland were favourable. Thirdly, the water distance for the force, and its subsequent supplies, to cross was the shortest available if the Pas de Calais were ruled out. Fourthly, the Germans were expecting the blow to fall across the Pas de Calais, and the Normandy beaches were correspondingly less heavily defended.

By 1944 an enormous Allied army had been built up in Britain –

Americans, British, Canadian, and French – and with supporting naval and air units it totalled nearly 3,000,000 men (**Map 1**). The assault forces, in essence the US First Army and the British Second Army, were to sail from their embarkation ports, assemble offshore, and make a landing on a front of four corps. Essential to the plan was the airborne operation by the US 82 and 101 Airborne Divisions and the British 8 Airborne Division. These were to be dropped right and left of the target beaches respectively and act as flank guards to the landings.

The whole operation was covered by the most elaborate programme of deception of the whole war. Every effort was made to persuade the Germans that the Pas de Calais was the real target. For every sortie flown west of Le Havre, two were flown north of it; for every ton of tombs dropped west of Le Havre, two were dropped to its north. In Kent, a likely stepping off point for a Pas de Calais crossing, dummy headquarters and railway sidings were built.

By the beginning of June, 1944, every precaution that could be taken to safeguard 'Overlord' had been taken. But one important and imponderable factor remained – the weather.

Across the channel the Allies were faced by Field-Marshal Gerd von Rundstedt, and more immediately by Army Group B (Rommel) and Seventh Army (Dollmann). Between them they could field thirty infantry divisions and six armoured divisions (**Map 2**). Many of the infantry divisions were 'coastal' or training divisions and of inferior quality. Moreover Rundstedt's Western

Command spread from the Arctic circle in Norway to the Mediterranean in France, and his relationship with his subordinates was complicated by Hitler's habit of bypassing him and issuing orders direct to his Army Group commanders. In fact, the Germans had no effective chain of command in the west, and this was to tell heavily against them when the moment arrived. The situation was further complicated by the fact that the Third Air Fleet, although stationed in France, came under Göring's command. It was virtually a paper organization anyway, having only ninety bombers and seventy fighters fit for action.

Perhaps the greatest weakness of the German position in the north of France lay in the topography itself The whole of Normandy is almost enclosed by the rivers Loire and Seine. To destroy the crossings on these rivers would virtually isolate all the forces in Normandy, and leave them only the small gap between Paris and Orleans through which to escape.

Below: A German sentry stands outside a coastal gun emplacement in France

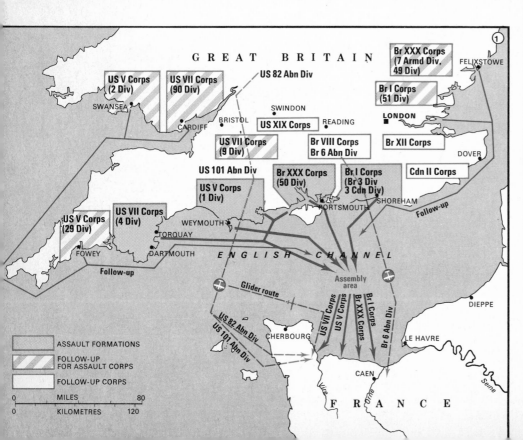

ASSAULT FORMATIONS

FOLLOW-UP FOR ASSAULT CORPS

FOLLOW-UP CORPS

Above: Spitfires flying on a mission prior to the D-Day landings

②

NORTH SEA

NETHERLANDS

347
16 GAF
719
165

19 Pz

GREAT BRITAIN

LONDON

712
48
87
19 GAF
331

GERMANY

BRUSSELS
1 SS Pz

BELGIUM

CALAIS
BOULOGNE

49 326
182
344 85
DIEPPE 245 2 Pz

ENGLISH CHANNEL

84 348
346 17 GAF

CHERBOURG

243 709
LE HAVRE
319
81 352 716 711
21 Pz 12 SS Pz

Fifteenth Army
(Salmuth)

116 Pz

OB West (Rundstedt)

Army Group 'B'
(Rommel)

PARIS

BREST

343 353
266 77
3
265 5

Seventh Army
(Dollmann)

Pz Lehr

LE MANS

ORLEANS

Loire

Seine

275
ST NAZAIRE

××××

××××

F R A N C E

SWITZ

158
17 SS Pz Gr

Army Group 'G'
(Blaskowitz)

189

First Army
(Chevallerie)

708

BAY OF
BISCAY

11 Pz

Saône

Rhône

ITALY

157

BORDEAUX

159

Nineteenth Army
(Wiese)

9 Pz

Garonne

××××

276

2 SS Pz TOULOUSE

271
277

338 244
242

MARSEILLES
TOULON

148

SPAIN

272

MEDITERRANEAN SEA

D-DAY

June 1944 opened with cold weather and high winds, a serious matter to the Allied planners. There were only a few days in each month on which the optimum conditions of moon and tide for the landings occurred, and the first week of June formed such a period. Command of the Overlord operation had been assumed by General Eisenhower earlier in the year, and the landing forces themselves were commanded by General Montgomery. The naval forces were commanded by Admiral Ramsay, and the air forces by Air Marshal Leigh Mallory.

Taking advantage of a break in the weather the landings went ahead on 6 June. Some 4,000 ships carried 176,000 troops and their material; 600 warships escorted the force; and 2,500 bombers and 7,000 fighter-bombers 'softened-up' the beaches and combed the skies. At 0200 hours the American and British airborne forces were dropped or landed on their targets. Tactical surprise was complete, and both airborne forces were able to consolidate a position. At 0314 hours the aircraft bombardment of the beaches began, augmented at 0550 hours by the guns of the 600 escorting warships. At 0630 hours the first waves went ashore (see map). In the west the US First Army tackled Utah beach

Cherbourg 13 miles

VALOGNES

MONTEBOURG

709 Inf Div

QUINNEVILLE

ST MARCOUF

RAVENOVILLE
919 Regt

LES DUNES DE VARREVILLE

Planned assault area

Merderet

ST GERMAIN DE VARREVILLE

1058 Regt

91 Inf Div

STE MÈRE ÉGLISE

LA MADELEINE

US 82 Abn Div

CHEF DU PONT

PONT L'ABBÉ

1057 Regt

ST MARIE-DU-MONT

VIERVILLE

POUPPEVILLE

US 101 Abn Div

Douve

6 Para Regt

ST CÔME-DU-MONT

BRÉVANDS

Part 914 Regt

Lessay 9 miles

ST JORES

CARENTAN

ISIGNY

SAINTENY

Taute

ST JEAN DE DAYE

St Lô 2 miles

Vire

US First Army
(Bradley)

US VII Corps
(Collins)

US V Corps
(Gerow)

US 4 Inf Div

US 1 Inf Div

US 12 Regt

US 22 Regt

US 8 Regt

US 2 Ranger Bn

Pointe du Hoe

GRANDCAMPS LES BAINS

115 RCT   16 RCT
116 RCT   18 RCT

Pointe de la Percée

VIERVILLE SUR MER

ST LAURENT

COLLEVILLE

STE HONORI

FORMIGNY

916 Regt

Aure

N 13

COLOMBIÈRES

30 Regt

Part 914 Regt

352 Inf Div

BLAY

LXXXIV Corps

LITTRY-LA-MINE

Forêt de Cerisy

Drôme

BALLEROY

BÉRIGNY

Legend

🪂 PLANNED AIRBORNE DROPPING AND LANDING ZONES

Utah ASSAULT AREAS

→ FIRST ASSAULT WAVES

←-- ATTACKS BY BRITISH 6 AIRBORNE DIVISION

⬭ HELD BY ALLIES AT 2400 HRS ON D-DAY

••• ALLIED OBJECTIVE AT 2400 HRS ON D-DAY

RCT US REGIMENTAL COMBAT TEAM

709 Inf Div SITUATION OF GERMAN UNITS AT DAWN ON D-DAY

▨ HELD BY GERMAN TROOPS AT 2400 HRS ON D-DAY

▶ COUNTERATTACKS BY 21 PANZER DIVISION

⊪ MAJOR GERMAN GUN BATTERIES

≈ FLOODED AREAS (PRAIRIES MARÉCAGEUSES)

0   MILES   5   10

0   KILOMETRES   10   15

(US VII Corps) and Omaha beach (US V Corps): in the east the British Second Army attacked Gold beach (British XXX Corps) and Juno and Sword beaches (British I Corps). On Sword, Juno, and Gold the British and Canadian divisions, using specialized armour to overcome specific obstacles, met stiff resistance in some places, but in most were able to press on towards Caen. The Bayeaux via Creuilly road was captured, and a counterattack by 21 Panzer Division was repelled.

In the west Utah beach was quickly overrun, contact was made with the airborne forces and a depth of six miles was reached. Only on Omaha beach did things go seriously wrong. The regimental combat teams of the US V Corps, deprived of full amphibious tank support by the rough seas, remained pinned down on the beach by the fire of the German 352 Division. Not until nightfall were they able to fight their way forward to the coast road.

By 2400 hours on D-Day the Allies had not attained their predetermined objectives, but, with the exception of Omaha, all the landings had secured comfortable beachheads, and, with the artificial harbours in position the flow of supplies and reinforcements could easily be maintained.

Cap de la Hague

AUDERVILLE

30 June
End of German resistance in Cotentin Peninsula

27 June
US VII Corps takes Cherbourg

Cap Lévy

Pt de Barfleur

BEAUMONT

AM 30 June

CHERBOURG

ST PIERRE-EGLISE

BARFLEUR

ST CROIX

Forte du Roule

21 June

BRILLEVAST

QUETTEHOU

ST VAAST-LA-HOUGUE

BRIX

Douve

4 Div

LES PIEUX

15 June

VALOGNES

QUINEVILLE

709 Div

OZEVILLE

BRICQUEBEC

9 Div

CRISBECQ

MONTEBOURG

4 Div

AZEVILLE

79 Div

Merderet

90 Div

243 Div

82 Abn Div

STE MERE EGLISE

9 Div

CARTERET

BARNEVILLE-CARTERET

ST SAUVEUR

82 Abn Div

Utah

US VII Corps

91 Div

101 Abn Div

GRANDCA
LES BAINS

9 Div

PORTBAIL

90 Div

US VIII Corps

2 Armd Div

29 Div

79 Div

353 Div

US VII Corps
(from Cherbourg)

83 Div

CARENTAN
11 June

ISIGNY
8 June

LA HAYE DU PUITS

17 SS Pz Gr Div
6 Para Regt

30 Div

3 Armd Div

35 Div

79 Div

8 Div

90 Div

4 Armd
Div

83 Div

ST JEAN-DE-DAYE

1 Div

2 and 3
Armd
Divs

LESSAY

243 Div   **353 Div**

2 SS Div

Taute

91 Div

PERIERS

17 SS Pz Gr
Div

US VII Corps

9 Div

Vire

29 Div

35 Div

LXXXIV Corps

9 Div

4 Div

30 Div

35 Div

5 Para
Div

352 Div

Seventh Army
(Dollmann)

Pz Lehr

MARIGNY

352 Div

ST LÔ
18 July

COUTANCES

COND
SUR-V

Avranches 35 miles

II Para Corps

THE BATTLE OF THE BUILD-UP

Rundstedt and Rommel were hampered by three important factors in any attempt to 'kill' the Allied invasion on the beaches. Firstly the Allies held total command of the air. Secondly since the beginning of 1944 the Allied bomber offensive had been geared to destroying communications, particularly rail communications, in the north of France. In this it had been successful, and this, combined with the efforts of the Maquis, made movement for the German forces very difficult. Thirdly Hitler himself still insisted that the real invasion would fall across the Pas de Calais, and he interfered with and hindered Rommel's attempts to mobilize reserves.

Nonetheless the Allies' breakout from their beachheads was a painful process. In the west the first task of Bradley's US First Army was to sever the Contentin peninsula, and then to capture Cherbourg, the Allies' first hope of a proper harbour (see map). By 17 June the US 9 Division had reached Carteret and Portbail, and by 21 June Cherbourg was besieged by 9 Division, 79 Division, and 4 Division of VII Corps. After a brief but bitter siege Cherbourg fell on 27 June, but so thoroughly had the Germans wrecked the harbour that it was unusable until August. Turning south VII Corps,

joined by VIII Corps, struck at Dollmann's Seventh Army and, by 24 July, had captured St Lô. The Contentin peninsula was occupied.

From Omaha beach the US XIX and V Corps had broken out southwards on 10 June, and by 17 June had reached Caumont on the Caen-St Lô road. On 19/22 June the Channel was swept by gales which destroyed the artificial Mulberry harbour on Omaha beach and badly damaged that on Gold. This inevitably set back Allied plans by reducing the flow of reinforcements and supplies. (The storm destroyed nearly five times as many landing craft as German fire had done on D-Day.)

Throughout June the British Second Army made slow progress towards Caen. It was, admittedly, part of the Allied plan that the advance on Caen should draw off most of the German opposition, leaving the Allied right free to wheel round south and east, but opposition was fiercer than expected.

HELD BY ALLIES AT 2400 HRS ON D-DAY
FRONT LINE ON MORNING, 10 JUNE
FRONT LINE MIDNIGHT 17 JUNE
FRONT LINE MIDNIGHT 30 JUNE
FRONT LINE MIDNIGHT 24 JULY
2 Div   326 Div   SITUATION OF ALLIED AND GERMAN FRONT LINE DIVISIONS AT MIDNIGHT 24 JULY
GERMAN COUNTERATTACKS

FLOODED AREAS (PRAIRIES MARÉCAGEUSES)
XXXX   BOUNDARY BETWEEN US FIRST ARMY AND BRITISH SECOND ARMY
ALLIED CORPS BOUNDARY

MILES   0 — 10
KILOMETRES   0 — 15

THE BATTLE FOR NORMANDY

The close-set hedges of the Normandy bocage favoured the defence, and of this the Germans were quick to take advantage. After heavy bombing that hindered rather than helped the attackers, Allied troops reached the outskirts of Caen on 13 July.

Reinforcements had now reached Rommel from the south of France, and this enabled him to regroup his armour for a decisive blow at the Allied armies. It was essential for Montgomery to prevent this, and accordingly he mounted two operations, Epsom and Goodwood, as a preventive strike against Rommel's forces (see previous pages). The first was a costly failure,

but Operation Goodwood (**Map 3**) was pushed forward against strong opposition and had the effect of pinning down German units around Caen.

On the left of the Allied front the Canadian II Corps fought its way into Caen street by street, and by 18 July was occupying most of the town.

During the next two days the remainder of the town fell. The British I Corps, bypassing Caen in a great sweep as part of Operation Goodwood, was brought to a halt by the guns of the 1 and 12 SS Panzer Divisions. By the 20th Caen had fallen, and the Allied front extended some miles beyond the town.

On 26 February 1944, Twelfth

Army Group forecast the progress to be
expected as the result of landings on
the Normandy beaches (**Map 1**).
They expected to reach Brest by
D+50, and Paris by D+90. Actual
progress was rather more modest.
By D+50 (27 July) only the Contentin
peninsula and the Normandy coast
were in Allied hands.

By the end of July the Allied
strength ashore was nearly 1,000,000
men, 150,000 vehicles, and a million
tons of supplies. They had lost about
122,000 men, as against German losses
of 114,000 plus about 41,000 prisoners.

The British and Canadian attacks
on and around Caen had drawn away
so many of the German forces on the
Allied right that, by the end of July,
Bradley's US First Army was in a
position to break out through the
German defences west of St Lô. On 25
July, after a prolonged air bombardment of a new kind called 'carpet'
bombing, the US VII, VIII, and
XIX Corps attacked (**Map 2**). The
VII Corps poured through the gap
caused by the bombing and in spite of
strong opposition had reached
Avranches by 30 July. German
counterattacks, ordered by Hitler
personally, failed to check this move.

Above: Canadian troops near Caen
Below: The ruins of Caen after its occupation

THE ANVIL LANDINGS

In yielding to Stalin's demand for a second front the Allies allowed themselves to lose sight of the fact that they already had a second front in Italy. From the first a strong school of thought among the Allied planners favoured the reinforcing of the Italian campaign with all the troops and supplies earmarked for a second front. There can be no doubt that with the extra strength in men, guns, aircraft, and landing craft, the war in Italy would have been transformed. An advance on Vienna and beyond would have been quite possible, and the German forces in the west could have been left to wither on the vine without incurring the cost of attacking them. This was very much a British idea, born of memories of the 'might have been' of Gallipoli, and it cannot be denied that behind it was a desire not only to defeat Germany, but to prevent the Russian armies establishing themselves too far to the west. This political motive was certainly present, but militarily the plan made sense. A move northward from the Po would have imperilled all the German forces in the Balkans, and if executed swiftly, might even have cut them off. The German forces in Italy itself could have been surrounded and destroyed by twin enveloping amphibious movements 'up the leg' of Italy. Germany, finding herself attacked through Austria, would have been compelled to transfer the bulk of her strength from the west to oppose such a move.

The American planners were deeply suspicious of this idea. They saw it as an attempt by the imperialist powers to involve American lives in political schemes of doubtful military value. In this they were backed by President Roosevelt who was anxious to go out of his way to please Stalin. Stalin, not unnaturally, wanted the Anglo-American effort made as far to the west as possible. To the Italian venture, therefore, the Americans opposed an exploitation of Overlord supported by an invasion of southern France, Anvil

(**Map 1**). Except that logistically Overlord was comparatively easy to support from England, this scheme had little to recommend it. The greatest possible distance was interposed between the invaders and their final objective; the enemy was attacked at a point where he was comparatively strong; and the troops earmarked for Anvil were virtually wasted – a sufficiently threatening advance across the north of France would have compelled the withdrawal of any forces in the south without the necessity of a supporting operation.

Nonetheless the Anvil plan was adopted. How far political or military considerations shaped this decision is not known, but with the abandonment of the plan for a campaign over the Alps towards Vienna and the Danube, a great opportunity was lost.

At 0800 hours on 15 August 1944, the US Seventh Army under Lieutenant-General Patch made landings in the South of France between Toulon and Cannes (**Map 2**). These landings were supported by airborne forces. The landings' object was to free Marseilles for supply purposes and to secure Eisenhower's southern flank. Opposition was light (only 183 men were killed in the landings) and, by last light on the 15th, 94,000 men and 11,000 vehicles were ashore. Immediately the French II Corps (General De Lattre Tassigny) was passed through Patch's forces and took up the advance.

While De Lattre's forces and the US 3 and 45 Divisions made west for Toulon, a task force under Butler headed north to Gap and then west to Montelimar, closing the trap on the German Nineteenth Army (Wiese). Much of Wiese's army managed to escape but Butler's artillery and Allied aircraft took a terrible toll. 15,000 German prisoners were taken and some 4,000 vehicles. At the same time De Lattre had captured Toulon and Marseilles taking 47,717 prisoners.

After these successes Patch's task

was simple. On 29 August he started out on the trek north up the Rhône valley. Contact with Patton's Third Army was made on 12 September. Patch's Seventh Army and the newly-formed French First Army became the US 6 Army Group under Lieutenant-General Devers.

Above: Landing craft set out for the shore as the invasion of southern France begins

Opposite: Allied paratroops dropping as part of the Anvil assault

②

12 Sept Contact by
Fr 2 Armd Div (US Third Army)
and part Fr II Corps

CHÂTILLON-
SUR-SEINE

Remnants of German First Army
retreat from south-west France

BELFORT

Seine

DIJON

BESANÇON
7 Sept

AUTUN

US
Seventh
Army

Saône

CHALON-
SUR-SAONE

PONTARLIER

BERNE

Route 6

SWITZERLAND

MÂCON

Lake Geneva

11 Pz
Div

BOURG
3 Sept

GENEVA

Fr II Corps

ANNECY

A
L
P
S

LYONS
3 Sept

CHAMBÉRY

F R A N C E

GRENOBLE
24 Aug

ITALY

US 36 Div

BRIANÇON

Butler
Task Force

Rhône

MONTÉLIMAR

GAP

11 Pz Div

Nineteenth Army
(Wiese)

DIGNE

Durance

Route Napoléon

0700 hrs, 15 August
US 1 Prov Abn Div drops.
Links up with US 36 Div later

AVIGNON

US 45 Div

US 3 Div

NICE

To
Sète

AIX

ORAGUIGNAN

Fr 1
Armd Div

LE MUY

CANNES

FRÉJUS

AUBAGNE

SAGAY

MARSEILLES
28 Aug

3 Alg Div

ST MAXIME

ST
RAPHAËL

Fr 9 Col Div

HYÈRES

ST TROPEZ

TOULON
28 Aug

1 Free
Fr Div

CAVALAIRE

LEVANT I

MEDITERRANEAN
SEA

PORT
CROS I

16 Aug
Fr II Corps (de Lattre)
passes through
US VI Corps

French Commandos

US 3 Div

US 45 Div

US 36 Div

French Commandos

US VI Corps
(Truscott)

FRONT LINE 28 AUGUST 1944
GERMAN COUNTER ATTACKS
LAND OVER 6000 FEET

'ANVIL' ('Dragoon')
0800 hrs, 15 Aug 1944
US Seventh Army (Patch)

0   MILES   60
0   KILOMETRES   100

237

THE BREAKOUT

After Bradley's advance on Avranches the Allied forces were reorganized. The US 12 Army Group was formed under Bradley comprising the US First Army (Hodges) and as from 1 August the US Third Army (Patton). The British forces became the British 21 Army Group under Montgomery, comprising the British Second Army (Dempsey) and the Canadian First Army (Crerar). Montgomery remained in overall command of Eisenhower's land forces until September.

On 1 August, Patton's Third Army poured through the Avranches gap. His armour overran Brittany (see inset) and swept south towards the Loire (**Map 1**). His infantry made for Le Mans. At the same time the US First, the British Second, and the Canadian First armies attacked south and east driving the German opposition before them. By 16 August the British and American forces in the north, and Patton's forces from the south had squeezed the German forces into a salient between Falaise and Argentan (**Map 2**). Through this gap the disorganized German Seventh and Fifth Panzer armies were escaping. Hitler's insistence on last-minute counterattacks had left these troops in a vulnerable position, and only some dilatoriness by the Allies allowed them to escape. As it was, by the time the pocket was closed by Canadian II Corps and US V Corps, some 50,000 Germans were captured and some 10,000 lay dead.

Kluge, who had replaced Rommel in July after Rommel had been wounded by Allied aircraft, was now in full retreat, with four Allied armies on his tail, making for the safety of the Seine crossings. Patton's armour reached the Seine at Fontainbleau on the same day that the Falaise gap was closed, and the US XV Corps established a bridgehead downstream of Paris. On the 25th the city was liberated. Kluge's reward for salvaging a remarkable proportion of Army Group B was to be replaced by Model.

The Allied breakout from Normandy was a remarkable military operation. It decisively defeated the German forces in Western Europe and should have opened the door for a pursuit to Berlin.

Above: American forces are greeted as they drive through a Normandy village

Below: Canadian artillery moves up to the front as the drive on Paris begins

GERMAN FRONT AT MIDNIGHT 16 AUGUST
GERMAN FRONT AT MIDNIGHT 19 AUGUST
ALLIED ATTACKS 17/20 AUGUST
GERMAN WITHDRAWAL ON NIGHT 19/20 AUGUST

THE DRIVE TO THE RHINE

Standing on the Seine, the German forces defeated and disordered, the problem that faced the Allies in late August 1944 was one of pursuit. Again the Allied commanders found themselves split, but this time it was not a simple split along lines of nationality. A straight pursuit by all four Allied armies was impossible. The supply demands would be far too great, and already the petrol situation was critical. But a strong thrust by a part of the Allied armies, through Belgium, encircling the Ruhr and on to Berlin might yield enormous benefits. Both Montgomery and Bradley favoured this plan, although neither was prepared to be subordinate to the other. Eisenhower, on the other hand, favoured a slow advance in line by all his forces. To a certain extent he was motivated by the need to keep the peace between his extremely fractious subordinates, but he also had military reasons for disliking the 'single strong thrust' plan. The German forces opposing him, although defeated, were still partially intact. Their chain of command remained, and their standards of morale and leadership were high. They were far from out of the game. Eisenhower feared that a deep thrust into Germany would expose flanks very vulnerable to attack by forces of this kind. A pencil-like thrust, as he described it, would stand too great a risk of being bitten off.

The maps (**1 and 2**) show the alternatives. It is easy with hindsight to accuse Eisenhower of being over-cautious. The Allied command of the air, and their enormous predominance on the ground, almost certainly outweighed the risks of the narrow front plan – a plan which held out the prospect of ending the war in 1944 with the Red Army still east of the Oder.

Broad front or narrow front, the Allies' most pressing need in August 1944 was a port. The 300-mile logistical haul from Normandy was stretched almost to breaking point. Over the Seine the Allies advanced rapidly (**Map 3**). By 4 September Brussels and Antwerp had fallen, and by the 15th the whole of Belgium and Luxembourg had been cleared. However this lightning advance by British Second Army was performed at the cost of the US First and Third Armies who found themselves short of petrol.

On 3 September Eisenhower assumed direct command of ground operations. Hitler recalled Rundstedt to command in the west two days later.

Although the Germans had been cleared from Antwerp they still commanded the Scheldt estuary. Also some time had to be devoted to clearing the Channel ports and eliminating the missile sites in the Pas de Calais area. These tasks were both discharged by the Canadian First Army by the end of September.

In spite of these checks, by 15 September the Allies stood on the borders of Germany. Since their landings in June they had put more than 2,000,000 men on French soil, and they had lost some 40,000 dead. German losses had been catastrophic – 500,000 from the field forces, and a further 200,000 from the coastal fortresses.

Left: Allied units arrive in Eindhoven

Opposite: US engineers bridging the Seine

240

FRONT LINE 25 AUGUST 1944
ALLIED SEINE BRIDGEHEADS
FRONT LINE 3 SEPTEMBER
FRONT LINE 15 SEPTEMBER
XXXXX ARMY GROUP BOUNDARY

MILES 0 _____ 80
KILOMETRES 0 _____ 140

NORTH SEA

GREAT BRITAIN

ENGLISH CHANNEL

DOVER
BRIGHTON

ROTTERDAM
Waal
NETHERLANDS
First Para Army
(Student)
Fifteenth Army
(Zangen)
GRAVE
NIJMEGEN
Maas
BREDA
EINDHOVEN
Walcheren
FLUSHING
ZEEBRUGGE
OSTEND
Meuse-Escaut Can
DUISBURG
ESSEN
DORTMUND
KREFELD
RUHR
DÜSSELDORF
DUNKIRK
CALAIS 30 Sept
GHENT
ANTWERP 4 Sept
GHEEL
Albert Can
HASSELT
MAASTRICHT
AACHEN
COLOGNE
BOULOGNE 22 Sept
Escaut
BRUSSELS 3 Sept
BELGIUM
LIÈGE
Army Group 'B' (Model)
Fifteenth Army (Salmuth)
LILLE
TOURNAI
NAMUR
Meuse
GERMANY
ARRAS
MONS
CHARLEROI
Sambre
Ardennes
BASTOGNE
PRÜM
Seventh Army (Brandenberger)
KOBLENZ
ABBEVILLE
Somme
CAMBRAI
US V Corps
Moselle
MAINZ
DIEPPE 1 Sept
ST VALERY
AMIENS
ST QUENTIN
Fifth Pz Army (Dietrich)
SEDAN
Meuse
LUX
LUXEMBOURG
TRIER
Army Group 'G' (Blaskowitz)
Br I Corps
Cdn II Corps
Br XII Corps
Br XXX Corps
RETHEL
Siegfried Line (West Wall)
LUDWIGSHAFEN
LE HAVRE 12 Sept
ROUEN
BEAUVAIS
COMPIÈGNE
SOISSON
Aisne
REIMS
THIONVILLE
VERDUN
SAARBRÜCKEN
Rhine
CAEN
Seine
LOUVIERS
VERNON
US XIX Corps
Oise
CHATEAU-THIERRY
Marne
CHÂLONS
METZ
SAAR
Cdn First Army (Crerar)
PARIS 25 Aug
US V Corps
EPERNAY
First Army (Knobelsdorff)
STRASBOURG
ARGENTAN
Br Second Army (Dempsey)
DREUX
MELUN
US XX Corps
US VII Corps
COMMERCY ST DIZIER
NANCY
21 Army Group (Montgomery)
US First Army (Hodges)
CHARTRES
Seine
NEUFCHÂTEAU
Fifth Pz Army (Manteuffel)
12 Army Group (Bradley)
FONTAINEBLEAU
US XII Corps
TROYES
US XV Corps
ÉPINAL
COLMAR
US Third Army (Patton)
CHAUMONT

THE ARNHEM OPERATION

After the liberation of Belgium, the 21 Army Group was faced by the complex of rivers and estuaries where the Rhine and the Meuse empty into the North Sea. To secure a continuous northward advance, Montgomery planned to drop three airborne divisions to capture the bridges at Veghel, Grave, Nijmegen, and Arnhem, creating an airborne corridor for Second Army, led by XXX Corps, to advance along. Planned for 17 September, the operation consisted of a landing by the US 101 Airborne Division at Veghel (**Map 1**), a landing by the US 82 Airborne Division at Grave, and a landing by the British 1

Airborne Division supported later by the Polish parachute brigade at Arnhem. The intention was to co-ordinate the advance of XXX Corps with these drops to achieve maximum surprise and dislocation.

The landings of 101 and 82 Divisions were successful and XXX Corps linked up with the airborne forces on schedule on the 18th. On the 20th the Nijmegen bridge fell to a combined attack by XXX Corps and 82 Division, but they could get no farther. The British 1 Airborne Division had encountered powerful opposition. Only one battalion got through to the bridge, and was instantly cut off. The remainder of the force was surrounded, but held out until the 26th. 2,200 survivors managed to escape, but 7,000 were left behind to be killed, wounded, or captured.

Many factors contributed to the British disaster at Arnhem. The major one was the readiness and flexibility of the German defence, but it must also be mentioned that the British airborne forces' doctrine of landing some distance from the objective was a risky one that threw away the surprise and shock that are the essence of airborne operations.

Before Antwerp could be of use to the Allies, the German forces in the Scheldt estuary had to be cleared (**Map 2**).

The Canadian First and British Second armies undertook this, and by 8 November the area was clear. Minor line mending took place around Venlo on the German border, and by the US First Army around Aachen. Bradley's 12 Army Group was enlarged by the arrival of the US Ninth Army (Simpson), and, to the south, Devers' 6 Army Group pushed through the Vosges mountains to the German border. By 15 December the Allies were poised for their next obvious objective – the crossing of the Rhine.

But German resistance west of the Rhine could be expected to be strong. Rundstedt's command, OB West, comprised Army Group H (Student), Army Group B (Model), Army Group G (Balck), and Army Group Oberrhein (Himmler). The broad front policy had given the Germans a breathing space, and they had used it to reorganize their defences.

Below: Allied paratroops dropping on Arnhem

OPERATION 'MARKET GARDEN ①

17 Sept 1944
Strong German forces block routes to bridge. PM, 2 Bn captures bridge but is cut off. Remnants of division withdraw across river to British lines on 25 Sept

20 Sept
Nijmegen bridge captured in joint attack by US paratroops and Br XXX Corps

PM 17 Sept
Bridge captured. Br XXX Corps links up with paratroops at 0820 19 Sept

17 Sept
All bridges captured. Br XXX Corps links up with paratroops PM 18 Sept

N

○ ALLIED AIRBORNE LANDINGS AT MID DAY 17 SEPT 1944

◀ MAIN GERMAN COUNTERATTACKS

0 — MILES — 10
0 — KM — 15

Above: German troops counterattack the British landings

②

NETHERLANDS
■ THE HAGUE
ROTTERDAM

Fifteenth Army (Zangen)
ARNHEM

Army Group 'H' (Student)

WALCHEREN

Neder Rijn
Waal
Maas GRAVE
NIJMEGEN
Reichs-wald
WESEL

Schelde

EINDHOVEN
VENLO
DUISBURG
KREFELD
The Ruhr
DÜSSELDORF

First Para Army (Schlemm)

Cdn First Army (Crerar)

Meuse-Escaut Can.
ROERMOND
XXXXX

ANTWERP NEERPELT
Albert Can.
Roer

Br Second Army (Dempsey)

GEILENKIRCHEN
COLOGNE

Army Group 'B' (Model)

21 Army Group (Montgomery)
■ BRUSSELS
MAASTRICHT

AACHEN
HÜRTGEN
Dams
BONN
REMAGEN
GERMANY

LIÈGE

Sixth SS Pz Army (Dietrich)

BELGIUM

NAMUR

US First Army (Hodges)

Fifth Pz Army (Manteuffel)

KOBLENZ

Ardennes

FRANKFURT
MAINZ

US Ninth Army (Simpson)

Seventh Army (Brandenberger)

Moselle
Rhine

Army Group 'G' (Balck)

LUX
■ LUXEMBOURG
TRIER

MANNHEIM

12 Army Group (Bradley)

Meuse

First Army (Knobelsdorff)

Saar

VERDUN
METZ
● SAARBRÜCKEN

KARLSRUHE

FRANCE

US Third Army (Patton)

XXXXX

NANCY

Moselle

STRASBOURG

Army Group Oberrhein (Himmler)

FRONT LINE 15 SEPTEMBER 1944
FRONT LINE 8 NOVEMBER
FRONT LINE 15 DECEMBER
ALLIED ATTACKS
ALLIED AIRBORNE LANDINGS
-XXXXX- ARMY GROUP BOUNDARY

0 MILES 80
0 KILOMETRES 120

US Seventh Army (Patch)

COLMAR

Nineteenth Army (Wiese)

6 Army Group (Devers)

MULHOUSE
BELFORT

Fr First Army (de Lattre)

SWITZ.

THE BATTLE OF THE ARDENNES

Poised for their attack toward the Rhine the Allies had entirely dismissed the possibility of a German offensive against them. Hitler, on the other hand, had determined to attack the Allies before they reached Germany. His plan (**Map 1**) was to break through the Allied front in the Ardennes, split the Americans from the British, and capture Antwerp, disrupting Allied supplies and destroying their armies piecemeal.

For this offensive Hitler had scraped together what was in effect his last remaining strategic reserve – twenty-four divisions, ten of them armoured deployed in the Sixth SS Panzer, Fifth Panzer, and Seventh Armies.

The offensive was daring and imaginative and came very close to success. One vital factor that the Germans lacked was air cover, and they were lucky that their offensive was covered by low cloud and heavy snowfall. On 16 December, eight Panzer divisions fell upon the US VIII Corps (**Map 2**). Tactical and strategic surprise was complete, and confusion was made worse confounded by the presence of English-speaking German soldiers in Allied uniforms behind the US lines. So great was the German success that Eisenhower was compelled to commit his reserves, the airborne divisions still resting after Market Garden. One of these, the US 101 Airborne Division, arrived in Bastogne just in time to be trapped by 15 Panzer Grenadier Division. By 20 December, Bastogne was encircled and the German forces stood ready to make for the Meuse.

But by 20 December the Allies were beginning to recover from their surprise. Eisenhower transferred command of all troops north of the 'bulge' to Montgomery, leaving only Patton's army under Bradley to the south. Despite the desperate defence of St Vith by the US 7 Armoured Division it fell on the 22nd, but the delay had been fatal to German plans. The 24th saw the high water mark of the German offensive. With empty fuel tanks and against stiffening opposition, the Ardennes offensive ground to a halt.

The Allies now proceeded to squeeze out the bulge. From the north Hodges' US First Army, and from the south Patton's Third Army closed in on the German salient (**Map 3**). The battle for Bastogne saw the last major effort by the Luftwaffe, with some 800 planes attacking airfields in France, Belgium, and Holland. It had no effect on the air offensive being conducted over the Ardennes in support of the ground forces. By 7 February the salient had been eliminated. Hitler's gamble had failed, due to the German's inability to overrun the Allied fuel dumps and thus replenish their tanks. The result was a delay of six weeks in the Allies' operations, and the loss of the only German forces that might have checked the coming Russian spring offensive.

Left: German troops pass a disabled US half-track

CROSSING THE RHINE

Above: US artillery shelling German positions across the Rhine

The tactical importance of the Rhine in 1945 was great enough, but this was enhanced by its symbolic importance. To both the Allies and the Germans it was the 'frontier' behind which lay the German heartland. The Allies could therefore expect the Germans to defend the Rhine, the most formidable water obstacle in Western Europe, with the utmost tenacity.

In early 1945 the flanks of the Allied armies had reached the Rhine in the north (Nijmegen) and in the south (Strasbourg). In the centre, however, the Ardennes offensive and the Siegfried Line had held back the Allied advance, and it was not until March that the Allies reached the Rhine along its whole length.

As the Allies approached the Rhine the hope grew that it might be possible to 'jump' a bridge intact but, even if this were to happen, there was no assurance that it would be in a vital or even useful quarter. All units, therefore, had to face the possibility of an opposed crossing of this wide, fast-flowing river. In the north, where Montgomery's 21 Army Group faced the widest stretch of the river, the defence could be expected to be at its hottest to deny the Allies access to the Ruhr and to the north German plain. In the south, however, where Devers' US 6 Army Group approached the Rhine between Strasbourg and Mannheim, the river, although narrower, was tricky and fast flowing. Also the Germans were able to control its flow by regulating dams on the east bank feeder rivers.

Then, on 7 March, the hoped-for happened. Speeding towards the Rhine, men of Hodge's US First Army captured intact the bridge at Remagen. Showing great flexibility and speed the Americans instantly exploited this opportunity, and by the evening of the 7th a substantial bridgehead had been established.

Useful though this was, however, it was not a decisive gain. The Remagen bridgehead could not be exploited alone. More substantial crossings were needed both up and down stream.

It was not until 22 March that a further crossing was made. On that day the US Third Army pushed its 5 Division across at Nierstein. On the following day after massive preparation British 51 (Highland) Division and Canadian 3 Division crossed near Rees and Emmerich. On the same day the US 9 Division crossed near Rheinberg.

These crossings were followed on 24/25 March by US 87 Division's successful storming of the river at St Goar. On the same day US 4 Armoured Division reached Darmstadt, and British and US airborne forces landed east of the Rhine and joined up with the advancing ground forces. On 26 March the US Seventh Army crossed near Worms and linked up with Patton's Third Army on the east bank. Finally on 27 March 80 Division of Third Army forced a crossing near Mainz and captured Wiesbaden.

The Allies had now cleared the Rhine from Nijmegen to Mannheim. From 31 March onwards the French First Army began to force crossings south of Mannheim, and by the first week in April the Germans had lost all their footholds on the east bank of the Rhine.

THE DRIVE INTO GERMANY

The Allied advance from the Rhine to link up with the Russian forces on the Elbe was marked in a few places by bitter opposition, but for the most part fighting was sporadic and isolated (map on right). Where a German officer of particularly determined character commanded seasoned troops,

a well organized and spirited defence could be expected. Most German units, however, leaderless, lacking air cover, often short of rations and ammunition, were only too thankful that they were facing the Americans and British and not the Russians, and they surrendered in increasing numbers. Town after town greeted the Allies with white flags. Communication and command in the German armies had broken down, and no airy talk by Hitler of a 'national redoubt' in the mountains could disguise this fact.

There is no doubt that during April the Allies could have reached both Berlin and Prague before the Russians, but, in keeping with undertakings made to the Russians, Eisenhower announced that the Allied advance would halt on the Elbe. Also, as the advance through Germany uncovered Belsen, Buchenwald, and other camps, the British and American attitudes to the Germans hardened.

By 7 May the 21st Army Group had cleared Holland and north Germany up to the Elbe and the Danish border; the 12th Army Group had cleared central Germany south of the Ruhr; and the 6th Army Group had driven through Bavaria and penetrated Austria. Small German pockets were left in the Ruhr itself, the Hartz Mountains, and on the north coast.

On 4 May General Montgomery accepted unconditional surrender of Admiral Dönitz's plenipotentiaries at Lüneberg Heath. On 7 May 1945 the war in Europe formally came to an end. There now remained the problems of what to do with Germany and what to do with the many thousands of Nazis, great and small. It was decided to divide Germany, and Berlin which fell deep within the Soviet area, into four zones each under one of the four major allies (**Maps 1 and 2**).

Below: US troops march through a devastated German town

DENMARK

BALTIC SEA

NORTH SEA

FLENSBURG

RÜGEN

KIEL

ROSTOCK

Kiel Canal

LÜBECK   WISMAR

7 May   SCHWERIN

WILHELMSHAVEN   HAMBURG
3 May

EMDEN   BREMERHAVEN

STETTIN

NEUSTRELITZ

GRONINGEN   OLDENBURG   18 Apr

BREMEN
26 Apr   Lüneberg   DANNENBERG   DÖMITZ

STARGARD

Weser   Belsen   ÜLZEN   WITTENBERG

Heath   TANGERMÜNDE

AMSTERDAM   Army Group 'H'
(Blaskowitz)   HANNOVER
10 Apr   US Ninth Army   BERLIN

NETHERLANDS   OSNABRÜCK   BRUNSWICK   POTSDAM   KUSTRIN

Twenty-fifth Army   MINDEN   4 Apr   MAGDEBURG   Twelfth Army   FRANKFURT

ARNHEM   Teutoburger Wald   HAMELN   G   E   R   M   A   N   Y
MÜNSTER   BARBY   ROSSLAU

First Para Army   Eleventh Army   BLANKENBURG   DESSAU

Cdn First Army
(Crerar)   WESEL   PADERBORN   Harz Mts   Brocken Pk   24 Apr   COTTBUS

Br Second Army
(Dempsey)   HAMM   LIPPSTADT   US First Army   Neisse

US Ninth Army
(Simpson)   ESSEN   DORTMUND   KASSEL   GÖTTINGEN   NORDHAUSEN   HALLE

21 Army Group
(Montgomery)   DUISBURG   BOCHUM   Ruhr   Sauerland   4 Apr   MERSEBERG   LEIPZIG

WUPPERTAL   GÖRLITZ

DÜSSELDORF   Fifteenth Army   Army Group 'B'
(Model)   Buchenwald   WEISSENFELS

COLOGNE   Fifth Pz Army   GOTHA   ERFURT   WEIMAR   ZEITZ   COLDITZ   DRESDEN

LIÈGE   BONN   JENA   USTÍ

BELGIUM   REMAGEN   Sieg   MARBURG   OHRDRUF   CHEMNITZ

Rhine   Lahn   GIESSEN   US Third Army   Mulde

KOBLENZ   FULDA 2 Apr   Thüringian Forest   Erzgebirge   KARLOVY VARY

12 Army Group
(Bradley)   Seventh Army   Seventh Army   PRAGUE

WIESBADEN   BAD ORB   HOF

LUX   Main   FRANKFURT   HANAU   HAMMELBURG   SCHWEINFURT   BAYREUTH   CZECHOSLOVAKIA

UXEMBOURG   TRIER   MAINZ   US Third Army
(Patton)   ASCHAFFEN-   WÜRZBURG   BAMBERG   PILSEN

OPPENHEIM   BURG   Spessart Mts   Odenwald   KITZINGEN 5 Apr

THIONVILLE   WORMS   US Seventh Army   4 Apr   NÜREMBERG   Bohemian Forest

(Patch)   MANNHEIM   Army Group 'G'
(Hausser)   FÜRTH   20 Apr   Vltava

SAARBRÜCKEN   Neckar   ANSBACH   18 Apr   CESKÉ
BUDEJOVICE   7 May

6 Army Group
(Devers)   First Army   HEILBRONN   Franconian Jura   REGENSBURG 26 Apr   Danube

KARLSRUHE   4 Apr   Löwenstein
Hills   US Seventh
Army   PASSAU

NANCY   8 Apr   PFORZHEIM   STUTTGART   ANSBACH   INGOLSTADT   Isar   LANDAU

Fr First Army
(de Lattre de Tassigny)   ESSLINGEN   KIRCHHEIM   DONAUWÖRTH   LANDSHUT
30 Apr

STRASBOURG   TÜBINGEN   DILLINGEN   AUGSBURG   Inn   LINZ
5 May

F   R   A   N   C   E   Swabian   Highlands   ULM 23 Apr   Dachau   BRAUNAU

COLMAR   Nineteenth
Army   EHINGEN   LANDSBERG   MUNICH
30 Apr   US Third Army

SIGMARINGEN   ROSENHEIM   SALZBURG
4 May

FREIBURG   Fr First Army   MEMMINGEN   US Seventh Army   BERCHTESGADEN
4 May

Schwarzwald   Lake
Constance   OBERAMMERGAU   KUFSTEIN   Enns

BASLE   FÜSSEN   GARMISCH-
PARTENKIRCHEN   KITZBÜHEL

BREGENZ   Oberjoch
Pass   INNSBRUCK   A   U   S   T   R   I   A   TAMSWEG

SWITZERLAND   Aarlberg
Pass   Fern
Pass   T   y   r   o   l
IMST   4 May

LANDECK   Brenner
Pass

A   L   P   S   KLAGENFURT

Resia
Pass   BOLZANO   I   T   A   L   Y   YUGOSLAVIA

US Fifth Army

OCCUPIED BY ALLIED FORCES, 28 MARCH 1945
BRITISH ATTACKS
US ATTACKS
FRENCH ATTACKS
GERMAN POCKETS
OCCUPIED BY RUSSIAN FORCES, 16 APRIL
CONCENTRATION CAMPS

0   MILES   120
0   KILOMETRES   200

THE
NAVAL
WAR

Opposite: Depth-charges being dropped
by a British escort vessel in the Atlantic

On land or in the air the Germans were formidable opponents. This was abundantly clear after the Polish campaign of 1939. Only at sea did the French and British allies enjoy the advantage. In the First World War unrestricted submarine warfare had wrought terrible havoc amongst the Allied merchant shipping in the Atlantic. In the Second the Germans lost no time in embarking upon a similar policy, indeed every U-boat fit for sea had been sent out before war was declared. But though they did a good deal of damage, and by March 1940 had sunk 222 ships totalling 764,766 tons, the Germans did not in fact have very many submarines when the war began, and during the first few months they lost eighteen, about one-third of their total. During that time only eleven new ones were commissioned. Later in the war Hitler gave a higher priority to their construction, and at one time or another they had 1,162 U-boats in service. Of these 785 were destroyed, 500 of them by British ships or aircraft.

The Germans were perhaps fortunate in that their High Seas Fleet had been scuttled in Scapa Flow at the end of the First World War. In consequence all their ships were of modern design, whereas the British, with their magnificent personnel, were handicapped by a lot of old iron. Of Britain's fifteen capital ships thirteen had been built before 1918. The ten *Queen Elizabeth* and R class battleships had all been designed before 1914. Not only were many of the British warships obsolescent they were by no means as numerous as could have been desired. The Norwegian campaign of 1940 highlighted this weakness, the legacy of a series of parsimonious governments. There was soon a serious shortage of destroyers.

A very serious weakness in the Royal Navy was the lack of aircraft-carriers and of modern aircraft. Off Norway, Crete, and Malaya the Royal Navy was to pay heavily for its neglect of the air arm. Naval officers were slow to realize that war is waged in three dimensions.

During the campaign in Norway the German surface fleet suffered very serious losses, so much so that it may be doubted whether Operation Sealion, the invasion of Britain was ever really a practical possibility. But with the fall of France the powerful and efficient French navy was lost to the Allies, and the entry of Italy into the war added to the Admiralty's problems. It was fortunate indeed that there were admirals of the calibre of Sir Andrew Cunningham, Sir Bertram Ramsey, and Sir James Somerville to weather the storms of those fateful days.

The British had expected the war to develop on much the same lines as that of 1914–18. An expeditionary force would be built up in France and the tasks of the Royal Navy, besides destroying the German fleet if it would come out and fight, would be to escort convoys of soldiers crossing the channel or supplies crossing the Atlantic. With the fall of France all this was changed. The Blue Water school had to face the fact that raids, landings and invasions were now inevitable. The idea was not popular in the Royal Navy. All the same British history was studded with combined operations – Gibraltar, Quebec, Aboukir Bay, the Dardanelles to name but a few. Amphibious warfare calls for special equipment and special techniques. At the outbreak of war the Royal Navy did have two landing craft, each capable of lifting a platoon. These were both lost in Norway, and it was not until late in 1940 that assault landing craft, carried by converted cross-channel steamers, came into service in any numbers.

Amphibious warfare makes special demands on planners and staff officers alike, for it has its own peculiar problems: where and when to land; naval gunfire support; the organization of ship to shore movement and so on. Techniques which had been mastered in the 18th century had been forgotten by the time of Gallipoli. The lessons of Suvla, Zeebrugge, and Ostend were by no means fresh in the memories of the senior officers of 1940. The achievement of Combined Operations Headquarters was not only in the sphere of planning but of training. To those who appreciate the complete neglect of preparation for amphibious warfare it is remarkable indeed that the defeats of 1940 should have been followed so soon by the landings in North Africa, Sicily, Italy, and Normandy.

As the war developed and one operation followed another the eyes of the public were constantly being focused on new problems, new crises. Dunkirk, the Battle of Britain, the various raids and landings: so far as the Admiralty was concerned there was always one deadly battle going on whose loss must mean defeat: the Battle of the Atlantic. In this long drawn out struggle each side in turn strove to work out new tactics. In 1939 Grand-Admiral Dönitz had published a book in which he forecast the tactics of the 'wolf-pack': German submarines would operate by night on the surface, in much the same fashion as torpedo-boats. The Admiralty does not appear to have given this book the attention it deserved. At first the British, instead of using the maximum number of vessels as escorts, spent a great deal of energy in hunting for U-boats in the open ocean. Few of the escorts had radar, and few had the speed to catch a submarine on the surface. Asdic which had now been introduced was designed to detect submerged submarines.

By mid 1941 escorts were becoming stronger and this compelled the U-boats

Above left: The British destroyer H M S *Eskimo* during a raid on the Norwegian coast

Above right: A U-boat in stormy seas

Opposite left: H M S *Furious* at speed in the Mediterranean

Opposite right: Sailors examine the hulk of the *Tirpitz* after she had been sunk by British bombers to attack in force. In June 1941 ten U-boats attacked south of Iceland. The Admiralty riposted by sending the escorts of two others to the relief of convoy HX 133. A protracted battle followed in which the Germans lost two submarines and the Allies five merchantmen. This action led to the evolution of 'support groups' a distinct tactical advance.

The invasion of Russia by drawing off German bombers to the eastern front led to a drop in the sinkings for July and August. American co-operation – even before Pearl Harbor – the build-up of Coastal Command, and the departure of U-boats to the Mediterranean, all conspired to reduce losses during the last quarter of 1941.

Another significant tactical advance was the introduction in December of the escort carrier, helping to close the 'air gap' in the Central Atlantic, which was out of range of land-based air cover.

The invasion of Russia had brought some easing of the pressure in the Battle of the Atlantic. The entry of Japan into the war was a grave setback. The Americans were now compelled to send numbers of their best warships to the Pacific. During the first four months of 1942 American losses on the east coast of the USA were very heavy, and included many tankers, in the period before they adopted the convoy system. 1942 was the worst year of the battle. U-boats accounted for 1,160 of the 1,664 Allied ships sunk – a total of 7,790,697 tons. But by the autumn the Allies navies had once more gained the upper hand, driving the U-boats southward to the Caribbean and the Gulf of Mexico and extending the 'Interlocking Convoy System'. British and Canadian escorts, now numbering some 450, were still too few for their tasks at a time when Dönitz had some 400 U-boats at his command. Despite the demands of Bomber Command, Coastal Command was gradually being given the long-range aircraft it needed to make its rôle decisive.

The climax of the Battle of the

Atlantic came in May 1943 when sinkings fell to fifty and cost the Germans, in all theatres, forty-one U-boats. Dönitz was compelled to withdraw his submarines from the North Atlantic. But the Germans were still producing forty U-boats a month including new types with a higher underwater speed. The introduction of the 'schnorkel' breathing-tube allowed them to recharge their batteries whilst submerged, thus helping to prevent their detection by radar.

June 1943 was a bad month for the Germans who lost seventeen U-boats without a single attack being made upon a North Atlantic convoy. Dönitz continued to probe far afield, and by using U-tankers or 'milch-cows' to support his submarines managed to cause casualties in the Indian Ocean and off the Brazilian coast.

Heavy German casualties between June and August, seventy-four U-boats sunk, were largely inflicted by Allied aircraft. In return the Germans managed to sink fifty-eight ships. Only in the Indian Ocean were they still scoring without unacceptable losses to themselves. There the demands of the Sicily and Italy landings had deprived the Eastern Fleet of sufficient escorts. In the autumn Dönitz tried to regain control in the North Atlantic, but despite some German success the Allies now had his measure.

Captain E. J. Walker (2 Escort Group) had devised tactics which are described by Captain S. W. Roskill, the Official Historian of the Royal Navy: 'His method was to station a "directing ship" astern of the enemy to hold Asdic contact, while two others, not using their asdics crept up on either side, to release a barrage of depth charges by signal from the directing ship at the critical moment. The U-boat thus never knew when the depth charges were released, and could not take avoiding action while they were descending.'

In October 1943 the Allies made an agreement with Portugal by which they

were enabled to set up naval and air bases in the Azores. At a time when long-range aircraft were proving their value as escorts this helped to tighten their grip on the battle. Already losses had fallen to a most gratifying extent. In September and October of 2,468 merchant ships crossing the Atlantic only nine were lost. In early 1944 matters improved still further: between January and March 3,360 ships crossed for the loss of three, whilst their escorts disposed of twenty-nine submarines.

Later in the year a kind of stalemate developed, for whilst the U-boats were not scoring heavily, and no longer operated on the surface in 'wolf-packs', their numbers were still rising, and continued to do so until in March 1945 they had 463. The Allied escorts found it extremely difficult to find the schnorkelling submarines. One (U-1199) remained submerged for fifty days!

By the end of the war Bomber Command had dropped such numbers of mines in the Western Baltic that the Germans were doing their training in Oslo Fjörd. When at last the Germans surrendered they still had 377 submarines: 221 were scuttled by their crews. In all the German U-boats had sunk 2,828 Allied or neutral ships of 14,687,231 tons. The British merchant navy, which in 1939 had comprised 9,488 vessels, totalling 21,215,261 tons, sustained losses amounting to 11,500,000 tons. During the war the Royal Navy lost 51,578 men, and the merchant navy 30,248. Of these the great majority lost their lives through U-boat action. The Germans for their part lost practically all their merchant navy to the Royal Navy and the RAF. Nor did many of their surface ships survive. The cruisers *Prinz Eugen* and *Nürnberg* were still fit for sea. *Hipper* and *Seydlitz* were scuttled. Bombing had accounted for *Emden*, *Köln*, *Lützow* and *Scheer*. The damaged *Leipzig* fell into the hands of the Royal Navy whilst the Russians captured the wrecked *Gneisenau* at Stettin, and the incomplete *Graf Zeppelin* at Gdynia.

THE BATTLE OF THE RIVER PLATE

Admiral Erich Raeder, commander-in-chief of the German navy, had decided to send the first of his commerce raiders, the pocket battleships *Deutschland* and *Admiral Graf Spee*, together with their supply ships *Westerwald* and *Altmark*, to their operational areas before the beginning of hostilities. *Graf Spee* sailed from Wilhelmshaven on 21 August 1939 and reached her waiting area in mid-Atlantic undetected, there to await the order to commence her mission. Though this was ostensibly commerce raiding, it was in fact more than this. Commerce raiding was only the secondary mission, the first being to post a threat to Allied sea communications, and thus dislocate Allied naval efforts against Germany by causing hunting groups to be set up at all points where the two raiders might strike. In this respect the Germans were remarkably successful.

Deutschland's commerce raiding activities were neither successful nor extended – she returned to port on 15 November 1939 having sunk only two ships of 7,000 tons – but *Graf Spee* had greater success (**Map 1**). Operating south of the equator, she was sent into action on 23 September, and opened her account by sinking the *Clement* off Pernambuco. The Allies were confused as to how many German raiders there were and set up five hunting groups in the South Atlantic on 5 October, the day that *Graf Spee* captured the *Newton Beech* north of Saint Helena. *Ashlea* and *Huntsman* followed in quick succession on 7 and 10 October, and then the *Trevanion* on 22 October. After this *Graf Spee* headed round the Cape of Good Hope to the Indian Ocean, where she sank the *Africa Shell* and stopped the *Mapia* on 15 and 16 November respectively, before heading back into the Atlantic once again. Here she sank the *Doric Star* on 2 December and the *Tairoa* on 3 December, before heading to the rich hunting grounds off the River Plate. *En route* she met and sank the

Streonshalh on 7 December. It was *Graf Spee*'s last success, bringing her tally to nine ships of 50,000 tons.

Commanding Force G, based on Port Stanley in the Falkland Islands, was Commodore H. Harwood with the heavy cruisers *Cumberland* and *Exeter* and the light cruisers *Ajax* and *Achilles*. At the time of the Battle of the River Plate, *Cumberland* was detached from the rest of the force, however. For some time Harwood had thought that Langsdorff, captain of the *Graf Spee*, would be attracted to the Plate, and so concentrated his three cruisers 150 miles off the mouth of the great river.

On 13 December Harwood's assessment was proved right for the pocket battleship was sighted. Though outgunned, Harwood had decided to attack immediately (**Map 2**). *Ajax* and *Achilles* were to go in from the west, and *Exeter* from the south, thus forcing Langsdorff either to concentrate his fire on one ship or group – leaving the other free to close right in – or divide the fire of his main battery, giving both the British subdivisions a better chance of closing and inflicting mortal damage. Langsdorff first chose the second, but soon directed the fire of his main battery on to *Exeter* alone. The German fire was formidably accurate, and the British cruiser was soon no

more than a battered wreck. *Exeter* was ordered to break off and make for the Falklands.

Graf Spee could now turn her attentions to the light cruisers, which continued the action alone, harrying the pocket battleship as she made for Montevideo. Langsdorff had decided to seek a temporary respite in this neutral port to have his casualties tended for and to make repairs before breaking out to Germany. *Graf Spee* reached Montevideo at midnight on 13/14 December, and there followed a spate of legal wrangles between the two belligerent powers and Uruguay about the terms of *Graf Spee*'s stay in port. British ruses finally persuaded Langsdorff that a far superior British force was now waiting for him outside territorial waters, and he decided not to throw away the lives of his crew in a futile battle. In fact only the two light cruisers were patrolling to seaward. Be that as it may, Langsdorff took *Graf Spee* out into Montevideo Roads on 17 December and there scuttled her. The crew were interned, and three days later Langsdorff shot himself.

Above: The German pocket battleship, *Admiral Graf Spee*

①

Iceland

24 Aug

FAEROE IS

WILHELMSHAVEN
21 August 1939
Graf Spee sails

LONDON

NORTH
AMERICA

NEW YORK

28 Aug

Force L
Dunkerque (B/c)
Béarn (A/c)
3 French cruisers

AZORES

GIBRALTAR

MEDITERRANEAN SEA

SUEZ

BERMUDA

ATLANTIC

Force F
Berwick (C)
York (C)

Forces M and N
Hermes (A/c)
2 French cruisers

AFRICA

West Indies

OCEAN

DAKAR

Force K
Renown (B/c)
Ark Royal (A/c)

**Record of the
Graf Spee's activities**
30 Sept   Clement sunk
5 Oct   Newton Beech boarded
7 Oct   ,,   ,,   sunk
7 Oct   Ashlea sunk
10 Oct   Huntsman boarded
17 ,,   ,,   sunk
22 Oct   Trevanion sunk
14 Nov   Holland sighted
15 Nov   Africa Shell sunk
16 Nov   Mapia stopped
2 Dec   Doric Star sunk
3 Dec   Tairoa sunk
7 Dec   Streonshalh sunk

6 Sept

FREETOWN

Equator

Force Y
Strasbourg (B)
Neptune (C)

INDIAN OCEAN

ASCENSION

10 Oct

PERNAMBUCO

30 Sept

5 Oct   7 Oct
17 Oct 7 Oct
ST HELENA

SOUTH AMERICA

22 Oct   2 Dec

Mozam-
bique

Madagascar

RIO DE JANEIRO

7 Dec   3 Dec

15 Nov

LOURENCO
MARQUES

14 Nov   15 Nov

MONTEVIDEO

River
Plate

✗ **13 December
'Battle of the River Plate'**

CAPE TOWN   SIMONSTOWN
Cape of Good Hope

2 Nov   20 Nov

Force G
Cumberland (C)
Exeter (C)
Ajax (C)
Achilles (C)

23 Dec 1939/21 Jan 1940
Waiting area 'Altmark'

Force H
Sussex (C)
Shropshire (C)

PORT STANLEY
Falkland Is

→ CRUISE OF THE GRAF SPEE
Force H BRITISH HUNTING GROUP
A/c = Aircraft carrier
B/c = Battle cruiser
C = Cruiser

Mercator's projection

②

✷ HITS ON EXETER
SMOKE SCREEN

0   NAUTICAL MILES   6

*Graf Spee retires to
Montevideo.
Arrives there midnight
13/14 December*

0730

0730

Ajax hit, two turrets
knocked out

Ajax fires
torpedoes

11,000 yds

0722

17,000 yds

0708

0700

0700

0730

0700

Graf Spee

0646

0800

**Ajax and Achilles
in pursuit**

0614

Opens fire on
Ajax and Exeter

0615

0636

0644

Achilles damaged

*Exeter retires badly
damaged and
firing one turret in
local control*

Fires torpedoes

2

Fires
torpedoes

2

Range
19,200 yds

Ajax flies off
aircraft

0630

19,400 yds

2

Ajax opens fire
Achilles opens fire

Exeter opens fire

0614

Smoke sighted to N West

To Falkland Islands

Exeter, Ajax and Achilles

THE RAIDERS

Early in the war with the voyages of the *Graf Spee* and the *Deutschland*, the German navy found out how much the conventional naval dispositions of their enemies were dislocated by the threat of surface raiders. This left considerable scope, if the dislocation could be increased by the use of disguised merchant raiders, for Germany's small but efficient regular forces to chip away at the Allies' naval superiority. Beside contributing towards this end, the merchant raiders would be able to take a worthwhile toll of Allied merchant shipping.

Work was put in hand soon after the beginning of the war to convert several merchantmen to the new role. Clearly armament was of prime importance, and all the raiders were fitted with between six and eight 5·9-inch guns, giving a firepower equal to most Allied light cruisers. Other armament consisted of cannon, torpedoes, mines, and spotter aircraft. Range was also of vital significance, and all the raiders were capable of staying at sea for about a year, receiving fresh supplies of food, ammunition, and fuel from supply ships that waited for them in designated areas. Finally, to avoid arousing suspicion, all the raiders were made to look inconspicuous as possible, and were fitted with equipment to enable their crews to alter salient features of their vessels so that the raiders might assume different identities at will.

Seven merchant raiders were sent on cruises varying in duration from four to eighteen months (**Map 1**):

Atlantis (known to the Germans as 'Ship 16' and the British as 'Raider C') sailed on 31 March 1940 and before being sunk by the British cruiser *Devonshire* on 22 November 1941, captured or sank twenty-two ships of 145,697 tons.

Orion (Ship 36, Raider A) sailed on 6 April 1940 and sank nine ships of 57,744 tons before returning to base on 21 August 1941.

Widder (Ship 21. Raider D) sailed on 6 May 1940 and sank or captured ten vessels of 58,645 tons before returning home on 31 October 1940.

Thor (Ship 10, Raider E) sailed on 6 June 1940 and before arriving home led an eventful career, which included engagements with the British armed merchant cruisers *Alcantara* and *Carnarvon Castle*, the sinking of a third, *Voltaire*, and the dispatch of eleven ships of 83,000 tons.

Pinguin (Ship 33, Raider F) sailed on 22 June 1940 and before being sunk by the British cruiser *Cornwall* on 8 May 1941 disposed of twenty-eight ships (including eleven whalers) of 136,551 tons.

Komet (Ship 45, Raider B) sailed from Germany on 9 July 1940 and sailed round the north of Russia to the Pacific with the aid of Russian icebreakers. Before returning to base she sank six ships of 42,959 tons.

Kormoran (Ship 41, Raider G) sailed on 3 December 1940 and sank or captured eleven ships of 68,274 tons before being sunk by the Australian cruiser *Sydney* on 19 November 1941.

All in all the German disguised merchant raiders proved remarkably efficient and economical weapons, dislocating Allied shipping seriously and inflicting considerable casualties.

German warships sent on raider missions were not as successful,

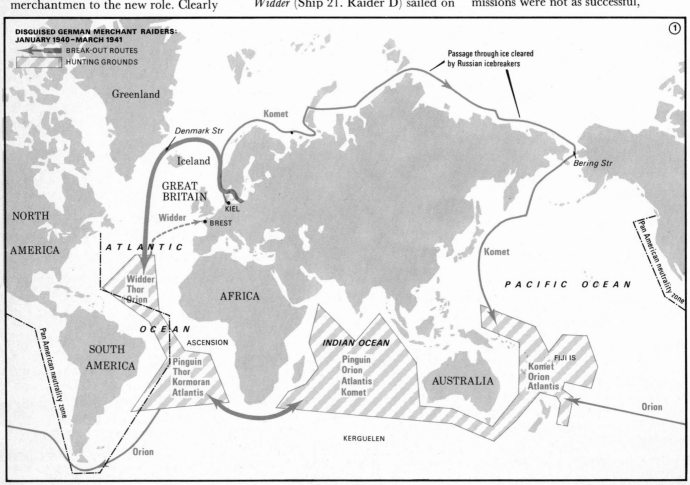

DISGUISED GERMAN MERCHANT RAIDERS: JANUARY 1940 – MARCH 1941

BREAK-OUT ROUTES
HUNTING GROUNDS

Greenland

Komet

Passage through ice cleared by Russian icebreakers

Denmark Str

Iceland

GREAT BRITAIN

KIEL

Widder

BREST

NORTH AMERICA

ATLANTIC

Widder
Thor
Orion

AFRICA

OCEAN

ASCENSION

SOUTH AMERICA

Pinguin
Thor
Kormoran
Atlantis

Orion

INDIAN OCEAN

Pinguin
Orion
Atlantis
Komet

KERGUELEN

AUSTRALIA

Bering Str

Komet

PACIFIC OCEAN

Pan American neutrality zone

Komet
Orion
Atlantis

FIJI IS

Orion

Pan American neutrality zone

however. Their range was limited, and they therefore had to act in the main shipping lanes, where the chances of meeting serious opposition in the form of Allied major units was much greater. As a further complication, Hitler ordered that they were to take no risks at all in the event of meeting such Allied opposition.

One really successful cruise was by the pocket battleship *Admiral Scheer* (**Map 2**). She sailed on 23 October 1940 and sank sixteen ships of 99,059 tons before returning home on 1 April 1941. She also sank the British armed merchant cruiser *Jervis Bay* on 5 November 1940.

The two battle-cruisers *Scharnhorst* and *Gneisenau* sailed from Germany on a raiding cruise on 21 January 1941, and in the course of the next two months, before returning to Brest on 22 March 1941, they cost the Allies twenty-two ships of 115,622 tons.

Other German surface raiders were the cruiser *Admiral Hipper*, which made two forays (30 November 1940 to 27 December 1940 and 1 February 1941 to 13 February 1941), in which she sank nine ships of 40,078 tons, and finally the battleship *Bismarck* and cruiser *Prinz Eugen* whose voyage is described later.

Below: The end of an Allied merchantman caught by a raider

THE NAVAL WAR IN THE MEDI- TERRANEAN

The naval situation in the Mediterranean was a difficult one for the Royal Navy: the Italian navy was modern in equipment and enjoyed a position from which it could bring superior forces to bear on either of the two major British forces in the Mediterranean, Force H at Gibraltar and the Mediterranean Fleet at Alexandria, a split which was inevitable but nonetheless very dangerous for the Royal Navy. In the centre, where it would have to take the full brunt of the Italian naval and air attack, was Malta, on which it was thought advisable to base only light and submarine naval forces. Commanding the Mediterranean Fleet, Admiral Sir Andrew Cunningham used his limited forces with great verve and aggression, constantly seeking for ways in which to whittle down the Italians' great superiority.

On 9 July 1940, while cruising off the coast of Calabria, Cunningham's three battleships, one aircraft-carrier,

five light cruisers, and several destroyers encountered an Italian force of two battleships, six heavy, and twelve light cruisers, and their destroyer escort. In the following action, one Italian battleship and a cruiser were severely damaged, with little or no loss to Cunningham's forces.

On 19 July the Australian light cruiser *Sydney* and four destroyers met two Italian light cruisers off Crete, and sank one of them.

The scales were not significantly altered, for all this, but Cunningham finally found a way of attacking the Italian fleet in harbour, with little danger to his own command. It was planned to launch twenty-one Fairey Swordfish torpedo-bombers to deliver a night attack on the Italian fleet in Taranto on the night of 11 November (**Map 1**). The strike was extremely successful, sinking the new battleship *Littorio* and two older but modernized battleships, very severely damaging two cruisers and two fleet auxiliaries. All

but two of the Swordfish returned to the carrier *Illustrious*. Cunningham's position was now far happier.

Above: Italian battleships firing on the British fleet

Below: A British cruiser lays a smoke screen during an engagement with the Italian fleet

① 2300, 11 Nov 1940
Main direction of Swordfish torpedo attacks

Mar Piccolo

Cruiser   Cruiser

Second wave

Torpedo nets

Mar Grande

TARANTO

Fiume
Zara   Duilio
Littorio   Cesare
Gorizia

First waves

San Pietro

Balloon barrage

Vittorio Veneto

Doria

San Paulo

Cavour

Diga di Tarantola

Oil storage depot

Diga di San Vito

◣ SHIPS CRIPPLED

0   1 MILE

A further heavy blow was inflicted on the Italian navy at the Battle of Cape Matapan on 28 March 1941 (**Map 2**). It was clear that an Axis invasion of the Balkans was imminent, and to bolster the Greeks, it was decided to ship in a contingent of British troops. These movements could not be concealed from the Axis, and the Germans urged the Italians to strike at the convoys carrying the troops with all the power they could muster. Cunningham realized that an Italian threat might emerge, and planned accordingly. Vice-Admiral H.D. Pridham-Wippell and his four cruisers were ordered to patrol to the south of Gávdhos, while the destroyer force in Piraeus was ordered to be ready to move south if needed. Naval and airforce strike aircraft were readied, and submarines were ordered to watch for an Italian force heading eastward.

On the evening of the 27th, RAF reports indicated a force of three Italian cruisers heading east, and Cunningham decided to put to sea from Alexandria with three battleships, one aircraft-carrier, and their destroyer escorts, at the same time summoning Pridham-Wippell to a rendezvous south of Crete. Air searches the next morning proved somewhat confusing, and it was uncertain how many battleships the Italians were using. In fact the force heading east was the battleship *Vittorio Veneto*, while the battleships reported south of Crete, heading south-west, were a group of three heavy and two light cruisers. Air strikes on *Vittorio Veneto* were launched, but only one torpedo hit was scored, at 1510. All the Italian forces were now heading for home at top speed. But at 1930 a torpedo hit on *Pola* stopped the Italian cruiser, and the heavy cruisers *Zara* and *Fiume* were sent back to help. Admiral Angelo Iachino, commanding the Italian force, thought that the British were still far to the east, whereas in fact they were not far behind, now closing on the three Italian heavy cruisers very swiftly. The battleship *Valiant* spotted the two returning Italian cruisers on radar, and Cunningham's battleships blasted them from the water at a range of 3,000 yards. The *Pola* was found and sunk later.

By now it was too late to catch *Vittorio Veneto*, and though a search was made for her, Cunningham soon realized the futility of this and ordered his scattered forces to rendezvous south-west of Cape Matapan before withdrawing.

Above: Italian cruisers under fire during the action off Cape Matapan

259

HUNTING THE BISMARCK

In the spring of 1941, two of Germany's newest surface units finished their trials and were judged ready for action. These were the superb battleship *Bismarck*, armed with 15-inch guns and protected by massive armour plate and first class internal compartmentalization, and the heavy cruiser *Prinz Eugen*, sister ship of the *Admiral Hipper*. Admiral Raeder decided that they could cut their operational teeth on a raiding sortie into the Atlantic.

On 18 May the two warships sailed from Gdynia for Bergen, where on the 21st they were spotted by RAF reconnaissance aircraft. Clearly the only reason for their presence in Norwegian waters could be a foray into the Atlantic, and all elements of the Royal Navy in the Atlantic and around Britain were warned to hold themselves ready for the inevitable battle.

On the same day that they were discovered, the two raiders, under the command of Vice-Admiral Günther Lütjens, put to sea in foggy weather and headed north to enter the Atlantic via the Denmark Strait. Although the British soon found out that the two German ships had sailed, it was not until late on 23 May that the cruisers *Suffolk* and *Norfolk*, patrolling in the Denmark Strait, spotted them and radioed a report. Vice-Admiral L. Holland, commanding the Battle-Cruiser Squadron (*Hood* and the new battleship *Prince of Wales*, which had not even been completed), altered course to intercept the German raiders.

The two forces met early the next morning, but as *Hood* closed on *Bismarck*, a shell from the latter plunged through the weak deck armour of the British battle-cruiser into one of the aft magazines. *Hood* blew up, and only three of her 1,500 man crew survived. *Bismarck* then turned her attention to *Prince of Wales*, scoring several hits on her and forcing her to break off the action, though not before one of the British ship's 14-inch shells had hit *Bismarck*, causing a tell-tale streak of fuel to leak from a ruptured tank.

Prince of Wales and the two cruisers continued to shadow the German squadron until the Home Fleet could close on it, but as *Bismarck* turned to head for Brest, *Prince Eugen* broke away south and finally returned safely to Brest on 1 June. Though contact with *Bismarck* was lost, a Catalina of the RAF spotted her in the morning of the 26th.

Force H, which was moving up north-east from Gibraltar, contained the carrier *Ark Royal*, and a torpedo strike by her Swordfish further damaged *Bismarck*, jamming her rudder and thereby sealing her fate. The next morning, the battleships *Rodney* and *King George V* arrived on the scene and started pouring heavy calibre shells on to the hapless *Bismarck*. The German battleship was soon a blazing wreck, but it was not until the cruiser *Dorsetshire* closed in and torpedoed her that she sank, taking with her all but 110 of her 2,300 man crew.

Opposite above: The *Bismarck* sets out from Bergen on her last voyage

Opposite below: *Bismarck* in action against HMS *Hood*. A photograph taken from the *Prinz Eugen*

THE CHANNEL DASH

German naval sorties into the Atlantic in 1941 had left three vital ships all but stranded in Brest: the battle-cruisers *Scharnhorst* and *Gneisenau* and the heavy cruiser *Prinz Eugen*. Hitler, obsessed by the idea that Norway was the 'zone of destiny' and that its invasion by the British was imminent, demanded against Raeder's better judgement that the squadron in Brest be brought home to Germany, and recommended that a quick dash up the Channel was the best way to achieve this. Since surprise was all important, the squadron would leave Brest at night, even though this meant that it would pass through the Straits of Dover in daylight.

German preparations, organized by Vice-Admiral Ciliax, were excellent: passages were swept through minefields and then marked so that the squadron could travel at top speed, and a permanent aerial umbrella was arranged with General Adolf Galland of the Luftwaffe. The British were aware that preparations for some venture were under way as the clearing of channels in the minefields had been observed, and therefore the ineptitude of their reaction when the day came is all the more to be condemned. Three air patrols by Coastal Command Hudsons fitted with air-to-surface radar were instituted to cover the night hours.

The German squadron's departure was delayed for more than three hours on 11 February, and it was not until 2245 hours that they sailed. The Hudson patrolling off Brest spotted nothing on its radar. In the second Hudson, north of Ushant, there was a radar failure. The German squadron did not get within range of the third Hudson's radar. And so, despite considerable German aerial activity being spotted by British surface radar, it was not until three Spitfires returned from patrol and their pilots were debriefed at 1130 hours on 12 February that any definite Intelligence of the breakout was received. Time was now of the essence, and it was decided to send all available aircraft into the attack as soon as they were ready. The Royal Navy 825 Squadron attacked at 1245 and all its aircraft were lost (its commander, Lieutenant-Commander E. Esmonde, was awarded a posthumous VC). Motor torpedo boat attacks also proved futile, as did all subsequent aircraft and destroyer attacks.

Although *Scharnhorst* hit a mine at 1431, she was soon making 25 knots again. The same happened to *Gneisenau* at 1955, but she too was only slightly damaged. However, when *Scharnhorst* hit a second mine at 2134 the damage was serious and she had to be left behind by the other two ships. However, she was able to limp on, and all three German ships reached port on the morning of 13 February.

Below: The German squadron in line ahead during the Channel Dash

Opposite: The German ships as they passed through the Straits of Dover

NORTH SEA

GREAT BRITAIN

North Coates
407 Sqdn
(6 Hudsons)

500 Sqdn (5 Hudsons)
Bircham Newton

Coltishall
42 Sqdn (14 T/Bs)
arrives 12 Feb

GREAT YARMOUTH

HARWICH
6 destroyers

LONDON

Manston
825 Sqdn (6 Swordfish)

217 Sqdn (7 T/Bs)
Thorney I

DOVER

86/217 Sqdn
(12 T/Bs)
St Eval

PORTSMOUTH

Straits of Dover

ENGLISH CHANNEL

CHANNEL
ISLANDS

CHERBOURG

LE HAVRE

1956/2156, 11 Feb

0530

0850

1042

0114

USHANT

0028

BREST

H3

Sealion

2356, 11 Feb/0028 12 Feb

Brittany

FRANCE

2134

1955

1832

1608

1545

1431

1245

BRUNSBÜTTEL

WILHELMSHAVEN

FRISIAN IS

TEXEL

AMSTERDAM

ROTTERDAM

OSTEND

CALAIS

BOULOGNE

AM, 13 Feb
Gneisenau and
Prinz Eugen arrive

AM, 13 Feb
Scharnhorst arrives

Scharnhorst hits
second mine

Gneisenau hits mine

Main attacks by
Hudsons and Beauforts

British destroyers
and Beauforts attack

Scharnhorst hits
first mine

Attacks by Swordfish
and MTBs

Spitfire identifies
German warships

German night-fighters
join squadron

Midnight, 12 May
Scharnhorst, Gneisenau,
Prinz Eugen and covering destroyers
sail

ROUTE TAKEN BY GERMAN SQUADRON
BRITISH AIRCRAFT AND SUBMARINE PATROLS

| 0 | MILES | 200 |
| 0 | KILOMETRES | 300 |

THE MALTA CONVOYS

Malta's position in the middle of 1942 was desperate – astride the Axis supply lines to North Africa, she was under continual air attack by the German and Italian airforces and supply convoys were suffering such heavy losses that they had had to be suspended. Although the success of missions ferrying aircraft in to the island's defences meant that Malta could continue her unequal struggle with the bombers of the Luftwaffe and Regia Aeronautica, it was abundantly clear that food and fuel for military and civilians alike had to be got in or the island would fall. It was decided that another attempt to pass a convoy through to Malta from the west should be made early in August. The importance of what was at stake can be gauged by the naval forces massed to protect this one convoy of fourteen merchantmen: two battleships, three aircraft-carriers, seven cruisers, thirty-two destroyers, and eight submarines, not counting lesser craft. At the same time, the aircraft-carrier *Furious* was to ferry more fighters in for the RAF squadrons on the island. The convoy left the Clyde on 3 August, escorted by Vice-Admiral E.N.Syfret's warships. Operation Pedestal was under way.

The convoy passed through the Strait of Gibraltar in fog early on the morning of the 10th. The same day a dummy convoy left Port Said, apparently for Malta, as a diversion, and then turned back the next day. As the Mediterranean fleet's other contribution to the operation, a cruiser force bombarded Rhodes on the 13th. But by the afternoon of the 10th the Axis had got wind of the main operation, and from the next morning onwards the convoy was constantly shadowed by reconnaissance aircraft.

During the afternoon of the 11th, *Furious* flew off her aircraft to Malta and turned back that same evening. But the Axis also made its first move, when a U-boat sank the aircraft-carrier *Eagle* at 1323. During the evening, a

first air attack was made, but no hits were scored on the convoy.

In the second Axis raid on the convoy on the 12th, the freighter *Deucalion* was damaged and had to leave the convoy, being sunk later that evening. In the afternoon the convoy passed through the main concentration of Axis submarines, one of which, the Italian *Cobalto*, was rammed and sunk by the destroyer *Ithuriel*. No Allied ships were lost. But in the evening the destroyer *Foresight* was badly damaged and had to be sunk, and the carrier *Indomitable* suffered three heavy bomb hits, which put her flight deck out of operation. Soon after this Syfret, as planned, turned back with the main covering forces, leaving Rear-Admiral H.M.Burrough to escort the convoy the rest of the way with his four cruisers. Two of these were hit by torpedoes at about 2000. *Nigeria* turned back to Gibraltar, but *Cairo* had to be sunk. The American tanker *Ohio* was hit at the same time but stayed with the convoy. Just at dusk, the convoy once again came under bombing attack, which cost it the merchantmen *Empire Hope* and *Clan Ferguson* sunk, while the *Brisbane Star* was hit but managed to reach Malta. The next casualty was the cruiser *Kenya*, torpedoed by the Italian submarine *Alagi*, but she managed to stay with the convoy.

At 0120 on the morning of the 13th the cruiser *Manchester* was hit by a torpedo, and was later scuttled. At the same time five merchantmen (*Santa Eliza*, *Wairangi*, *Almeria*, *Lykes*, and *Glenorchy*) were lost, the result of the convoy having become stretched out by the attacks of the previous afternoon and evening. Soon after dawn the air attacks were renewed, resulting in the loss of the *Wairanama* and further damage to the *Ohio*, which was disabled in a later attack, during the course of which the *Rochester Castle* and *Dorset* were also hit. Soon afterwards, light forces from Malta met the main body of the convoy, which now consisted

only of *Port Chalmers*, *Melbourne Star*, and *Rochester Castle*. Behind them *Dorset*, *Ohio*, and *Brisbane Star* struggled to make port, though the first two were again damaged by bombs, *Dorset* sinking. The gallant *Ohio* and her precious fuel cargo were finally towed into Valletta on the 15th. Her master was awarded the George Cross.

And so ended Operation Pedestal. Five of the fourteen merchantmen got through and enabled Malta to hold on and even strike back, but nine others had been sunk, together with one aircraft-carrier, two cruisers, and a destroyer, with a further carrier and two cruisers severely damaged.

Above: British aircraft-carriers forming part of the escort of a Malta convoy

Opposite: The destroyer HMS *Malcolm* passes through a convoy

1915, 12 August Second air attack	1215, 12 August Deucalion damaged, sunk later	1600, 12 August Italian submarine Cobalto sunk	1840, 12 August Foresight sunk, carrier Indomitable damaged. Main covering force ('X') withdraws as planned	2000, 12 August Cairo, Clan Ferguson & Empire Hope sunk. Nigeria, Brisbane Star, Kenya & Ohio damaged	Night, 12/13 August Santa Elisa, Wairangi, Almeria, Lykes & Glenarchy sunk. Manchester damaged, sunk later. Rochester Castle damaged	0800, 13 August Waimarama sunk, Ohio damaged	1125, 13 August Rochester Castle & Ohio damaged. Dorset damaged, sunk later	1900, 13 August Merchant ship straggler sunk by German aircraft

THE ARCTIC CONVOYS

In conditions far different to the Mediterranean convoys, the Arctic convoys also provided tales of great heroism under savage attack and appalling weather as Allied seamen struggled to push supplies through to Russia. The convoys were begun in August 1941 shortly after Germany invaded Russia and continued until September 1943 (**Map 1**). During the summer, when the edge of the pack ice retreats northward, convoys could stand off further from the German-occupied coastline of Norway and that of her ally Finland, with all their air bases, but then the length of the day made them relatively

easy prey for the U-boats. During the winter the ice edge moved south again, driving the convoys in closer to the air bases, but shorter days meant that the threat of U-boats was lessened. Allied air bases, being on the outside of the great curve described by Scandinavia, could not cover the convoys the whole way, there being a considerable gap between Jan Mayen Island to north of Murmansk.

In these waters, however, there occurred one of the war's most tragic episodes, the loss of Convoy PQ–17, which sailed for Russia on 27 June 1942 with thirty-six merchant ships. Because of the threat posed by German heavy units based in northern Norway, the convoy was given a heavy escort. Close cover was provided by four cruisers and three destroyers, as far as Bear Island. Distant cover was provided by two battleships, one carrier, two cruisers, and fourteen destroyers. Close escort was provided by three minesweepers and four trawlers, which sailed with the convoy. The long-range escort, of six destroyers, four corvettes, and two submarines, joined the convoy on 30 June.

The next day the convoy was spotted by U-boats and aircraft, but U-boat attacks were all driven off. The next afternoon PQ–17 passed the homeward

bound QP–13. An air attack was beaten off that evening, by which time the close cover was 40 miles to the north of the convoy. Then in fog the convoy lost its shadowing aircraft as it turned east to pass just north of Bear Island. Meanwhile, back in Britain, air reconnaissance had revealed that the German heavy surface ships had left their southern bases.

Early on the 4th a German aircraft spotted the convoy through the fog and torpedoed a merchantman. An air attack at 0830 cost the convoy two ships, but a third managed to keep up, though damaged. Meanwhile, *Tirpitz*, *Scheer*, and *Hipper* had reached Altenfjord, but Hitler's standing orders forbade their dispatch towards the convoy. The First Sea Lord, Sir Dudley Pound, who was controlling the operation from London, thought it inevitable that the German surface vessels would move out to intercept the convoy, and as the distant cover had been withdrawn according to plan, the convoy and the close cover would be destroyed. He thus ordered the distant cover to return. However, as they were still some 800 miles from Archangel, their destination, Pound thought that the individual ships of the convoy might be able to evade the German raiders if they scattered, and he ordered them to do this at 0936 hours on 4 July. The long-range escort, except for the submarines, left the convoy to rendezvous with the close cover. The commander of the long-range escort, Commander J.E.Broome, wished to rejoin the convoy, but the commander of the close escort, Rear-Admiral L.H.K.Hamilton, under the impression that he was moving back to join up with the Home Fleet, as a result of poorly worded messages from the Admiralty, would not let him do so. The convoy was now scattered and defenceless.

The reason for the 'scatter' order, the presence and imminent threat of three major German ships, in fact materialized on the morning of the 5th: the three ships sailed from Altenfjord, but on receipt of the news that U-boats and aircraft were dealing satisfactorily with the scattered remnants of the convoy they turned back.

The four days from 5 to 8 July were terrible ones for the convoy, with most of its ships sunk. One of many notable feats was that of the armed trawler *Ayrshire*. She led three merchantmen up into the ice, where they painted their upper works white and waited for the crisis to pass before making for Archangel. Only eleven of the original

thirty-six merchantmen made Russia. Among the cargo lost were 3,350 vehicles, 430 tanks, 210 aircraft, and 99,316 tons of other cargo.

Right: A near miss on an Allied destroyer

Below: A convoy enters Archangel harbour

MERCHANT SHIPS SUNK BY U-BOATS AND BOMBERS

MERCHANT SHIP RUN AGROUND

✈ GERMAN AIR BASES

MILES 0 — 200
KILOMETRES 0 — 300

SPITZBERGEN

HOPE I

Ayrshire escorts Silver Sword, Troubadour and Ironclad through ice barrier to Novaya Zemlya and Archangel

Bolton Castle — Washington
Paulus Potter
Earlston — Pankraft
Empire Byron — River Afton
Carlton
Aldersdale — Daniel Morgan
Honomu — Zaafaran
Fairfield City
Peter Kerr
Sunk 5 July

2215 4 July PQ-17 scatters

ROUTE OF PQ-17

BEAR ISLAND

Cruiser and destroyer escort head South

B A R E N T S   S E A

Pan Atlantic

Hartlebury
Winston Salem
Olopana
John Witherspoon
Alcoa Ranger
Sunk 6/8 July

Novaya
Zemlya
Matochkin Strait

Afternoon, 5 July Tirpitz, Scheer, Hipper and 6 destroyers sail

North Cape

Alten Fjord

2130, 5 July Operation abandoned due to success of attacks by German bombers and submarines on PQ-17

LOFOTEN ISLANDS
TROMSO
✈ BARDUFOSS
✈ BANAK
NARVIK
NORWAY
KIRKENES
PETSAMO

KOLGUEV I

Hoosier
El Capitan   **Sunk 10 July**

Cape Kanin

SWEDEN
FINLAND
MURMANSK
RUSSIA
IOKANGA
To White Sea & Archangel

BATTLES OF THE BARENTS SEA

After the disaster of PQ–17 and the savaging that the next Arctic convoy, PQ–18, received, there was an interval before Russian convoys were resumed, with a different code (JW) and different tactics, whereby instead of one large convoy there would be two smaller ones (A and B), much easier to handle and defend. The new system got off to a flying start when the first such convoy, JW–51A, got through without loss. As soon as it arrived off Murmansk, its escort of the two cruisers *Sheffield* and *Jamaica*, under Rear-Admiral R.L.Burnett, turned back to meet the second instalment of the convoy, JW–51B, which was at present escorted by six destroyers under Captain R.Sherbrooke.

A U-boat, however, spotted JW–51B and radioed a sighting report. Raeder saw this as a golden opportunity to test *Lützow*, with a view to sending her on a raid into the Atlantic if she was successful. The German plan was simple and could have been effective but for the crippling tactical restrictions imposed on all surface ship actions by Hitler. The force was to consist of the heavy cruiser *Hipper*, the pocket battleship *Lützow*, and six destroyers, commanded by Vice-Admiral Oscar Kummetz. *Hipper* would take on the escort, while *Lützow*, commanded by Captain Stänge, destroyed the convoy. Though Kummetz was ignorant of the presence in the area of Burnett's cruisers and a covering force of one battleship, one cruiser, and three destroyers commanded by Vice-Admiral Sir Bruce Fraser, the plan started auspiciously enough. The German squadron sailed 30 December 1942 and approached the convoy the following morning. Seeing the convoy to the south of himself, Kummetz turned towards it, but was spotted by the destroyer escort, one of which started to lay a smoke screen between the Germans and the convoy while the others made dummy attacks on *Hipper*. The latter turned away but then decided to try another attack. Sherbrooke had meanwhile sent two of his destroyers back towards the convoy to deal with the German destroyers, which were closing in, and thus found himself in dire straits as *Hipper* returned to the fray, severely damaging *Onslow*. Kummetz once again withdrew. Burnett, meanwhile, had seen the gun flashes to the south and was closing as fast as he could. But the other half of the German pincer, *Lützow*, now appeared from the south, with no British destroyers between herself and the convoy. However, she too turned away, uncertain whether she was about to meet friend or foe.

Above: The *Scharnhorst* in Norwegian waters

Opposite right: HMS *Sheffield* seen from *Duke of York* during the hunt for the *Scharnhorst*

0929
Cruisers open
fire on Scharnhorst

1221
Cruisers fire on
Scharnhorst again

BEAR ISLAND

0628

0339
Convoy JW-55B

0730
Bey orders
destroyers
to fan out

0929

0339
Cruisers Norfolk,
Sheffield, Belfast
(Burnett)

Burnett's cruisers
shadow Scharnhorst

ARCTIC OCEAN

0339
Scharnhorst
(Bey)
with 5 destroyers

1820
Scharnhorst damaged,
stops firing

1650
Duke of York and
Jamaica engage
Scharnhorst

1945
26 December 1943
Scharnhorst
torpedoed
and sunk

North Cape

0339
Duke of York, Jamaica
(Fraser)
with 4 destroyers

NORWAY

Hipper now returned, sinking the destroyer *Achates* before flinching away from the threat of torpedo attack, only to find herself caught between Burnett's cruisers and the destroyers. Three hits were soon scored on *Hipper* before two German destroyers were met. One of these was sunk. To the south again, Stänge at last opened fire on the convoy, but was then foiled by a smoke screen laid by the destroyers. Kummetz then broke off the action and ordered his ships to retire to the south.

The Germans had had all the advantages: superior firepower, surprise, and all the tactical advantages. But yet they had thrown them all away by poor co-ordination and lack of initiative, especially by the destroyer captains. Hitler, quite rightly, was incensed and ordered the major units of the surface fleet to be scrapped. Raeder managed to dissuade him, but felt obliged to resign. He was succeeded as commander-in-chief of the German navy by Admiral Karl Dönitz.

Almost exactly a year later, the German navy suffered another major reverse in the north. The battle-cruiser *Scharnhorst* sailed from Altenfjord on 25 December 1943 to intercept Convoy JW-55B, which was escorted by fourteen destroyers, and covered by

Admiral Burnett's cruisers *Belfast*, *Sheffield*, and *Norfolk*, which had the double task of protecting the westbound RA–55A and the eastbound JW–55B. Distant cover was provided by Sir Bruce Fraser with the battleship *Duke of York*, the cruiser *Jamaica*, and four destroyers. Rear-Admiral Erich Bey took *Scharnhorst* and her five escorting destroyers due north. At about 0730 on the 26th Bey ordered his destroyers to fan out and search to the south-west, and then lost touch with them. *Scharnhorst* was on her own from now on.

At 0840 *Belfast* picked up *Scharnhorst* on her radar and then illuminated her with starshell at 0924. Burnett's squadron opened fire at 0929, but *Scharnhorst* hauled round to the south and withdrew from the cruisers before trying to work her way round to the north-east. This move was spotted by *Belfast*'s radar, but the German ship was considerably faster in the prevailing seas, and Burnett decided to keep himself between the convoy and where he expected the German ship to reappear.

Burnett's move was proved right shortly after noon when *Belfast* once again picked up *Scharnhorst* by radar. A short action ensued in which both sides received damage. *Scharnhorst* then broke away to the south – exactly

where Fraser's force was waiting for her. *Duke of York*'s radar picked up the German ship at 1617. *Belfast* illuminated her with starshell at 1650 and *Duke of York* and *Jamaica* immediately opened fire. Try as she might, *Scharnhorst* could not escape the sandwich she was in between Fraser and Burnett. *Duke of York*'s 14-inch shells, plunging down steeply at long range, tore through the German ship's deck armour. She was soon reduced to a wreck and sank at 1945. The surface threat to the Arctic convoys was over.

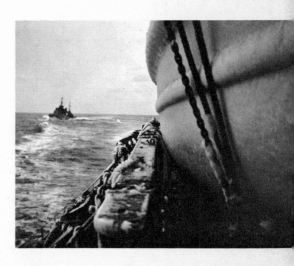

THE EARLY COMMANDO RAIDS

With the realization in the middle of 1940 that the fall of France almost certainly precluded the use of major military forces on the European continent for some time to come, it was decided to raise a force of men who, with special training and equipment, would make small forays against German-controlled installations on the continent. These would have the dual purposes of keeping up British morale by showing that some military effort was being made, and of keeping German forces that might have been used profitably elsewhere tied up guarding installations that might be raided (**Map 1**).

The first target for the Commandos, as they became known was the fish oil factories of the Lofoten Islands (**Map 2**). Some 500 commandos from Nos 3 and 4 Commandos sailed from Scapa Flow in two converted cross-Channel steamers under the command of Brigadier J.C.Haydon on 1 March 1941, escorted by five destroyers under Captain C.Caslon. On 4 March the attack went in, meeting no opposition until it had landed. All the fish oil installations were destroyed, 200 German prisoners were taken, 300 Norwegian volunteers were picked up, and the navy sank the fish factory ship *Hamburg* and numerous small cargo ships.

The next raid was carried out by a predominantly Canadian force. This was the destruction of the coal installations on Spitzbergen (**Map 1**). The force, under the command of Rear-Admiral P.Vian sailed for the island on 19 August. All went smoothly. Stocks of coal were burnt, the installations destroyed, three colliers captured and sent to Britain, and the Norwegian inhabitants of the island evacuated. Vian sailed for home on 3 September, *en route* encountering the German training ship *Bremse*, which he sank.

The next raid was planned as a bigger affair. The major landings were to be made on Vaagsö Island, with subsidiary landings on Maaloy Island (**Map 3**). The main force sailed from Scapa Flow on 21 December 1941 under Rear-Admiral L.H.K.Hamilton, escorted by a cruiser and eight destroyers. One of the two troop transports broke down, so the main operation was confined to small landings and the capture of two

small coasters. All the forces were back in Scapa by 1 January 1942. The secondary landings had greater success, however. Coastal batteries were silenced by bombing and gunfire, and the landing parties destroyed all the German installations on the island, while the navy disposed of some 16,000 tons of shipping. All the Vaagsö forces returned to Scapa by 28 December.

On 27 February 1942, an important raid was made on a German radar station at Bruneval on the northern coast of France (**Map 4**). Parachutists were dropped just inland from the site, captured the station, took parts for examination by British scientists, destroyed the rest of the station, and were then evacuated by the Navy. British casualties were three killed and seven wounded.

An altogether more ambitious Commando operation was launched in May 1942. Japanese operations in the Indian Ocean had led to fears that

England map showing THRUXTON, LONDON, PORTSMOUTH, Bruneval, LE HAVRE, FRANCE, ENGLISH CHANNEL, CHANNEL IS.

0 MILES 100

④

Bruneval map:

Radio-location device destroyed

Paratroops evacuated

Isolated house

La Presbytère

Road block

House

Paratroops land

Assembly point

BRUNEVAL

0 MILE ½

☐ BLOCKHOUSE
● MACHINE-GUN POST
xxxxx BARBED WIRE

Madagascar map:

COMORO IS

5 May 1942 Force 121 (Sturges) 17, 29 Bde Groups and No 5 Commando

DIEGO SUAREZ   Cape Amber

ANTSIRANE 7 May

AMBILOBE

7 S Afr Bde

MOZAMBIQUE

10 Sept 29 Bde lands, re-embarks for Tamatave later

MAJUNGA

ANDRIBA

22 E Afr Bde

MAINTIRANO

MADAGASCAR

MOZAMBIQUE CHANNEL

MORONDAVA

TANANARIVE 23 Sept

ANTSIRABE

18 Sept 29 Bde

TAMATAVE

INDIAN OCEAN

10 Sept

MANANJARI

FIANARANTSOA

AMBALAVAO

IHOSY

TULÉAR

6 November Vichy French commander surrenders

29 Sept S African bn

FORT DAUPHIN

0 MILES 400

0 KILOMETRES 600

29 Sept

⑤

Madagascar, part of the Vichy French Empire, might be captured and used as a base for attacks on Allied sea routes from Suez to the Far East and Australia. Between 5 and 7 May a force under the command of Rear-Admiral E.N.Syfret attacked and took the port of Diego Suarez in the extreme north of the island (**Map 5**). But on the 29th a Japanese aircraft was spotted over the harbour and the next day the battleship *Ramillies* was damaged in Diego Suarez by a midget submarine, this leading to the notion that the Japanese had a secret base on the island. In fact both craft had been launched from a submarine. It was, however, decided to overrun the rest of the island.

This proved a difficult undertaking. The conquest did not get under way until September, and it was not until 6 November that the Vichy French governor capitulated to the troops under Lieutenant-General Sir William Platt. The island was handed over to the Free French early the following January.

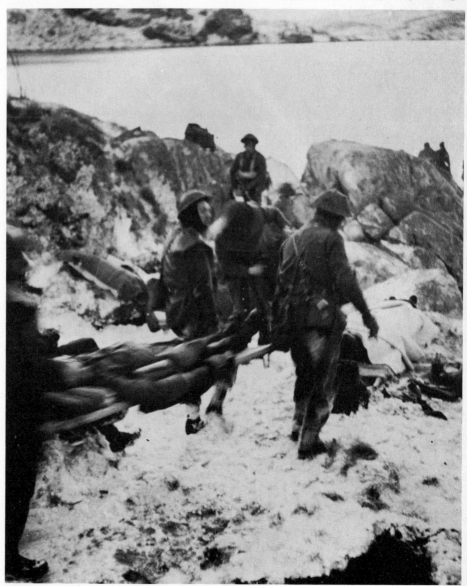

Above: British commandos attacking under cover of a smoke screen during the Vaagsö operation

Right: Commandos withdrawing from Måaloy

271

THE RAID ON ST NAZAIRE

The threat that the new German battleship *Tirpitz* might, like her sister ship *Bismarck*, break out into the Atlantic was a constant worry for the Admiralty at the beginning of 1942. But there was only one place in which so large a vessel could be dry-docked in France, and if this dock should be destroyed, the Admiralty thought that there was a good chance that *Tirpitz* might not attempt the breakout. The dock in question was the Normandie dock in St Nazaire, and a bold scheme to destroy it was set in motion.

The plan was for an old destroyer, one of the fifty 'four-stackers' provided by the Americans, to be lightened so that she could steam straight up the Loire regardless of sand banks and ram the outer lock gate. Later, explosive charges in her bows would go off, destroying the outer gate entirely. The escort force of one motor gun boat as headquarters ship, sixteen motor launches, and one motor torpedo boat. Troops were to be landed from the expendable destroyer, *Campbeltown*, and from the motor launches to carry out other demolition work before being evacuated.

The force left Falmouth on 26 March 1942. By 0130 on the 28th the force had got within two miles of its objective without being spotted, but then it was illuminated by German searchlights. The defence was confused by fake identification signals, and several minutes passed before the Germans opened fire. At 0134 *Campbeltown* rammed the lock gate and stuck fast, while the commandos she was carrying stormed ashore. The smaller craft had a more difficult time of it, however. The Germans were now fully alert, and of the landings planned (the right hand column at the Old Entrance and the left on the Old Mole), only three craft succeeded, including MGB 314, the headquarters craft. The evacuation was a confused affair, and many commandos were left behind.

Campbeltown blew up just before mid-day as a large party of German officers was inspecting her, and completely destroyed the lock gate. The primary task of the operation had been achieved. Fourteen small craft were lost, and total losses were 144 dead and missing. Five Victoria Crosses were awarded.

BASSIN DE PENHOUET

SWING BRIDGE

SLIDING GATE

FORME ECLUSE (Normandie dock)

CONTROL POSTS FOR GATES

(Under construction)

DOCK PUMP HOUSE

SLIDING GATE

0134, 28 March 1942 Campbeltown rams dock gate

SWING BRIDGE

OLD ENTRANCE

A

BASSIN DE ST NAZAIRE

SUBMARINE PENS

SEARCHLIGHT

BLOCKHOUSE

IRON BRIDGE

THE OLD MOLE

Motor Gun Boat 314

R I V E R   L O I R E

SOUTH LOCK

Old Town

B   Lighthouse

A A GUNS

Campbeltown

Avant Port

Motor launches before taking up attack positions at points A and B

0 YARDS   200   400   600

MTB 74

GREAT BRITAIN

1400 26 Mar   FALMOUTH

English Channel

FRANCE

Atlantic Ocean

ST NAZAIRE   Loire

NANTES

THE DIEPPE OPERATION

The large-scale landing at Dieppe on 19 August 1942 was an altogether different matter. It was felt that with large numbers of troops ready for action in the British Isles, a reconnaissance in force might be made on to the continent of Europe. The raid would provide battle experience for the troops and provide much useful information on German defensive methods. This latter would prove very useful in planning the D-Day landings.

The site selected was Dieppe, as it was typical of German defended localities the destruction of whose port and defence installations would be worthwhile, but was still within the range of fighters operating from England. The troops chosen for the raid were from 2 Canadian Division, commanded by Major-General J.H. Roberts, with commandos providing the two flank forces that were to land on either side of the town and silence the coastal batteries which would otherwise seriously jeopardize the whole operation. The total land forces amounted to slightly over 6,000 men, carried in nine landing ships escorted by eight destroyers.

The outer flank attacks were to silence the heavy batteries at Vasterival and Berneval, the inner ones those at Pourville and Puys, all at dawn. The main assault was to follow 30 minutes later. All German forces in the area were to be destroyed by the combined land forces before the town was evacuated.

Indications that the raid was going to fail started with the first landings: the eastern outer flank could not silence the guns that were its objective. The eastern inner flank assault was late, surprise was not obtained, and the force was pinned down as soon as it landed. Greater success was obtained on the other flank, however. There the commandos silenced their objective and then withdrew successfully. The inner flank made some progress inland but was then halted by German reinforcements. As the advance by the main assault from the town failed to materialize, the inner flank force had to pull back.

The main landings proved an almost total failure. The landing craft were met by a withering hail of fire, which pinned them down on the beach, and the tanks that did manage to scale the sea wall and reach the promenade were halted there by German obstacles. From that moment onwards the enterprise was doomed. The Canadians fought with enormous courage, but were in a hopeless position. The evacuation started at 1100 hours, and by 1300 what remained of the force started to sail back to England.

The raid had proved an appalling blunder, whose sole mitigating factor had been the lessons learnt. In particular that any attempt to capture a port by direct assault would certainly fail, and that any landings on the continent of Europe must be made over the open beaches. Canadian casualties were 3,363 out of 4,961, the commandos lost 247 out of 1,057. The Navy lost a destroyer and thirty-three landing craft, together with 550 men, and the RAF lost 106 aircraft and 190 men. German casualties were only about 600.

THE WAR IN THE AIR

If a single bomb drops on Berlin
you can call me Meyer!
Hermann Göring

Opposite: USAAF Liberators
during a raid on Tours

On 11 June 1917 a formation of fourteen Gothas dropped 118 high explosive bombs on London, killed and wounded 588 people, scored a direct hit on Liverpool Street Station, and convinced General Smuts, the *eminence grise* of the British Government in two world wars, that the air arm 'can be used as an independent means of war operations'. This view was shared by the Italian Brigadier-General Giulio Douhet whose *The Command of the Air* (1921) had a wide influence among the airmen of all the great powers, as well as upon influential authors such as H.G.Wells. It was Douhet's thesis that once the airforce has won command in the skies control of land and sea must follow as the night the day. In Britain men like Trenchard and Harris subscribed whole-heartedly to this view. In Germany it had the support of Göring, and in America of Mitchell. Above all it was a view widely accepted by press and public in all the countries that were to be involved in the Second World War. The techniques that were to permit the North Vietnamese to survive the recent attentions of the US Air Force were as yet unimagined.

During the Second World War both sides made effective use of the air arm, yet on the whole desire seems to have outrun performance. The Germans were, at least at first, too much inclined to regard the Luftwaffe as a form of close support artillery. The Allies whose Bomber Command was a weapon of relatively slow growth, expected from it a weapon of precision which could destroy selected targets in the German economy. Instead of a rapier they found they had armed themselves with a bludgeon.

At the Washington Conference on the Limitation of Armaments (1922) it was agreed that 'Aerial bombardment for the purpose of terrorizing the civilian population, or destroying or damaging private property not of a military character, or of injuring non-combatants is prohibited' (Article 22, Part II). From the very first day of the Second World War this article was a dead letter for bombing, aimed at getting the enemy population on to the roads so as to obstruct troop movements, was a deliberate part of the German *Blitzkrieg*. The Luftwaffe and notably the Stuka dive-bomber played a vital part in the conquest of Poland, the Low Countries, and France. When the Battle of Britain began German air power was at its height: Field-Marshals Kesselring and Sperrle could dispose of 2,830 aircraft and neither they nor their followers foresaw much difficulty in their two-fold task of denying the English Channel to

Allied shipping and of destroying the Royal Air Force. The latter with fifty-five fighter squadrons, a strength of 600 or 700 planes seemed to everyone but themselves to be hopelessly outmatched. The disparity in numbers was offset to some extent by the development of radar, which helped the defenders to differentiate between genuine and feint attacks and to deploy accordingly.

Meeting a resistance at once more efficient, determined, and flexible than they had expected, the Germans allowed themselves to be deflected from the objectives they had set themselves, and embarked on the series of operations known to history as the London blitz. In its first three months they killed 12,696 Londoners, but on 12 October Hitler found himself compelled to cancel Operation Sealion, the plan to invade England.

Slowly the initiative began to pass to the Allies. As early as 1940 the British, who then had only a very small bomber force, made concentrated attacks on Mannheim, Bremen, Wilhelmshaven, Kiel, and other targets. In March 1941 they devoted much attention to the *Scharnhorst* and *Gneisenau* at Brest. It was a relief to the RAF when the two battle-cruisers escaped up the Channel, and they were able to turn their attentions to German targets once more.

When after two and a half years of war Sir Arthur Harris took over Bomber Command he found that his total force was only 378 serviceable aircraft. It would be another year before the Americans could develop their potential strength to the full. At this time the RAF was receiving about 200 new bombers each month, and could not, therefore, afford heavy casualties. Successful attacks on Lübeck and Rostock raised the morale of Bomber Command. By May 1942 when the first of the 'thousand bomber raids' was mounted, bomb damage in Germany already equalled that inflicted on England. It was now that the real Bomber Offensive began. It had the effect of compelling the Germans to redeploy much of the Luftwaffe to defend their industry. When the German army invaded Russia in 1941 50 per cent of their aircraft were there in support. By the end of 1943 only 20 per cent were available for army co-operation.

In August 1942 the British improved the accuracy of their concentrated bombing by the introduction of the Pathfinder Force. By December Harris had at his disposal an average front-line strength of about 340 aircraft, including some 260 heavy bombers. The Lancaster bomber,

with four engines and capable of taking the 22,000-lb. 'Grand Slam' bombs, was now in service.

The Casablanca Conference of January 1943 outlined the strategy for the Combined Bomber Offensive: 'The progressive destruction and dislocation of the German military, industrial, and economic system, and the undermining of the morale of the German people to a point where their capacity for armed resistance is fatally weakened.' What this meant is explained by 'Bomber' Harris himself who wrote: 'After the extent of devastation in a number of towns had been compared with the loss of output in these towns over a period of months, a definite correlation was found between acreage of concentrated devastation and loss of man hours; . . .'

On the night 5/6 March the Battle of the Ruhr began when 442 aircraft made a severe and successful attack on Essen. On the night 16/17 May No. 617 Squadron breached the Möhne and Eder Dams releasing some 330,000,000 tons of water and flooding parts of Kassel.

At the end of July 7,196 tons of bombs were dropped on Hamburg, causing 80,000 casualties, destroying 6,200 acres of the built-up area and knocking out the city economically. The great shipbuilding yards, which had produced so many U-boats were severely damaged. A million of the inhabitants fled, and in the words of Colonel Adolf Galland: 'A wave of terror radiated from the suffering city and spread throughout Germany.' Everywhere people were saying 'What happened to Hamburg yesterday can happen to us tomorrow'. The famous fighter ace adds that 'in the wide circle of the political and military command could be heard the words: "The war is lost." ' But though Speer, the minister for war production, thought that six more such attacks could bring Germany to her knees, it somehow did not come to pass: at least not yet.

Meanwhile at Peenemünde the Germans were working on the second of Hitler's famous secret weapons – the V-2 – an 80-ton rocket with with a warhead containing ten tons of explosives. Its development was seriously delayed by an attack by 600 aircraft (17/18 August) which killed many of the staff and caused heavy damage.

The American 8th Air Force now made its debut in Europe. It believed in daylight precision bombing by Boeing B-17 'Flying Fortresses', which might or might not have fighter escort. Casualties were heavy from the first but the raid on the great German ball-bearing factory at Schweinfurt (14 October) was a disaster. Once past Aachen the Fortresses were beyond the range of fighter cover, and though they did much damage, sixty were shot down and 138 damaged out of 291 aircraft taking part. The Americans now realized that they must have a long-range fighter and with truly amazing drive had the P.51 Mustang in service only two months later. The Mustang, turned down by the USAAF in 1940, was given a Rolls Royce engine and was superior to the German fighters not only in speed, manoeuvrability, and range, but in numbers. By the end of the war 14,000 had been produced.

The Battle of Berlin, sixteen attacks on the German capital, made up Bomber Command's offensive in the bitter winter of 1943–1944. Perhaps 14,000 people were killed and 3,000,000 made homeless: 5,000 acres of the city were devastated. Gradually the German night fighters got the upper hand and the battle cost the RAF 300 aircraft.

Strange though it seems the Luftwaffe was still growing in strength and from February to April 1944 the Allies gave first priority to bombing the German aircraft industry. By dispersing their plant the Germans managed to save about 80 per cent of their production.

From April to September 1944 support of Operation Overlord, the Second Front, had priority, and the consequent lull in strategic bombing gave German industry six months in which to make up for the heavy damage during the previous year.

In the summer of 1944 thirty-seven Allied divisions drove sixty German divisions out of France, destroying their Seventh Army, 500,000 strong. The disparity on the ground was offset by almost complete superiority at sea and in the air.

The pre-D-Day bombing of the French railway system, and the destruction of bridges over the Rivers Seine and Loire made the movement of German reinforcements to the bridgehead area both slow and hazardous. Command of the air made it possible to secure the flanks of the lodgement area by dropping three airborne divisions.

In June 1944 the Allies were able to turn their attention to a massive attack on German oil production. This was remarkably effective. The production of aviation gasoline was reduced from 170,000 tons a month in June 1944 to 52,000 tons in March 1945. Training became impossible and numbers of aircraft were actually grounded for lack of fuel. The army suffered as badly as the Luftwaffe.

The Bomber Offensive's last great spectacular raid was also its most

Bombs dropped on German targets
Thousand tons

Aircraft production
(German) Thousands

Tank production
(German) Thousands

Oil poduction
(German) Million metric tons

controversial: Operation Thunderclap. On the night of 13/14 April 1945 800 bombers attacked Dresden, by far the biggest German city which was still undamaged. Its pre-war population was 630,000 and there were some 200,000 refugees. The casualties were somewhere between 250,000 and 400,000. Dresden, besides its industrial importance, was the centre of communications for the southern sector of the Eastern Front. It is easy to condemn such destruction but it must be remembered that the unconditional surrender of Germany still lay some three months in the future.

The Bomber Offensive, whilst undoubtedly effective was extremely costly. Bomber Command is thought to have lost 7,122 aircraft, with 55,573 aircrew and 1,570 ground staff killed, 22,000 wounded and 11,000 captured. The USAAF lost 23,000 aircraft and suffered 120,000 battle casualties.

The USAAF also mounted another major air offensive, this time in the Pacific against Japan. The main problem here was the great distances from US held territory to the target area. On 18 April 1942 Major Doolittle had led a raid on Tokyo in which his bombers were launched from the aircraft carrier *Wasp* off the coast of Japan and then flew on to land in China. Although this

raid caused little material damage it had a profound effect on Japanese civilian morale. It was not until 1944 when the Mariana islands had been taken that the Americans had bases from which their Superfortress bombers could strike at Japan directly. The early high-level, unescorted attacks suffered terrible losses, but once tactics had been changed to lower-level attacks with incendiaries, and fighter escorts could be provided from Okinawa, the US 20th Air Force was able to devastate the industrial towns of Japan, and have a truly major effect upon Japan's ability to rearm and support her forces.

Above: Four diagrams showing the relative ineffectiveness of the Allied campaign. Only on oil did the bombing have a significant effect in decreasing German production

THE BOMBER OFFENSIVE ON GERMANY

The first major Allied air raid of the war took place in the spring of 1940, but it was not until late 1943 and the widespread entry into action of American 8th Air Force units that the grand strategic bombing offensive can really be considered to have got into its stride. It was only in the spring of 1944 that the increasing range of escort fighters allowed deep penetration raids over the whole of Germany.

At first results matched the weakness of the effort made by the Allies. But with increasing experience, the introduction of new aircraft and electronic aids, and the growth of the number of aircraft available, that the success rate improved. RAF Bomber Command, using the greater number of aircraft, concerned itself mostly with area bombing of Germany's urban areas by night; the US 8th Air Force, however, concentrated on precision bombing of specific military targets by day. Initial heavy losses slowed down the American effort, but the arrival of long-range fighter escorts (see map) enabled heavy raids to be conducted deep into Germany. The effect of most of the early raids is still a moot point, but with the major effort being made on transport systems and oil production towards the end of the war, the Allies at last found and destroyed targets that considerably shortened the war. The following are some of the raids that marked turning points in the bombing offensive.

The first truly strategic air raid took place on 15/16 May 1940, when ninety-nine RAF aircraft bombed the Ruhr, losing one of their number. Damage caused was very slight.

The night of 16/17 December 1940 witnessed the RAF's first night area raid, when 134 aircraft bombed Mannheim. Three aircraft were lost, and again damage was slight, as the bombing was extremely inaccurate.

Lübeck was visited on 28/29 March 1942 by 234 British bombers, of which twelve were lost. The raid was the first to see the widespread use of incendiary bombs, and though extensive material damage was caused, war production was back to normal after only one week.

The city of Cologne was the next target to witness a milestone in bombing history: on the last night of May 1942 it received the first '1,000-bomber raid'. The very bottom of Bomber Command's barrel was scraped to gather the necessary aircraft, and 1,046 were despatched. Of these, forty were lost and 116 damaged. Half the target area was destroyed, under 500 Germans were killed, but 40,000 were made homeless. Reconstruction work was remarkably swift.

The American 8th Air Force entered the lists on 17 August 1942, when twelve Flying Fortresses attacked the marshalling yards near Rouen. Damage was slight, but the Americans lost no aircraft and as a result committed themselves firmly to this pattern of day precision bombing.

The 8th Air Force despatched 291 bombers to attack the Schweinfurt ball-bearing factory on 14 October 1943. Damage to the factory held up production for a short time, but American losses were crippling: sixty destroyed and 138 damaged. This destroyed the theory that the bomber 'boxes' could fight their way through unescorted, and the American effort was held up until adequate escort fighters were available.

Berlin was raided by 444 RAF bombers on the night of 18/19 November, and serious damage was caused, with RAF losses only nine. This was the first of sixteen major raids on the German capital, which almost completely destroyed it.

With the arrival of escort fighters the 8th Air Force could resume its efforts, and on 8 March 1944 590 bombers attacked the Erkner ball-bearing factory in Berlin. Damage held up production considerably, and the Americans lost thirty-seven aircraft.

On 30/31 March 1944 Bomber Command attacked Nuremberg with 795 aircraft, and suffered the heaviest defeat in its history. Damage caused was not very extensive, but ninety-five bombers were lost and seventy-one damaged. After this, the British abandoned area raids on distant objectives.

Bomber Command did not restrict itself entirely to area bombing, as the raid on the Dortmund–Ems Canal on the night of 23/24 September 1944 proves. 141 aircraft took part, and 14 were lost, but eleven 12,000-lb. 'Tallboy' bombs were used, and a six-mile stretch of the canal emptied of water.

The most controversial raid of the European war took place on 13/14 February 1944, when 805 Bomber Command aircraft destroyed some 1,600 acres of Dresden, together with an unknown number of civilians (estimates vary between 35,000 to 135,000). British losses were eight aircraft. The city, which was of no conceivable military value, was attacked by 400 8th Air Force aircraft the next day.

KEY BOMBING TARGETS

Industrial

1 Le Mans (aircraft)
2 Paris
3 Rouen
4 Siracourt (V-bombs)
5 Lottinghem
6 Mimovecques (V-bombs)
7 Watten
8 Wizernes (V-bombs)
9 Lille
10 Brussels (aircraft)
11 Rotterdam
12 Amsterdam (aircraft)
13 Le Havre
14 Boulogne
15 Dunkirk
16 Metz
17 Emden (U-boats)
18 Wilhelmshaven (U-boats)
19 Vegesack (U-boats)
20 Bremen (aircraft)
21 Hamburg
22 Flensburg (U-boats)
23 Kiel (U-boats)
24 Lübeck
25 Hannover
26 Brunswick
27 Magdeburg
28 Oschersleben (aircraft)
29 Dessau (aircraft)
30 Essen
31 Dortmund

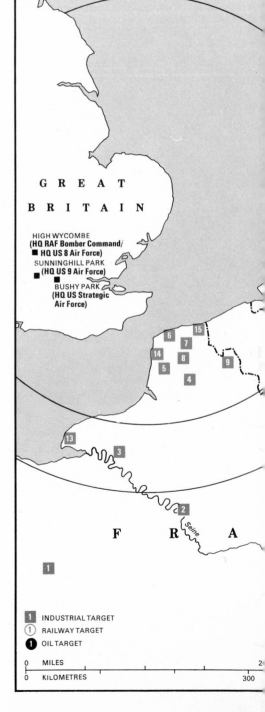

GREAT BRITAIN

HIGH WYCOMBE
(HQ RAF Bomber Command/
■ HQ US 8 Air Force)
SUNNINGHILL PARK
■ (HQ US 9 Air Force)
BUSHY PARK
(HQ US Strategic Air Force)

FRA

Seine

1 INDUSTRIAL TARGET
① RAILWAY TARGET
● OIL TARGET

0 MILES 2
0 KILOMETRES 300

32 Duisburg
33 Düsseldorf
34 Cologne
35 Bonn
36 Möhne Dam
37 Wuppertal
38 Eder Dam
39 Sorpe Dam
40 Kassel (aircraft)
41 Leipzig
42 Dresden
43 Liegnitz
44 Berlin
45 Rostock
46 Peenemünde
   (V-bombs)
47 Stettin
48 Erfurt
49 Gotha (aircraft)

50 Schweinfurt
   (ball-bearings)
51 Fürth
52 Nuremberg
53 Regensburg
   (aircraft)
54 Augsburg (aircraft)
55 Munich
56 Ulm
57 Stuttgart
58 Ludwigshafen
59 Saabrücken
60 Bochum
61 Karlsruhe
62 Friedrichshafen
63 Chemnitz
64 Prague
65 Wiener Neustadt
   (aircraft)

Railways
1 Frankfurt
2 Hanau
3 Aschaffenburg
4 Koblenz
5 Oberlahnstein
6 Giessen
7 Siegen
8 Schwerte
9 Soest
10 Hamm
11 Löhne
12 Osnabrück
13 Rheine
14 Bielefeld
15 Altenbecken
   Neuenbecken
16 Seelze
17 Lehrte
18 Hameln

19 Paderborn
20 Bebra
21 Stendal
22 Halle
23 Gera
24 Breslau
25 Minden
26 Mulhouse
27 Freiburg
28 Offenburg
29 Rastatt
30 Karlsruhe
31 Heilbronn
32 Treuchtlingen
33 Pasing
34 Munich
35 Rosenheim
36 Salzburg
37 Strasshof
38 Würzburg

39 Mannerheim
40 Darmstadt
41 Mainz
42 Bingen
43 Vienna
44 Munster

Oil
1 Wesseling
2 Reisholz
3 Dülmen
4 Gelsenkirchen
5 Salzbergen
6 Nienburg
7 Farge
8 Heide
9 Hitzacker
10 Dollbergen
11 Derben
12 Pölitz

13 Salzgitter
14 Lützkendorf
15 Leuna
16 Ruhland
17 Böhlen
18 Rositz
19 Mölbis
20 Zeitz
21 Brüx
22 Neuburg
23 Freiham
24 Linz
25 Moosbierbaum
26 Korneuburg
27 Floridsdorf
28 Schwechat
29 Lobau
30 Ploesti

THE BOMBER OFFENSIVE ON JAPAN

As the Japanese homeland could only be attacked at long range, for lack of bases close to the islands of the Japanese archipelago, a special aircraft was needed, and this was found in the Boeing B-29 Superfortress, operating for the most part from huge airfields constructed in the Marianas islands. Initially, the success rate was not good, as the Japanese defences proved to be more efficient than anticipated, and bombing accuracy severely troubled by the high winds at the bombing altitude of 30,000 feet, the effect of ice on instruments and performance, and fog at ground level. Losses were running at the

unacceptably high rate of 6 per cent. The 20th Air Force's new commander, General Curtis Le May, set about overcoming these difficulties. The answer involved a complete reappraisal of American bombing tactics: instead of high altitude raids with high explosive, the new tactics called for low level raids with incendiaries.

Success was immediate. The first raid, on Tokyo, was carried out by 334 B-29's, dropping some 1,667 tons of incendiaries from 7,000 feet. Fifteen square miles of the city were destroyed. The next four raids proved the success of the new tactics. Operating at the new altitude, the B-29's could carry about three times the bomb load they had at 30,000 feet, but raided at night to avoid the worst efforts of the Japanese anti-aircraft fire. In all, 9,365 tons of incendiaries were dropped, gutting 32 square miles of urban areas. Losses were reduced dramatically: of the 1,595 sorties despatched, only twenty-two aircraft were lost, a loss rate of only 1·4 per cent. With the arrival of the first escort fighters operating from Iwo Jima on 7 April, American losses fell still further, and with the constantly growing number of B-29's available, Japanese industry suffered mortal blows in the

period of total American air superiority between May and August 1945.

The Japanese continued to resist, however, and it was not until the awesome import of the two Atom bomb raids had been digested that the Japanese sued for peace.

Below: USAAF Superfortresses releasing incendiary bombs over Yokohama

B-29 TARGETS IN JAPAN: FEB/AUGUST 1945

MAIN INCENDIARY (FIRE RAID) TARGETS *

OTHER INCENDIARY TARGETS *

X X X   MINE LAYING AREAS

ATOMIC BOMB ATTACK

* FIGURES SHOW PERCENTAGE OF URBAN AREA DESTROYED

| 0 | MILES | 150 |
| 0 | KILOMETRES | 200 |

KOREA

Second atomic bomb dropped on 9 August (95,000 casualties)

SHIMONOSEKI   UBE 23
MOJI 27
YAWATA   KOKURA
FUKUOKA 22
SASEBO 48
OMUTA 42
OITA 25
KUMAMOTO 20
NAGASAKI
Kyushu
IZUMI
KAGOSHIMA 44

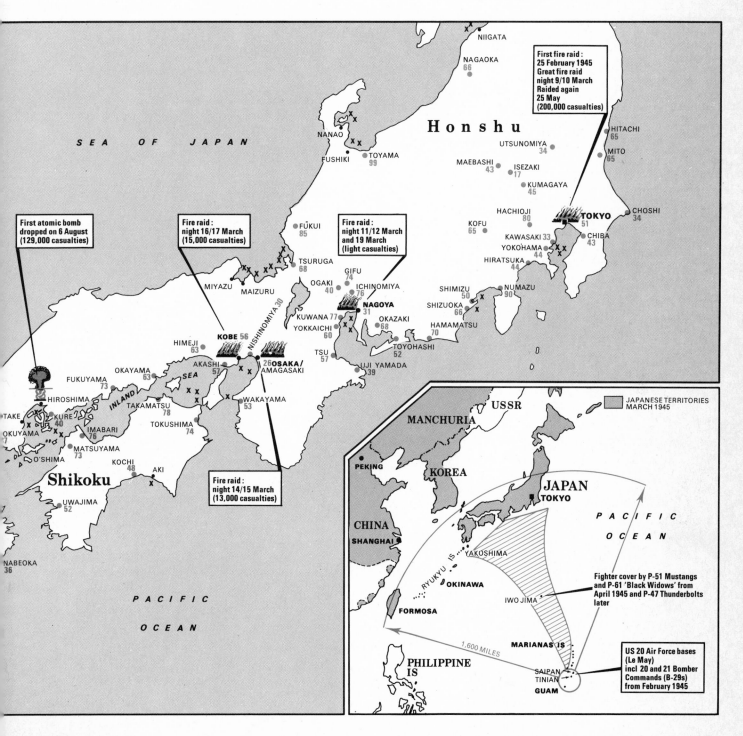

SEA OF JAPAN

Honshu

First fire raid:
25 February 1945
Great fire raid
night 9/10 March
Raided again
25 May
(200,000 casualties)

NIIGATA

NAGAOKA
66

HITACHI
65

UTSUNOMIYA
34

MITO
65

NANAO

TOYAMA
99

MAEBASHI
43

ISEZAKI
17

CHOSHI
34

FUSHIKI

KUMAGAYA
45

HACHIOJI
80

TOKYO
51

KOFU
65

KAWASAKI 33

CHIBA
43

FÚKUI
85

YOKOHAMA
44

First atomic bomb
dropped on 6 August
(129,000 casualties)

Fire raid:
night 16/17 March
(15,000 casualties)

Fire raid:
night 11/12 March
and 19 March
(light casualties)

HIRATSUKA
44

TSURUGA
68

GIFU
74

SHIMIZU
50

NUMAZU
90

MIYAZU

OGAKI
40

ICHINOMIYA
76

SHIZUOKA
66

MAIZURU

NISHINOMIYA 30

NAGOYA
31

KUWANA 77

OKAZAKI
68

HAMAMATSU
70

HIMEJI
63

KOBE 56

YOKKAICHI
60

OSAKA/
26 **AMAGASAKI**

TOYOHASHI
52

AKASHI
57

TSU
57

UJI YAMADA
39

FUKUYAMA
73

OKAYAMA
63

INLAND

SEA

TAKAMATSU
78

WAKAYAMA
53

HIROSHIMA

TAKE

KURE
40

TOKUSHIMA
74

OKUYAMA
7

IMABARI
76

MATSUYAMA
73

O'SHIMA

Fire raid:
night 14/15 March
(13,000 casualties)

KOCHI
48

AKI

Shikoku

UWAJIMA
52

NABEOKA
36

PACIFIC

OCEAN

JAPANESE TERRITORIES
MARCH 1945

USSR

MANCHURIA

KOREA

PEKING

JAPAN
TOKYO

PACIFIC

CHINA

OCEAN

SHANGHAI

YAKOSHIMA

RYUKYU IS

OKINAWA

IWO JIMA

Fighter cover by P-51 Mustangs
and P-61 'Black Widows' from
April 1945 and P-47 Thunderbolts
later

FORMOSA

1,600 MILES

MARIANAS IS

PHILIPPINE
IS

SAIPAN
TINIAN
GUAM

US 20 Air Force bases
(Le May)
incl 20 and 21 Bomber
Commands (B-29s)
from February 1945

INDEX

283